《多彩中国节》丛书编委会

Editorial Committee of the Colorful Chinese Festivals Series

丛书主编　彭新良

The Spring Festival

汉英对照

春节

张跃　李曦淼　等　编著
王竹青　译

全国百佳图书出版单位
时代出版传媒股份有限公司
安徽人民出版社

图书在版编目（CIP）数据

春节：汉英对照 / 张跃，李曦淼等编著；王竹青译．-- 合肥：安徽人民出版社，2018.8
（多彩中国节丛书 / 彭新良主编）

ISBN 978-7-212-10023-0

Ⅰ．①春… Ⅱ．①张… ②李… ③王… Ⅲ．①春节－风俗习惯－中国－汉、英 Ⅳ．① K892.18

中国版本图书馆 CIP 数据核字 (2018) 第 005203 号

《多彩中国节》丛书

春节：汉英对照
CHUNJIE

彭新良　**丛书主编**
张跃　李曦淼　等　**编著**　　王竹青　**译**

出 版 人：徐　敏　　**选题策划：**刘　哲　陈　娟
出版统筹：张　旻　袁小燕　　**责任编辑：**汪　龙
责任印制：董　亮　　**装帧设计：**陈　爽　宋文岚

出版发行：时代出版传媒股份有限公司 http://www.press-mart.com
安徽人民出版社 http://www.ahpeople.com
地　　址：合肥市政务文化新区翡翠路 1118 号出版传媒广场八楼
邮　　编：230071
电　　话：0551-63533258　0551-63533259（传真）
印　　刷：安徽联众印刷有限公司

开本：880mm × 1230mm　1/32　**印张：**10.125　**字数：**290 千
版次：2018 年 8 月第 1 版　2018 年 9 月第 1 次印刷

ISBN　978-7-212-10023-0　　**定价：**40.00 元

代　序

我们共同的日子

个人一年一度最重要的日子是生日，大家一年一度最重要的日子是节日。节日是大家共同的日子。

节日是一种纪念日，内涵多种多样。有民族的、国家的、宗教的，比如国庆节、圣诞节等。有某一类人的，如妇女、儿童、劳动者的，这便是妇女节、儿童节、劳动节等。也有与人们的生活生产密切相关的，这类节日历史悠久，很早就形成了一整套人们约定俗成、代代相传的节日习俗，这是一种传统的节日。传统节日也多种多样。中国是一个多民族国家，有 56 个民族，统称中华民族。传统节日有全民族共有的，也有某个民族特有的。比如春节、中秋节、元宵节、端午节、清明节、重阳节等，就为中华民族所共用和共享；世界文化遗产羌年就为羌族独有和独享。各民族这样的节日很多。

传统节日是在漫长的农耕时代形成的。农耕时代生产与生活、人与自然的关系十分密切。人们或为了感恩于大自然的恩赐，或为了庆祝辛勤劳作换来的收获，或为了激发生命的活力，或为了加强人际的亲情，经过长期相互认同，最终约定俗成，渐渐把一年中某一天确定为节日，并创造了十分完整又严格的节俗，如仪式、庆典、规制、禁忌，乃至特定的游艺、装饰与食品，来把节日这天演化成一个独具内涵、迷人的日子。更重要的是，人们在每一个传统的节日里，还把共同的生活理想、人间愿望与审美追求融入节日的内涵与种种仪式中。因此，它是中华民族世间理想与生活愿望极致的表现。可以说，我们的传统——精神文化传统，往往就是依靠这代代相传的一年一度的节日继承下来的。

然而，自从20世纪整个人类进入由农耕文明向工业文明的过渡，农耕时代形成的文化传统开始瓦解。尤其是中国，在近百年由封闭走向开放的过程中，节日文化——特别是城市的节日文化受到现代文明与外来文化的冲击。当下人们已经鲜明地感受到传统节日渐行渐远，并为此产生忧虑。传统节日的淡化必然使其中蕴含的传统精神随之涣散。然而，人们并没有坐等传统的消失，主动和积极地与之应对。这充分显示了当代中国人在文化上的自觉。

近10年，随着中国民间文化遗产抢救工程的全面展开，国家非物质文化遗产名录申报工作的有力推动，传统节日受到关注，一些重要的传统节日被列入了国家文化遗产名录。继而，2006年国家将每年6月的第二个周六确定为“文化遗产日”，2007年国务院决定将3个中华民族的重要节日——清明节、端午节和中秋节列为法定放假日。这一重大决定，表现了国家对公众的传统文化生活及其传承的重视与尊重，同时也是保护节日文化遗产十分必要的措施。

节日不放假必然直接消解了节日文化，放假则是恢复节日传统的首要条件。但放假不等于远去的节日立即就会回到身边。节日与假日的不同是因为节日有特定的文化内容与文化形式。那么，重温与恢复已经变得陌生的传统节日习俗则是必不可少的了。

千百年来，我们的祖先从生活的愿望出发，为每一个节日都创造出许许多多美丽又动人的习俗。这种愿望是理想主义的，所以节日习俗是理想的；愿望是情感化的，所以节日习俗也是情感化的；愿望是美好的，所以节日习俗是美的。人们用合家团聚的年夜饭迎接新年；把天上的明月化为手中甜甜的月饼，来象征人间的团圆；在严寒刚刚消退、万物复苏的早春，赶到野外去打扫墓地，告慰亡灵，表达心中的缅怀，同时戴花插柳，踏青春游，亲切地拥抱大地山川……这些诗意化的节日习俗，使我们一代代人的心灵获得了美好的安慰与宁静。

对于少数民族来说，他们特有的节日的意义则更加重要。节日还是他们民族集体记忆的载体、共同精神的依托、个性的表现、民族身份之所在。

谁说传统的习俗过时了？如果我们淡忘了这些习俗，就一定要去重温一下传统。重温不是表象地模仿古人的形式，而是用心去体验传统中的精神与情感。

在历史进程中，习俗是在不断变化的，但民族传统的精神实质不应变。这传统就是对美好生活的不懈追求，对大自然的感恩与敬畏，对家庭团圆与世间和谐永恒的企望。

这便是我们节日的主题，也是这套《多彩中国节》丛书编写的根由与目的。

中国56个民族是一个大家庭，各民族的节日文化异彩纷呈，既有春节、元宵节、中秋节这样多民族共庆的节日，也有泼水节、火把节、那达慕等少数民族特有的节日。这套丛书选取了中国最有代表性的10个传统节日，一节一册，图文并茂，汉英对照，旨在为海内外读者通俗、全面地呈现中国绚丽多彩的节庆文化和民俗文化；放在一起则是中华民族传统节日的一部全书，既有知识性、资料性、工具性，又有可读性和趣味性。10本精致的小册子，以翔实的文献和生动的传说，将每个节日的源起、流布与习俗，图文并茂、有滋有味地娓娓道来，从这些节日的传统中，可以看出中国人的精神追求和文化脉络。这样一套丛书不仅是对我国传统节日的一次总结，也是对传统节日文化富于创意的弘扬。

我读了书稿，心生欣喜，因序之。

冯骥才

（全国政协常委、中国文联原执行副主席）

Preface

Our Common Days

The most important day for a person is his or her birthday while the most important days for all are festivals, which are our common days.

Festivals are embedded with rich connotations for remembering. There're ethnic, national, and religious ones, such as National Day and Christmas Day; festivals for a certain group of people, such as Women's Day, Children's Day, and Laborers' Day; and those closely related to people's life and production, which enjoy a long history and feature a complete set of well-established festive traditions passed on from one generation to another. These are so-called traditional festivals, which vary greatly, too.

China, consisting of 56 nationalities, is a multi-ethnic country. People in China are collectively called the Chinese nation. So it's no wonder that some of the traditional festivals are celebrated by all nationalities while others only by certain nationalities, with the representatives of the former ones being the Spring Festival, the Lantern Festival, the Dragon Boat Festival, the Tomb-Sweeping Festival, and the Double Ninth Festival, etc. and that of the latter being the Qiang New Year, a unique festival for Qiang ethnic group. Each of ethnic groups in China has quite a number of their unique traditional festivals.

The traditional festivals have taken shape in the long agrarian times when people were greatly dependent on nature and when life was closely related to production. People gradually saw eye to eye with each other in the long-term practicing sets of rituals, celebrations, taboos as well as games, embellishments, and foods in a strict way and decided to select some days of one year as festivals with a view to expressing their gratitude to nature, celebrating harvesting, stimulating vitality of life, or strengthening bonds between family members and relatives. In this way, festivals have evolved into charming days with unique connotations. More importantly, people have instilled their common aspirations and aesthetic pursuits into festive connotations and rituals. To put it simply, festivals are consummate demonstrations of Chinese people's worldly aspirations and ideals, and Chinese people's spiritual cultures are inherited for generations by them.

Nevertheless, the cultural traditions formed in the agrarian times began to collapse with human beings being in transition from agrarian civilization to industrial one, esp., in China, whose festive cultures were severely hammered by modern civilization and foreign cultures in nearly one hundred years from being closed to opening up to the world. Nowadays, people strongly feel that traditional festivals are drifting away from their lives and are deeply concerned about it owing to the fact that dilution of traditional festivals means the fall of the traditional spirit of Chinese people. Of course, we don't wait and see; instead, we cope with it in a positive way. This fully displays the contemporary Chinese people's cultural consciousness.

In recent ten years, the traditional festivals have been earning more and more attention and some significant ones are included to the list of the National Heritages with the vigorous promotion of China's Folk Heritage Rescue Program and China's intangible cultural heritage application; for example, China set the second Saturday of June as "Cultural Heritage Day" in 2006; the State Council decided to list three significant traditional festivals as legal holidays—the Tomb-Sweeping Festival, the Dragon Boat Festival, and the Mid-Autumn Festival in 2007. These measures show the state gives priority to and pay tribute to the inheritance of public traditional cultures.

Holidays are necessary for spending festivals which will be diluted otherwise; however, holidays don't necessarily bring back traditional festivals. Since festivals, different from holidays, are equipped with special cultural forms and contents, it's essential to recover those traditional festive customs which have become stranger and stranger to contemporary Chinese people.

In the past thousands of years, our ancestors, starting from their aspirations, created many fine and engaging traditions. These aspirations are ideal, emotional, and beautiful, so are the festival traditions. People usher in the New Year by having the meal together on the New Year's Eve, make moon cakes by imitating the moon in the sky, standing for family reunion, or go to sweep the tombs of ancestors or family members for commemorating or comforting in the early spring when the winter just recedes and everything wakes up while taking spring hiking and enjoying spring scenes by the way. These poetic festive customs greatly comfort souls of people for generations.

As for ethnic minority people, their special festivals mean more to them. The festivals carry the collective memory, common spirit, character of their ethnic groups as well as mark their ethnic identities.

Are the traditional festive customs really out-dated? We're compelled to review them if we really forget them. What matters for review is not imitating the forms of the ancient Chinese people's celebrations but experiencing essence and emotions embedded in them with heart and soul.

Traditions have evolved with history's evolving, but the traditional national spirit has never changed. The spirit lies in people's never-ending pursuit for beautiful life, consistent gratitude and awe for nature, constant aspiration for family reunion and world harmony.

This is also the theme of our festivals and the root-cause of compiling the series.

The Chinese nation, featuring its colorful and varieties of festive cultures, boasts the common festivals celebrated by all nationalities, such as the Spring Festival, the Lantern Festival, the Mid-Autumn Festival, and the ethnic festivals, such as the Water Splashing Festival (Thai people), the Torch Festival (Yi people), Naadam (Mongolian nationality). This series, selecting the most typical ten festivals of China, with each festival being in one volume with figures and in both English and Chinese, unfolds the colorful festive and folk cultures in an engaging and all-round way for appealing to foreign readers. If put together, they constitute a complete set of books on Chinese traditional festivals, being instructive and intriguing. The ten brochures elaborate on the origins, distribution, and customs of each festival in an engaging way with figures, tales, and rich literature. Chinese people's spiritual pursuit and cultural veining can be tracked in this series, serving as a summary of Chinese traditional festivals and innovative promotion of them.

I went over the series with delight, and with delight, wrote the preface, too.

Feng Jicai

CPPCC National Committee member

Former Vice-president of the China Federation of Literary and Art Circles

目 录

Contents

引 言

在中国人的传统纪年方法中，将一年分为春、夏、秋、冬四个季节，但采用的是农历表述方式。农历的十一月和十二月分别称为“冬月”和“腊月”，为一年中最寒冷的月份。而农历的第一个月，按照习惯称为“正月”，意味着一年之首春季的到来。

春季是四季之首，此时冰雪消融、春色满园、大地复苏、百花齐放。“一年之计在于春”，中国人以最大的热情迎接春天的到来：千家万户打扫房前屋后，穿上新衣新鞋，用新面貌迎接新一年的到来；准备最精美、最丰盛的饮食欢庆上一年的丰收；用最隆重的礼节祭拜先祖和上天诸神，感谢他们的眷顾，并期盼新一年里依然佑庇自己；无论身处何地都要返回家中与亲人团聚，放松劳碌了一年的身体；举行丰富多彩的娱乐活动，尽情享受民间习俗带来的愉悦。在中国传统文化中，这就是春天里的节日，中国最为隆重、节日氛围最浓厚、影响范围最大、喜庆时间最长的节日——春节。

“百节年为首”，春节的时间正好处于农历旧年与新年交替之际，因此又被形象地称为“过年”，即从腊月过渡到了正月，辞别旧岁，喜迎新年。

春节在中国不同时代有不同的名称。尧舜时期被称为“载”，有万象更新的寓意；先秦时期被称为“上日”“元日”“改岁”等；西汉、东汉时期又被称为“三朝”“岁旦”等；魏晋南北朝时期被称为“元辰”“元首”“岁朝”；到了唐宋元明期间，被称为“元旦”“岁日”等；而在清代一直被称为“元旦”或“元日”。在这些称谓中，以“元旦”使用最为普遍、时间最长久。民国时期，将“元旦”改称为“春节”。中华人民共和国成立后，采用世界通用的公元纪年。为了区分阳历和阴历两个“年”，又因一年二十四节气的“立春”恰在农历年的前后，故把阳历（公历）一月一日称为“元旦”，农历正月初一正式改称“春节”，一直沿用到现在。

春节的出现体现了中国人以四季更替变化的规律为依托，以自然为取向，尊重自然进而由物喻人的人文情怀。春节中所进行的一系列祭祀、娱乐活动也反映出了中国人家庭和谐、邻里和睦的社会逻辑以及中华民族勤劳、朴实、热情的民族性情。春节不仅凝聚了历代中国人对美好生活的追求与向往，也是中华民族共同认同的文化记忆，维系着中华民族的情感与统一。

Introduction

According to Chinese traditional way of numbering the years, a whole year could be divided into four seasons. The eleventh and twelfth lunar month was called "Dong Yue" and "La Yue" which are the coldest time of a year. While the first month of the lunar New Year, known as "Zheng Yue", means the coming of spring, which is regarded as the head of seasons.

As the head of seasons, spring watches the ice melting down, trees waking and flowers blooming. The whole year's work depends on a good start in spring,as a Chinese proverb goes. To offer a warm-hearted welcome to spring and to celebrate the harvest of last year, every family sweeps the house, wears new clothes. They prepare most delicious food to worships ancestors and gods in most solemn manners, thanking for their protection and whishing for their future blessing in the coming year. On such a big occasion every family member returns home to a reunion party where he or she could relax his or her yearly toiled body. A variety of recreational activities will be held to make the festival enjoyable and colorful.This is a festival in spring. Traditionally, this festival is the longest and happiest, most important and most influential holiday among Chinese circle.

It is true that "Chinese Spring Festival is ahead of all other holidays in China." the festival happens to be on the turning point of the past year and the new year in lunar calendar. That is why it is also called as "Chinese New Year". People indeed welcome a NEW year and bid a farewell to an Old year when the Spring Festival goes from "La Yue" to "Zheng Yue".

Chinese New Year had different names at different times. Back to the Yao and Shun period it was called "Zai", which implied that all things would take on a new start. In the Pre-Qin Dynasty "Shang Ri", "Yuan Ri", "Zheng Dan", and "Gai Sui". In Western Han and Eastern Han Dynasty it was "San Zhao"or "Sui Dan". In the Wei and Jin Southern and Northern Dynasties it was entitled as "Yuan Chen", "Yuan Ri", "Yuan Shou"and "Sui Chao". It was alluded toas "Sui Ri" till the Tang Song Yuan Ming four dynasties. Asin the Qing Dynasty, "Yuan Dan" or "Yuan Ri"was so named. Of all those appellations, "Yuan Dan" was mostly accepted for the longest time. During the period of the Republic of China, "Yuan Dan" was changed into "Spring Festival". The People's Republic of China has adopted-international chronology. In order to differentiate the two New Yearsin the solar and lunar calendars, and also because of that "Li Chun" in the TWENTY-FOUR SOLAR TERMS being around the lunar New Year, people named the first day of the first lunar month Spring Festival and January 1st in solar calendar was declared as "Yuan Dan".

Chinese respect nature and tend to their humane feelings in accordance with the law of the changing of seasons. Theirenthusiasm and energy are evoked with the coming of the Spring Festival. And a series of worship and recreational activities also display their eager desires for harmonious family and peaceful community. And Chinesepeople'sindustrious and optimistic temperament could be demonstrated to the full length in these traditional events.In a word, the Spring Festival is not only a holiday that could embody people's hopes and wishes for a better life, but also serves as commoncultural memory for all Chinese, abroad or home, or more accurately, as a bond of love to unite them as one unified people.

第一章 春节起源与传说

春节，即农历岁首的第一个节日，在中国民间被习惯性地称为“过年”。

一般认为，春节起源于上古尧舜时代。当时的人们为了答谢保佑他们一年农事顺利的神灵，便在四季走完一个轮回、新的轮回即将开始时，用上一年人们所收获的最好的食品献祭给神灵，报答神灵的恩赐。同时，人们也通过各种狂欢娱乐活动来庆祝丰收。中华民族五千年历史长河中，中国新年的礼俗经历了萌芽、基本形成、裂变和转型等发展阶段，中华民族的传统文化在春节中得以延续了数千年，而且在不同时期具有时代特征的社会文化也通过春节为后人所了解。

一、春节的起源

春节最本质的含义是中华民族先民在长期的生产实践中对农作物四季生长规律的认识和对天体运行变化规律的了解，因此，春节又被当作“年”的别称，作为时序循环周期的记载。

○中国春节特色剪纸

1. “年”的来由

对于“年”这样一个时间节点，在中国不同朝代被赋予了不同的称谓。《尔雅·释天》中有记载：“夏曰岁，商曰祀，周曰年，唐虞曰载。”由此可见，中国文化中关于“年”的概念在夏商（公元前2070—公元前1046）时期就已经出现了。然而，“年”最初的含义并不是时间概念，而是源自于农业生产。在古代，农作物的生长周期一般都为一年左右，所以“年”最初的含义是谷物收成的意思。一年是根据谷物的播种和收获周期而确定的，反映了“年”与农作物收成之间的密切关系。

作为一个传统的农业国，农业生产对中国社会的影响超过了其他任何方面。可以说，中国传统文化各个方面的形成均与农事农耕相关。农作物生长的完整周期伴随着春夏秋冬的轮回，从春天播种、秋天收获的长期农事耕作规律实践中，先人们对寒来暑往的变化、气候阴晴雨雪的交替反复以及农作物的生长成熟都逐渐有了一些理性的认识。通过观察，发现了四季交替及天体运行与农作物生长之间的关系，在这个基础上逐渐总结出了一套测定和计算时间的方法，用天干、地支记录年、月、日，并通过制定历法的形式将农时以节气的形式在历法中加以明确。

然而，古代中国的历法也随着朝代的更迭、帝王的易姓而不同。每一次改朝换代，天子们为了证明他们的权力是上天所授予，都要把月份的次序更改一次，历代历法变更后都将每年的第一个月称为“正月”，剩下的十一个月依次顺延。因此，在中国历史上便出现了夏朝用春季的第一个月（孟春）作为正月，商朝用冬季的最后一个月（腊月）作为正月，而到了秦朝则将冬季的第一个月作为正月。汉朝沿用秦朝的历法，由于感到历法与天体运行规律出入太大，汉武帝命公孙卿、司马迁、邓平等人创《太初历》。该历以夏朝历法的正月作为一年之首，并将二十四节气修订入历法之中。自汉朝以后，虽然历代都对历法进行过修订，但都以《太初历》为蓝本，以春季的第一个月为岁首。太初历一直沿用至清末，共延续了两千多年，至今中国民间都把太初历称作“夏历”。有了固定的历法，人们根据历法中的二十四节气安排农事，以年作为计时单位。春夏秋冬周而复始便是一年，冬是旧岁的末尾，春是新年的伊始，而分隔新年旧岁的日子便是“过年”。随着年历的确定，每年新旧年岁交替时的年节——“春节”也就随着一年一度固定的日子延续了下来。

2. 年终腊祭

与上面“年”为“五谷皆熟”的说法不同，中国民间还有“年”与“围猎祭神”相关的解释。

在中国古代，人们对自然规律及其运作方式的认识并不是很充分，尤其是在农业生产中。由于生产力低下，人们只能更多地求助于鬼神等超自然力量来确保农业上的丰收。因此，在一年农事结束、新年旧岁交替之时，人们便要到野外猎取各种野兽，用最好的粮食做成丰盛的饮食款待神灵，报答神灵一年的恩赐，并祈求神灵在新的一年里继续让人们享受恩泽，来年五谷丰登，家人平安吉祥，这种习俗称为“腊祭”。

腊祭风俗最早始于周代（公元前 11 世纪中期—公元前 256），是一年岁终的隆重祭祀活动。东汉为腊祭准备的打猎选在新旧年岁交接之时。在这个时候，人们用通过打猎所获得的猎物祭祀先祖神灵，报答神灵对他们的恩赐。人们选在一年之中的最后一个月进行围猎，并在那时举行腊祭，因此一年之中的最后一个月也就被称为“腊月”。对于腊祭时的盛况，在《礼记·杂记下》孔夫子与子贡的对答中也可略见一斑。孔圣人的弟子子贡观看了腊祭时的盛况，孔子问他：“腊祭的时候你兴奋吗？”子贡回答：“举国上下的人们都为之而疯狂。”

○腊祭

腊祭的不断发展演变，使每年最后一个月所进行的集体捕猎行动逐渐淡化，但是现在人们还是习惯把腊月腌制的猪肉称为“腊肉”。而在腊月用丰盛的祭品祭祀先祖神灵的仪式也被保留了下来。无论官宦还是平民之家，每年年底都要举行一次岁终之祭。其规模的盛大、内容的繁复为节庆之最，并逐渐演变为春节习俗而延续至今。

二、有关春节的传说

春节对于中国人是如此重要，不仅前人留下了大量的史籍文献，在民间也流传着众多饶有趣味且富有寓意的传说，丰富了春节的文化内涵。

在春节的各种传说中，不仅对春节的起源进行了神圣化和夸张化的描述，也为人们在节日期间的种种行为和活动安排了生动而有趣的解释。通俗易懂的传说与神话构成了春节活动的一部分，每年春节时分，家中长辈都要向好奇而天真的孩子们讲述“年兽”“灶王爷”的故事。春节的传说正是以这样的方式在中国人中一代一代传递，深深内化于每个人心中。

1. 万年历

《万年历》是传说中最为古老的一部太阳历，据说其编撰者是一个名叫万年的青年，为了纪念他编撰这部历法的功绩，人们便以他的名字命名这部历法为《万年历》。

传说在商朝，历法与时令很混乱，有一个叫万年的樵夫便想制定一部历法将节令定准确。虽然他苦苦思考，但一直都找不到计算时间的方法。一天，万年到山上去砍柴，累了就坐在树荫下休息。他呆呆地望着树影，心里依然在想着如何将节令定准确的事情。时间在推移，太阳也由东向西慢慢移动，不知不觉中已经过了大半个时辰。突然间，万年发现地上的树影已经不在之前的位置，而是悄悄移动了方位并且比之前长了很多。万年心中一动，他想到何不用影子的移动和长短变化来计算时间。万年回家后,立即找来一个圆盘，在上面标刻上了十二个时辰，在圆盘中心竖立了一根又粗又长的针。他将这个圆盘放在太阳下，根据阳光照射在针上所投射下日影的位置来指示当时的时辰，以此测定一天的时间，这个圆盘后来被人们叫作“日晷”。虽然在白天日晷能很准确地指定时间，但是到了晚上或是阴雨天，日晷就失去了作用。万年也发现了日晷的缺点。

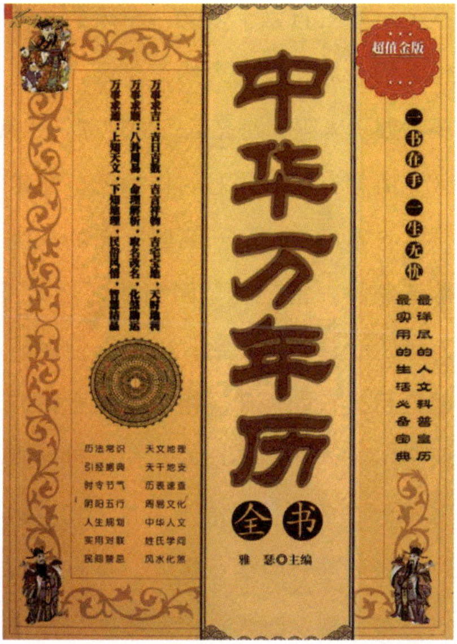

○中华万年历，中国古代的一部百科全书

又一天，万年在山边泉眼喝水。他看见泉水从山崖上一滴一滴有节奏地往下流，有节奏的滴水声深深印入他的心，也启发了他的灵感。回家后，他便动手制作了一个有五层的漏壶，利用漏水的方法来计算时间。这样一来，不管阴晴雨雪都能很好地掌握时间了。有了日晷和漏壶这些计时的工具，万年观察天时节令方便了许多，他观察起来也更用心了。经过日复一日的观察，几年后万年发现，差不多每隔三百六十多天，白天的长短就会重复一次，而且春夏秋冬也轮回一周，每隔大约三十天，月亮也就阴缺一次。万年发现，只要掌握了太阳和月亮运行的规律，也就掌握了节令的时间。

商朝当时的国君叫作祖乙，他常常为百姓不能掌握节令变换耽误了农事而苦恼。一名叫阿衡的大臣为了讨好天子，建议他登天坛敬天祭神。祖乙听了阿衡的话，率领百官前往祭天，但无济于事。万年听说这件事之后，便带着他发明的日晷和漏壶去觐见祖乙，说明日月运行的规律。祖乙听后觉得万年说得很有道理，于是把万年留了下来，并在天坛前建起了日月阁，筑起了日晷台和漏壶亭，还派了十二个童子服侍万年并供其差遣。他要求万年在这里专心研究时令，测准日月运行规律，确定准确的晨夕时间，创建历法，为黎民百姓造福。一天，祖乙派阿衡前往天坛探望万年并了解他制定历法的情况，当阿衡登上天坛时，见石壁上写着一首诗：

日出日落三百六，周而复始从头来。

草木荣枯分四时，一岁月有十二圆。

阿衡知道万年对节令的推算已经有了初步的成果，非常忐忑，担心万年制定出准确的历法后得到天子祖乙的重用，使他受到冷落。此时万年的成就已经威胁到了阿衡的地位。于是，阿衡花重金收买了一名刺客，谋划行刺万年。然而，万年废寝忘食地研究时令，几乎从不走出日月阁，阿衡只好让刺客在夜深人静的时候用弓箭刺杀万年。一天夜里，刺客来到日月阁，在远处挽弓射杀万年。只听“嗖”的一声，万年的胳膊中箭，这时服侍万年的童子们也发现了刺客。童子们高喊捉拿刺客，守卫的兵士及时抓住了刺客，并将他呈送天子。祖乙知道是阿衡的诡计后，将他关入了大牢，并亲自前往日月阁探望受伤的万年。借此机会，万年也把自己最新的发现报告给了祖乙。他说：“现在申星追上了蚕百星，星象复原，子时夜交，旧岁已完，正是十二个月满。旧岁已完，希望天子定个节名吧。”祖乙说：“春为岁首，就叫春节吧。”祖乙见万年为了制定历法日夜劳碌，且又受了箭伤，心中恻隐，便请万年入宫调养。万年认为他现在所制定以太阳运行为依据的历法依然不够严谨。他必须留在日月阁直到制定出准确的历法。数十年之后，万年所制定的历法终于完成了，而万年也成了一个白发苍苍的老人。当他把历法献给祖乙时，国君深受感动，便将这部历法以万年的名字命名，定名为《万年历》，并封万年为“日月寿星”。

自此之后，人们为了纪念德高望重的万年，在过年时都要在家里挂上万年的画像，也叫作“寿星图”。

2. 送灶神

灶神俗称“灶王爷”，全名是“东厨司命九灵元王定福神君”。在中国不同的地方又被叫作“灶王”“灶君”“灶君公”“灶公灶母”“司命真君”“九天东厨烟主”“护宅天尊”等。灶神是中国古代传说中掌管百姓饮食的神灵，也是厨房之神。

○灶神

灶神的说法起源很早，商朝时民间已经在供奉灶神了。《礼记·祭法》中已经提到了西周的国君为百姓设立了七个祭祀神灵的地方，其中有一个便是祭祀灶神的。而且根据等级的不同规定了人们可以祭祀的神灵数量，地位越高，祭祀的神灵就越多，而对于普通百姓来说，他们只需要祭祀一个神灵，那便是灶神。

中国传统文化认为，衣食住行是百姓生活的基本需要，因此作为掌管百姓饮食的神灵，灶神在百姓生活中的地位十分重要。早在秦汉时期，灶神就已经被列为最主要的五种需要祭祀的神灵之一，灶神和门神、井神、厕神、中溜神共同负责家家户户的平安。

然而，灶神之所以为人们所敬重，不仅因其掌管人们的饮食、赐予人们生活便利，也是玉皇大帝派遣到凡间督察善恶的神灵。他的职责是监督人们的言行举止，在一年将尽的时候上天向玉皇大帝禀报每家人一年来的所作所为。相传，灶神的左右侍奉着两个神灵，一位手捧“善罐”，另一位则捧着“恶罐”。他们随时将每家人的善行恶举分别保存在这两个罐中，并在年终时向玉皇大帝报告。每年农历十二月廿四日就是灶神离开人间上天的日子，所以民间又把这一天称作“辞灶”，这一天家家户户都要“送灶神”。

关于灶神的来历，有这样一个传说。

古代有一户姓张的人家，他们是兄弟两人。哥哥是泥水匠，弟弟则是画师。哥哥最为拿手的活计是制作灶台，他做的灶台结实耐用，在周边一带非常出名，街坊邻居都夸他手艺高，尊称他为“张灶王”。他不仅制作灶台的手艺高，而且还有一个爱好，就是到别人家制作灶台的时候，无论遇到人家有什么纠纷他都爱管闲事，无论是婆媳吵架还是邻里争执他都能很好地调解，使双方都感到满意，因此左邻右舍有了矛盾都要找他调解，大家都很尊敬他。

张灶王 70 岁的时候去世了，他去世那天正好是农历腊月二十三日的深夜。张灶王一去世，张家就乱成了一锅粥。张灶王是一家之主，家里的大事小事都是由他决定的，现在他离开了人世，而弟弟只会作诗绘画，从未管过家事。这时，弟弟的妻子闹着分家，而弟弟手足无措，整日愁眉苦脸。一天，弟弟想到了一个好主意，在腊月二十三日哥哥张灶王去世一周年忌日的深夜，他把全家人都叫醒，告诉他们哥哥显灵了。他将全家人都叫到了厨房，在被油烟熏得黑漆漆的墙壁上若影若现的烛光中显现出了张灶王和他妻子的容貌，这时全家人都惊呆了。弟弟告诉家人说，他梦见哥哥和嫂子都已经变成了神仙，玉皇大帝封哥哥张灶王为“东厨司命九灵元王定福神君”。弟弟还说哥哥在梦中说，他的家人平时好吃懒做，不敬不孝，闹得家神不得安宁，而且现在还要闹分家。哥哥知道后很生气，准备上天禀告玉皇大帝，让玉皇大帝在大年三十的晚上下界惩罚他们。

家人听了这番话后都非常害怕，忙着对张灶王显灵的墙跪地磕头，并取来张灶王平时爱吃的甜食供上，恳求他饶恕家人的过错。从此以后，张灶王的家人再也不敢撒泼吵闹，全家人和和睦睦地平安相处，安宁度日。这件事也传到了街坊邻居们的耳朵里，他们知道后一传十、十传百，都悄悄到张家来一探究竟。其实，腊月二十三日那天晚上在墙壁上显灵的灶神，是弟弟事先画在上面的，他打算假借哥哥显灵来镇住家人，让他们不再争执，没想到这个办法非常灵验。然而当乡亲们向他打听的时候，他只能假戏真做，将画好的哥哥画像分送给邻居们。如此一来，家家户户都在厨房的墙上贴上了张灶王的画像，每年都在腊月二十三日晚上给张灶王上供，祈求合家平安。岁月流逝，渐渐形成了一种习俗，人们将张灶王亲切地叫作“灶王爷”。

周朝以后，周朝国君将祭祀灶王爷列入了宫廷的祭典之中，在全国立下了祭祀灶神的规矩，流传至今。

3. 三尸神

每到小年，除夕将近，百姓们都纷纷开始打扫房前屋后的卫生，清除积攒了一年的污垢尘土，这样的活动被叫作“扫尘”。

关于扫尘的习俗，据说源自这样一个传说：

古人认为，每个人的身上都附有一个叫作“三尸神”的神灵。他就像影子一般和每一个人形影不离，无论人们走到哪他都跟随在人们左右。与其他庇佑人们平安的神灵不同，三尸神是一个非常爱搬弄是非而且喜欢阿谀奉承的神。每到年终，他都会上天向玉皇大帝造谣生事，把人们的品性德行和人间风气描绘得丑陋不堪。时间一长，在玉皇大帝的印象里，人间就是一个肮脏不堪、充满罪恶暴戾的世界。

有一年年末，三尸神又向玉皇大帝谎报，人们在人间诅咒上天的神灵，正组织力量准备和天庭对抗。得知这个消息后，天庭震怒，玉皇上帝下旨要三尸神迅速下界查明人们犯上作乱的事情，凡是怨恨、亵渎神灵的人家，要三尸神将他们的罪行写在屋檐下面。为了不让人们提早得知天庭对他们的惩罚，还要让蜘蛛张网掩盖这些记号。他又命令王灵官在除夕之夜下界，凡是遇到留有记号的人家便一个不留，满门抄斩。三尸神见这个计谋可以得逞，兴冲冲地飞到人间，不论是非对错，他在每家人的屋檐下都做了记号，希望玉皇大帝将人间的百姓都赶尽杀绝。

正当三尸神认为计谋即将得逞的时候，有一户人家的灶王爷发现了三尸神的企图。他大惊失色，随即召集来各家的灶王爷，商量如何对付三尸神的计谋。经过一番商议，灶王爷们想出了一个好办法。他们托梦告诉百姓们，等到十二月二十三日灶王爷上天之后，大家都必须清扫家中尘土，掸去墙角屋檐下的蜘蛛网，擦拭门窗桌椅，要把家里打扫得干干净净，否则灶王爷就不回到这户人家中。出于对灶王爷的敬仰和爱戴，大家都把自家的宅院都打扫得干干净净。等到王灵官奉旨下界惩罚人们的时候，发现根本找不到三尸神所留下的记号。他看到的只是家家户户窗明几净、灯火通明，人们欢声笑语、祥和无比，三尸神的诡计也就不攻自破了。王灵官十分纳闷，只好无功而返。等到回到了天界，王灵官将他在凡间的所见所闻都一一禀报给玉皇大帝，玉帝这才得知其实人间祥和安定，百姓们安分守己。玉皇大帝大为震怒，下令将三尸神掌嘴三百，囚禁在天牢永不见天日。由于这次劫难多亏了灶王爷的及时发现和搭救，人们为了感激灶王爷，每年在灶王爷上天后都热火朝天地打扫家里的卫生，好让灶王爷回家后能干干净净地住下来。

4. 除夕与守岁

除夕指的是一年之中最后一天的晚上。因为除夕是在农历十二月三十日（个别年份，一年最后一天是十二月二十九日），因此那天又被称作“年三十”。除夕是春节整个节日过程中最为重要的一天。那天晚上，人们往往通宵都不睡觉，家人亲戚们聚在一起，在欢笑声中熬到新的一年太阳升起之后，因此又被称作“守岁”。

守岁的习俗在中国最早见于南北朝时期。相传在除夕那天，人们都要点起油灯、蜡烛通宵守夜，烛光从旧的一年一直燃烧到新的一年，象征着上一年的瘟邪病疫由于畏惧光亮而被困在了过去一年里，无法在新的一年中危害百姓。这一习俗，表现了老百姓在新的一年里对新气象的期待与渴望。

在中国民间，流传着关于除夕和守岁的这样一个传说：

在远古的洪荒时代，深山密林里生活着一种名叫“夕”的怪兽。夕相貌狰狞、生性凶残，平时都躲在深山之中。每年到了大年三十这天晚上，夕便跑出深山，到村寨中吞食牲畜，伤害人命。天亮之后又躲回山林，直到第二年的大年三十才会再次出现。因此，每到大年三十这一天，百姓都要收拾行装，扶老携幼逃往他处以躲避夕的伤害，直到第二天鸡鸣破晓才敢返回村庄。

○传说中的怪兽“夕”

有一年，又到了大年三十，百姓们都在收拾细软、牵牛赶羊、关门锁窗，准备出逃躲避夕，村中到处人马嘶鸣，一片忙乱恐慌的景象。就在乡亲们准备逃离村子的时候，从村外走进来一个十一二岁的小孩，长得白白嫩嫩、漂亮可人。小孩遇到老婆婆就问，大家为什么如此惊慌。老婆婆无奈地告诉小孩，夕又要来作乱了，并劝那个小孩跟他们一起出去躲避夕。小孩听完老婆婆的话后笑着说，夕没有什么可怕，只要让他在老婆婆家待一晚上，就一定能把夕赶跑。老婆婆看小孩虽然年纪不大，但是气宇轩昂，可她仍然不能相信小孩子能有这么大的本事把夕赶跑。老婆婆依然劝小孩跟他们一起出逃，小孩笑而不语。无奈之下老婆婆只好让小孩留在她家中，自己避难去了。老婆婆走后，小孩便开始装扮老婆婆的屋子，他在门口贴上大红纸，在门前生了一堆火并准备了大堆竹子，之后小孩便点亮了屋子里的所有蜡烛、油灯，身披红袍等着夕的到来。

半夜时分，夕闯进了村子，发现村子里有与以往不同的气氛。村中老婆婆家门口红通通的，屋内灯火通明。夕看到之后浑身颤抖，怪叫一声便向老婆婆家扑去。接近门口的时候，门前传来了噼噼啪啪的爆响声。夕停住了脚，犹豫不前。这时，小孩身披红袍从屋内冲了出来，将一根根点燃的竹子向夕扔去。夕怪叫一声落荒而逃。自此，夕再也不敢到村庄里面来为非作歹，原来夕最怕红色、爆响声和火光了。

第二天，人们回到村中发现小孩安然无恙，都觉得很诧异。这时，小孩在乡亲们面前幻化成一缕青烟缓缓向天上飘去。天上传来了小孩的声音，说他本是天界紫微星，因为看到乡亲们年年为夕所伤害，决心帮助乡亲们赶走夕，因此变做小孩来到凡间。乡亲们才恍然大悟，看到老婆婆家门上贴着红纸，门口火堆里没有燃尽的竹子依然在噼啪作响，屋内油灯还发着微弱的余光，乡亲们便明白了用这些办法便可以赶走夕。这件事一传十、十传百，很快在周围的村子里传开了，人们都知道了驱赶夕的办法。因此，每到大年三十，家家户户都要在自家的门上贴上红纸，燃烧竹子并穿上红艳艳的新衣服，到了第二天还要出门向亲戚朋友互相道贺，庆祝他们没有被夕伤害。由于

○放爆竹成为了春节的重要习俗

小孩是在大年三十的晚上除掉了夕，此后人们便将大年三十晚上称作“除夕”。

虽然夕被赶走了，但是乡亲们担心有一天夕会卷土重来。到了大年三十晚上，人们虽然不再出门躲避夕，但是家家户户仍然早早地做好晚饭，熄火净灶，把牛羊拴好，天不黑就将自家的大门紧紧关闭，躲在家里吃年夜饭，并在夕出没的那个时辰在院子中点燃竹子。这天晚上，乡亲们也不敢睡觉，都围坐在一起闲聊，一直等到天亮，直到第二天鸡叫之后才高高兴兴地打开大门。

守岁的习俗一直流传至今。如今竹子变成了鞭炮，亲戚朋友之间的互相道贺也被人们叫作“拜年”，但是紫微星赶跑夕的故事仍然在民间流传。

5. 春联

春天是一个万象更新的季节，而庆祝春天到来的节日——春节，也象征着百姓在新年里有新的开始。春节到来的时候，老百姓们都要将家中的物件清洗置换一新，贴上新的春联和门神画像就是新年里一项重要的活动。

春联的种类较多，依其使用场所，可分为门心、框对、横批、春条、斗斤等。其中，门心贴于门板上端中心部位；框对贴于左右两个门框上；横批贴于门楣的横木上；春条根据不同的内容，贴于相应地方；斗斤也叫“门叶”，为正方菱形，多贴在家具、影壁中。每副春联都有横批。春节普天同庆，各家各户除了门口要贴春联外，猪舍、鸡鸭舍等处也要贴对联，寓意六畜兴旺，内容一般为“鸡鸭满圈，牛羊成群，六畜兴旺”等。院子里的大树需贴上“树大根深”，院子里的墙面需贴上“春光明媚”，家里靠炕的墙上需贴上“幸福健康”，厨房里需贴上“勤俭节约”等，到处都是红红的春联。

春联以工整、对偶、简洁、精巧的文字描绘春节，抒发美好愿望，是中国特有的文学形式。

在世界纪录协会所收录世界最早的春联中，唐代刘丘子于开元十一年(723)所撰的“三阳始布，四序初开”，可以说是中国的第一副春联。

春联，起源于桃符（悬挂在大门两旁的长方形桃木板），直到宋代，春联仍称“桃符”。每到除夕之日，家家户户挂桃符，在桃木板上写对联。

○春联

关于桃符，在专门记录中国古代神话的《山海经》里，讲述了这样的故事：

很久以前，在东海风景秀丽的度朔山上，生长着一片桃林。其中有一棵桃树巨大无比，树根虬结有劲，枝繁叶茂。它的枝叶覆盖了三千里地域，传说只要人们吃了这棵桃树上结的桃子便能成为神仙。这棵桃树树根下有一个洞，那是通往鬼蜮的大门，门口由神荼和郁垒两个神灵守护。每晚鬼魂们就从这个门里走出来，到外面游荡。树枝上栖息着一只金鸡，每当天空渐白，金鸡长鸣，在外游荡的鬼魂必须赶回来。这时神荼和郁垒便在门口检查鬼魂们在晚上出去游荡时有没有做伤天害理的事情，如果被发现有，神荼和郁垒便将其捉起来，用芒苇做的绳子捆好送去喂虎，因此天下的鬼魂都害怕神荼、郁垒。而老百姓为了防止鬼魂混进家伤害自己，便用桃木刻成神荼、郁垒的模样挂在自家门口，以驱赶鬼魂。后来人们直接在桃木板上写上神荼和郁垒的名字，认为这样同样可以镇邪去恶，而桃木板也就被人们称为“桃符”了。

宋代以后，随着门神和象征喜气吉祥的红纸的出现，桃木板渐渐退出历史舞台，改为“春贴纸”和“春联”。

“春联”一词的出现，是在明代初年，春节贴春联的民俗也在明代开始盛行。

明朝开国皇帝朱元璋（1328—1398）酷爱对联，不仅自己挥毫书写，还常常鼓励臣子书写。他在定都金陵（现在的南京）以后，命令大臣、官员和一般老百姓在除夕前都必须书写一副对联贴在门上。春节期间，他喜欢穿便装出巡，挨家挨户欣赏对联取乐。当时的文人也把题联作对当成文雅的乐事，写春联一时成为社会风尚。

关于春联的得名和推广，是朱元璋采取行政命令的办法颁布御旨才得以在家家户户推广开来的。

有一年除夕前，他颁布御旨，要求金陵家家户户都要用红纸写成春联贴在门框上，来迎接新春。大年初一早晨，朱元璋微服巡视，挨家挨户察看春联。每当见到写得好的春联，他就非常高兴，赞不绝口。在巡视时见到一家没有贴春联，他很是生气，就询问原因。侍从回答说：“这是一家从事杀猪和劁猪营生的师傅，过年特别忙，还没有来得及请人书写。”朱元璋就命人拿来笔墨纸砚，为这家书写了一副春联：“双手劈开生死路，一刀割断是非根。”写完后就继续巡视。过了一段时间，朱元璋巡视完毕返回宫廷时，又路过这里，见到这个屠户家还没有贴上他写的春联，就问是怎么回事。这家主人很恭敬地回答道：“这副春联是皇上亲自书写的，我们高悬在中堂，每天要焚香供奉。”朱元璋听了非常高兴，就命令侍从赏给这家三十两银子。

作为春联的一部分，家家户户在屋门、墙壁、门楣贴上大大小小的“福”字，也是中国民间由来已久的风俗。关于“福”字，过去多指福气、福运，现在则解释为“幸福”，寄托了人们对幸福生活的向往，也是对美好未来的祝愿。在民间，人们为了更充分地体现这种向往和祝愿，干脆将“福”字倒过来贴，表示“幸福已到”“福气已到”，因为汉语中“倒”与“到”同一个音。

○“福”字意味着幸福、安康

不过，据说这也与明朝的一个故事有关。明太祖朱元璋当年用“福”字作暗记准备杀人。好心的马皇后为消除这场灾祸，令全城大小人家必须在天明之前在自家门上贴上一个“福”字。马皇后的旨意没人敢违抗，于是家家门上都贴上了“福”字。但是有户人家不识字，竟把“福”字贴倒了。第二天，皇帝派人上街查看，发现家家都贴了“福”字，其中有一家把“福”字贴倒了。皇帝听了禀报后大怒，立即命令御林军把那家满门抄斩。马皇后一看事情不好，忙对朱元璋说：“那家人知道您今日来访，故意把‘福’字贴倒了，这不是‘福到’的意思吗？”皇帝一听有道理，便下令放人，一场大祸终于消除了。从此人们便将“福”字倒贴起来，一求吉利，二为纪念仁慈的马皇后。

“福”字除了单独成字张贴外，还被精做成各种图案，如寿星、寿桃、鲤鱼跳龙门、五谷丰登、龙凤呈祥等。

6. 门神

贴门神的习惯也是伴随着桃符生成的。据《淮南子》说，这种“桃符是用一寸宽、七八寸长的桃木做的；在桃木板上写上神荼、郁垒二神的名字，悬挂在门两旁，或者画上这两个神像——左神荼、右郁垒。

大门上贴门神，目的是让一切妖魔鬼怪都望而生畏，不敢进到家里来。门神一般是善于捉鬼的人物，如天师钟馗等。他们相貌凶恶，怒目圆睁，手持各种法器，随时准备捉住敢于上门的鬼魂。唐朝以后，除了以往的神荼、郁垒二将外，门神的形象逐渐演变为秦叔宝和尉迟敬德两位唐朝开国大将。

相传，玄武门之变后，唐太宗李世民大肆屠杀李建成与李元吉的家人，上至白发苍苍的老人，下至没满周岁的婴儿，一个都没有放过。虽然李世民顺利坐上了皇位，但是被他杀害的冤魂常常夜里来搅扰，他晚上睡觉时经常听到卧房外有冤魂呼喊、抛砖扔瓦的声音。他夜夜做噩梦，梦到他的哥哥、弟弟向他索命。李世民心中十分害怕，彻夜难眠，弄得后宫不得安宁。李世民将这些异状告诉了大臣们，这时将军秦叔宝走上前，说自己一生杀人无数，被他杀的人尸体堆积如山，从来不怕这些小鬼，他愿意和尉迟敬德在夜晚身着戎装侍奉在李世民左右。鬼魂果然惧怕两位大将，不敢再来搅扰，李世民得以安心入睡。然而时间一长，两位大将夜不能寐最终病倒了，李世民也觉得让他二人整夜守候在他左右也十分辛苦，于是命令画工将他二人戎装怒发、手持兵刃的形象画下来，悬挂在两扇宫门上，用来震慑妖魔鬼怪。

自此，春节时在大门贴上秦叔宝和尉迟敬德的画像便在民间逐渐演变为广为流传的习俗。

○贴门神

Chapter One

The Origin and Legends of Chinese New Year

Chinese New Year is the first festival in lunar calendar. Chinese folks habitually referred to NewYear as "Guo Nian(Spending the year)".

It is generally accepted that Chinese New Year originated in the Yao and Shun period. In order to pay respect to the gods who granted people a smooth farming harvest, theyoffered the best of harvest to sacrifice to the gods at the time whenfour seasons completed a cycle and a new cycle was about to begin. At the same time, people enjoyed a variety of carnival entertainment to celebrate the harvest. These primitive practices gradually developed into a set of custom or tradition through such a long history of 4000 years. Chinese traditional culture has been handed down in the celebration of the Spring Festival. And more importantly, social cultural characteristics of different times are also revealed in the process of Chinese New Year. Andfuture generations could explore more from close inspection.

1. The Origin of the New Year

Cycling is the basic meaning of the Spring Festival. Chinese ancestors understood gradually in the long-term labor that the growth of the crops in four seasons is relevant to the movement of the celestial bodies. Therefore, the Spring Festival,or New Year, is regarded as a record of time cycle.

It has been given different names in different dynasties in China. Erh Ya(ancient book containing commentaries on classics, names, etc)-Shi Tian(interpret the sky)recorded that Chinese New Year was called "Sui""in the Xia Dynasty, "Si" in the Shang Dynasty, "Nian" in the Zhou Dynasty and "Zai" in the Yao and Shun Period. In this sense, New Year as a new term has emerged since the Xia and Shang Dynasties (2070 BC~1046 BC). But the original meaning of "New Year" was not referred to as time but connected with agricultural production. In ancient times, the growth cycle of crops finished in about one

Chinese paper-cut for the Spring festival

year, so "New Year" always carries the connotation of harvest. And in agricultural era,a year is often determined by a cycle of grain planting and reaping. The close connectioncouldthusbe revealed to the full length between Chinese New Yearand harvest .

China was a traditional agricultural country. No any other industries than agriculture could have such greater influence upon social life. It can be said that all aspects of traditional culture were closely related with farming. A full cycle of crop growth corresponds toa cycle of seasons.From the long-term agricultural farming practiceour forefathers came to form a rational understanding about the change of seasons, a climate shift and the growth of the crops. Through observationthey found out the fundamental relationship between alternating seasons, celestial runs and growth of crops. On this basis they summed up a set of method measuring and calculating time. And they recorded year, month and day in use of the Heavenly Stems and Earthly Branches Methodology till they eventually made a calendar and settled down the framing seasons.

However, ancient Chinese calendar was changing all the time with the changes of dynasties. The emperor who took the throne changed the order of the month at his will to prove the divinity of his given right. The first month changed was always known as "the first month of the Lunar Year", and the other eleven followed in a certain sequence. In Chinese history, Xia Dynasty used the first month of the spring (Meng) as the beginning of the year. Shang Dynasty used the last month of winter (the twelfth lunar month) as the first month while Qin Dynasty employed the first month of the winter as the first month of the year. Han Dynasty followed Qin's calendar. As the calendar did not fit celestial laws well which governed the operation, Wu Di the Emperor of the Han dynasty ordered Gong Sunqing, Si Maqian, and Deng Ping to create a new calendar named Tai Chu.In this new calendar the first month of Chinese lunar calendar was set as the beginning month of a new year and twenty-four solar terms were included in it. Later dynasties all made some modification, but the rule that the spring was the beginning of year remained today. The Taichu calendar has been used up to 2000 years till the end of the Qing Dynasty. Chinese folk regardedthe Taichu calendar as "traditional Chinese lunar calendar".With the calendar fixed, people could arrange their farming production in time according to 24 solar terms. Four seasons in order constitutes a year with winter as the endingand spring as the beginning. The transitional days from the old year to a new year are so-called "Chinese New Year" or "the Spring Festival". Spending the festival happily has been a traditional custom.

1.1 Hunting and sacrifice at the end of a year

Besides "Barns of Ripe Grains", Hunting and sacrifice was another event related to the origin of Chinese New Year.

In ancient China, people didn't know much about the law of nature and didn't know how to take advantage of it in their farming work. Productivity wasso low that people had to turn to god and other supernatural forces for help. They prayed to the god that god could bestow a bumper harvest to them. Therefore, after finishing theirfarming, or on the transitional days from the old year and the new year, men went into the wild to hunt all kinds of beasts. The hunted animals could be cooked as supplementary food and meanwhile they were made rich food along with best crops as sacrifice to god and ancestors so that people could repay the gift given by gods. They prayed to the gods that they would continue to allow people to enjoy the grace ofa big harvest, peace of family and good fortune in the coming year. And this practice was known as the December Festival or Hunting Festival.

December Festival first started in the Zhou Dynasty (mid-11th century BC - 256 BC). Generally, it was a grand sacrifice offering event which took place in the end of a year. In the Eastern Han Dynasty, December was the best month for hunting as it was hardest time for these wild animals to take moves. Preys were easier to kill and were offered at last to worship gods and ancestors. For this reason December, the twelfth lunar month, is also known as "the month for hunting".The grand occasion of December Festival could be seen in an interesting dialogue inRites Miscellanies last part. Confucius' student Zigong watched the December festival in person and Confucius asked him, "Are you excited at the sight?"Zigong replied, "Sir, the whole nation has got crazy."

Hunting and sacrifice

The time flied and massive hunting sports in the last month gradually stepped out of the stage of history. But people are still accustomed to regard the pickled pork in the "La" month (hunting month) as "La meat" (the meat from hunted animals). The ceremony of god and ancestors worship has been kept till today. Regardless of courtiers or civilian, each family held a year-end sacrifice with the biggest scale and the most complicated rules. The sacrifice gradually evolved intothe Spring Festival.

2. Legends of Chinese New Year

No any other festival in China could be so important like Chinese New Year. Chinesepredecessors had left a lot historical literature to record it. In the folk culture, there are so many legends which are interesting and colorful, enriching the cultural connotation of the Chinese New Year.

These stories provide some divine and exaggerated descriptions about the originality of Chinese New Year. At the same time,vivid and interesting explanations for all the activities during the festival are also given out in details.Easy-to-understandlegends and myths constitute a part of the Spring Festival activities. EverySpring Festival, family elders will be telling stories to the curious and naive children about the "beast of Nian(Year)", the story of the "kitchen god". The legends of the Spring Festival arepassed down through generations in such a way and will be deeply rooted in their memory.

2.1 Perpetual Calendar

According to the legend, Perpetual Calendar is the oldest solar calendar. It is said that the editor was a young man named Wan Nian (in English: Perpetual). In order to commemorate his achievements, people named the calendar after his name.

Legend says inShang Dynasty, people don't know how to time day and night due to calendar confusion.A woodcutter named Wan Nian (Perpetual) wanted to make a calendar in which seasons will be set accurately. Although hethought long and hard, he had not a method of computation. One day, Wan Nian(Perpetual) went into the mountains to cut firewood. Feelingtired, he sat under atreeto rest. He blankly looked at the shadows but he was still thinking about how to give the accurate record of time. An hour went by slowly, and the sun

Perpetual Calendar, an encyclopedia in ancient China

moved slowly from east to west, While Wan Nian still sat thinking of something. Suddenly, Wan Nian (Perpetual)found the shadows of the trees were no longer where they were and a lot longer than it was an hour before. Wan Nian (Perpetual) had a brainwave at that time---whynot use the movement and the length change of the shadowto calculate the time? Wan Nian(Perpetual) got a disc immediately after he went home, engraving it with24 subareas.Wan Nian(Perpetual) set a thick and long needle in the center of the disk. He put the disc in the sun and employed the position of the needle's shadow casted to denote hours one single day. That disc was latercalled a "sundial". Though it worked very well during the day, it failed at night or on cloudy days. Wan Nian(Perpetual) also found this shortcoming himself.

Another day, Wan Nian(Perpetual) was drinking water from a spring in the hillside when he saw and heard water drops dripping down one after another from the cliff. The rhythmical dripping sound impressed Wan Nian so much and thus inspiredhim to make new timing equipment. After he returned home, Wan Nian(Perpetual) made a five-leveldrip vessel or clepsydra which could keep up with time by a leaking. In this way,people can track the time accurately no matter what kind of weather they came across. With the sundial and clepsydra timing tools, observingtime andseasons became far more convenient for Wan Nian(Perpetual), and he worked on it more carefully than ever. After a long observation of a few years, Wan Nian(Perpetual) eventuallyfound that the daytime of same length would always appear around every 360more days and the new four seasons would come along after the same term. Discoveries made through moon watch revealedthat the moon wanes approximatelyeverythirtydays.Wan Nian(Perpetual)concluded that if the secret of time and other natural phenomena came to be revealed, we should first understand the run of the sun and the moon.

Then there was a monarch named by Zu Yi. He was always distressed by the fact thathis people delayed the agricultural time for not knowing the rule of the seasons. In order to curry favor with the monarch, a senior Minister named E Heng suggestedthe monarch shouldvisit the Temple of Heaven to do a ritual in honor of the gods. Zu Yi followed his ideas and then led officials of all ranks and prayed, but the ritual was done in vain. Having heard of these, Wan Nian(Perpetual) took the sundial and clepsydra to visit the King. After hearing detailed explanations, the King was convinced. Wan Nian stayed to go on with his research and observations. The monarch built hima sun-and-moon pavilion, a sundial pedestal and a clepsydra pavilion before the Heaven of Temple. He even sent twelve lads at the service of Wan Nian(Perpetual), who was instructed to concentrate on seasonal research and to measure accurately the cycles of the sun and moon in order to ensure accurate measurement of morning and evening. The king expected him to find out the rule of calendar for the sake of all people. One day, E Hengwas sent to the Temple of Heaven to seeinto the progress.When E Hengcame to the Temple of Heaven, he saw a poem on the rock wall which says:

The Sunrise and sunsetcirculates every 360days, which repeats from the light to the dark; plants bloom and then die through four seasons, there are 12 full moons in a year.

Realizing how important the preliminary data Wan Nian(Perpetual) made are, E Heng was rather disturbed.E Heng worried that he would lose the king's trust and favor when Wan Nian(Perpetual)mightone day make an accurate calendar and be ranked higher. Fear that Wan Nian's achievement of (Perpetual)might threaten him, E Heng spent a large amount of money hiring an assassin to kill his target. Wang Nian knew nothing about the murder but absorbed in his research in the pavilion as if he had forgotten everything except his work. The killer had to carry a long weapon and threw it with a great force at him from a long distance. An arrow pierced into Wan Nian(Perpetual)'s arm. The young lads who was at service detected the assassin and shouted loudly to warn the guards. The killer was captured finally andwas taken to Zu Yi. Now everything had been brought to light and Zu Yi put E Heng in jail. He paid a visit to Wan Nian(Perpetual) in person, who reported his latest discovery to Zu Yi. Here is what he said.

"Now the Star Sheen overtook the Star silkworm. All the stars restore into where they were. The old cycle will come to an end and 12 months has gone at the turning point of this night. Your Majesty should give it a name". ZuYi said, "thespring is the beginning of the year, then I declare it the Spring Festival."Considering that Wan Nian worked day in night and his wound was still severe, Zu Yi felt so pitiful that he invited Wan Nian to nurture in his palace for a while. But Wan Nian declined with a reasonable explanation that the calendar made on the basis of the sun is not precise enough. He must stay in his workshop until all the problems solved and an accurate calendar was born. Decades later, the calendar had been finished and Wan Nian became white-headed. When he dedicated his work to the King, the King was greatly moved that he named the calendar after Wan Nian (English: Perpetual) and entitled him sun and moon god of longevity.

Since then, in honor of virtuous Wan Nian, every family hangs his picture at the Spring Festival.

2.2 Sending the Kitchen God off

The Kitchen God is commonly known as "the Kitchen Lord", and his full name is "DingFu the Emperor". In some other places he is also worshiped as the king of stove, lord of the stove, lord of smoke and yard-guard god, etc. In ancient Chinese legend, The Kitchen God is the spirit in charge of the diet of mortal people.

The Kitchen God was worshipped early and the Shang Dynasty saw the folk pay their respect to the god. The book Ritesrecords that the monarch of Western Zhou Dynasty set up seven sacrifice and trial places, in which one was established for the Kitchen God worship. At that time, the number of God you can worship depends on your social status. The

Kitchen God

higher ranked officials can have more God to worship. While the commons needed to offer their respect only to one God---the Kitchen God.

The earliest description of the God was found in Zhuang Zi•Da Sheng that the God wore a bun on his head. In the Tang Dynasty, we had a more specific and detailed statement about him. A man named XuanYing the Taoist priest gave such a picture. The Kitchen God was wearing fiery red clothes, so pretty as a young beauty.After the Wei and Jin Dynasty, kitchen god gothis own name. Du Yuqing of the Sui Dynastyquoted The Stove Bookin his A Treasury of Jade Candle that the God's family name was Su and his full name was Su Jili. While in the Tang, Duan Chengshi claimed in his book You Yang Za Cu•Nuo Gao that the Kitchen God was named Zhang Dan or Zhang Huai.

Kitchen God or King of Stove

Chinese traditional culture laid stress on the basic necessities such as clothes and food. The Kitchen God thus plays an important role in people's life as a god in charge of food. As early as in Qin and Han dynasties, the God was among the most important five gods, and the rest four were Well God, Door God, Toilet God and Zhong Liu God. They were together to guard people's safety and peace of family.

Besides the factor mentioned above, the Kitchen God was awed by all not only because of his duty over people's diet but also due to the fact that he was sent by the Jade Emperor to supervise man's evil deeds. He recorded what people had done this year and reported all to the Emperor at the end of the year. It is said that there were two gods accompanying the Kitchen God, one holding a tank which contains good deeds while the other holding a tank for evil things. The Kitchen God would bring all his records to the Heaven when he left the earth on December 24, which later was settled down as the day for human being to bid farewell to the Kitchen God. And every family surely needed to hold a respectful ritual to send the Kitchen God off.

Here is a legend of the God's origin.

Once upon a time, there were two brothers in a family. The elder brother was a plasterer while the younger brother served as a painter. The elder Brother was adept in making stoves. The stoves he had made always were of good use in a long time, so he came to be known as "king of the stove" by neighbors. Besides his splendid hearth-making skills, he also developed an interesting hobby-- he loved to settle all kinds of disputes whether between a woman and her mother-in-law or involved neighborhood. His mediation was effective and usually satisfactory to every side so that he was asked to intervene in more problems when people cannot settle them down by their own. Gradually, the elder brother had gained his reputation as a good mediator and well respected by the community.

The elder brother died at the age of 70 on that day that happened to be the lunar month, 23. His death caused a disorder as the family lost its head. The younger brother only knew painting and writing. His wife asked for a partition and wanted to move out of the big family with the share of their property. The younger brother felt unhappy and gathered his brows into a frown all day. Suddenly, a good idea struck him. On the night of his brother's one-year anniversary, he woke up every family member and told them that his brother would make his presence. He brought them to the Kitchen. On the black oily walls appeared the faces of the elder brother and his wife's under a flickering light. Everyone froze with a shock. At this time the younger brother told that he had a dream in which his brother and his sister-in-law had been among immortals. The Jade Emperor entitled him as "Ding Fu the Emperor". The brother warned his family that they did nothing but ate a lot and showed no piety to the god and the seniors. And now they were bold enough to argue and break up. The brother was in such anger that he would report their deeds to the Emperor to punish them severely on the day of 30th this month when the Emperor descended into the world of man.

The Family listened to the words and was afraid. They knelt down to kowtow and some hurried to offer the sweet food the brother usually loved eating to beg his forgiveness. Since then, scream and quarrel never had been heard again and the whole family restored to their previous peace. The neighbors heard of the story and retold it to each other. They paid a secret visit to the younger brother to find out what was going on. As a matter of fact, the figure looming on the wall that night was a picture that the brother had painted. He intended to use it and a story to cease all the disputes in his family. Now the villager asked for his brother' pictures, and he had to give them some. In this way, every household plastered the portrait of the elder brother on theirkitchen walls. They offered delicious food

Paying respect to Kitchen God or King of Stove

as sacrifice and prayed a happy new year. Years passed and the custom came into being. People worshipped "theKing of Stove" as "the Kitchen God"

From the Zhou Dynasty, the sacrifice to the Kitchen God had been a court ritual and the rule to make a sacrifice to the Kitchen God began then.

2.3 The Evil Spirit

When the "Small Year" near New Year's Eve is approaching, people start cleaning their houses to remove yearly dirt and dust, and this is called "dust sweeping".

The custom of sweepingis said to start from such a legend.

The ancient people believe that each person was possessed by a spirit named San Shi. The spirit acted asan inseparable-shadow wherever peoplego. Unlike the other virtuous spirits or gods, the spirit liked to stir up trouble and was good at flattery. At the end of the year, theywouldgo to the Jade Emperor to spread rumors, portraying the moral of the world as the ugliest. His descriptions cast a shadow over the Jade Emperor that he considered the world of the human to be a filthy one full of crime and violence.

At the end of one year, the evil Spirit lied to the Jade Emperor again that mankind was cursing the Gods and organizing a confrontation against the Gods. When the Jade Emperor heard the news, his thunder-like fury was kindled. He decreed that the Spirit identified as soon as possible those people who were to be rebellious against him. These who harbored resentment and profane to the heaven shall be noted down under their eaves. In order to keep people remain unaware of the punishment, spiders' network was used to cover up these marks. The Jade Emperor also ordered the Chief General in heav-

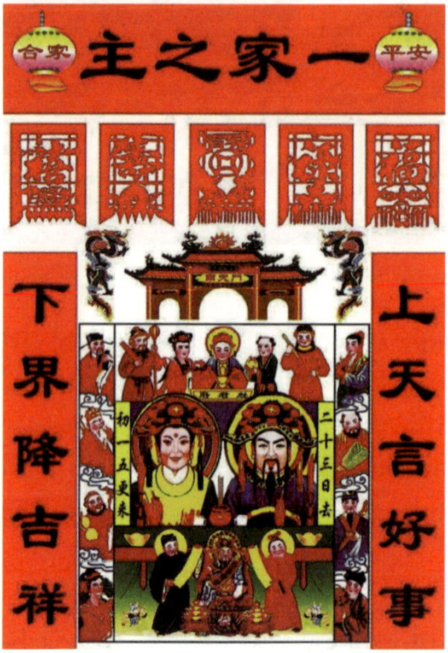

The kitchen God Who Will Guard family's safety

ento descend to the man's world on New Year's Eve and execute the whole family of every marked household. The spirit was so excited to see his trickery work. He flew to the earth to mark every household regardless of theirright doings or wrong doings.The only thing he wanted is that the man would be eradicated from the world.

When the Spiritgloated over his oncoming success, one Kitchen God found outhis plot. This Kitchen God was so shocked that he immediately summoned the other Kitchens to discuss how to deal with the tricks. After a deliberation, the Kitchensagreed on an idea. They appeared in people's dreams and requested people to do a thorough cleaning of their houses on the day of 23rd of last Moon of the lunar calendar, when they were to leave for the heaven. People were told to sweep all the dust in the house, brush off all the spider's nets under the eaves and clean all the tables and windows. If they kept everything dirty, the Kitchen God would never come back to their house. Out of affections for the Kitchen, people cleaned up their houses carefully. When the Chief General in Heaven went down to the man's world, the marks that ought to be left by the evil spirit were gone. The Chief General just saw nothing but a tidy, illumining and harmonious world with joy and laughter. He returned to the Heaven with confusion. He reported what he had seen and heard down there to the Emperor. Till then the Emperor realized that he had been fooled by the evil spirit. As a result of the Emperor's wrath, the Spirit was sentenced hundreds of slaps and life in prison. In order to thank timely rescue from the Kitchen Gods, and more importantly, to invite the god to live in a new and cleaner environment, people were always occupied with housing sweeping and cleaning when the god parted.

2.4 New Year's Eve and Staying up Late

New Year's Eve refers tothe night of the last day of a year. As the result, the day was called "Nian San Shi" according to Chinese convention. (it means the last day of twelfth lunar month for a year, most of them fall on the 30thday of lunar December and very few on the 29th.) New Year's Eve is the most important day of the Spring Festival. People usually do not sleep and family members gather together to stay up all night in laughter till the sun risestomorrow. This is also known as staying up all night.

This custom in China was first observed in the Northern and Southern Dynasties. According to the legend, on New Year's Eve, peoplelit oil lamps and candles all night to keep wake. The light of the candle illuminating over night symbolizes that the plague and evil epidemic in the previous year were trapped in the past so that they could not annoy people in the coming year. People's expectations and desire for a new life can be revealed in the custom.

The story below related to the custom spread far and wide among the folks.

In prehistoric and chaotic times, there lived a monster called Xi in the mountain forests.Xi lookedbeastly and he was ferocious. He was usually hid in the mountains and only emerged to prey on livestock and people on New Year's Eve. When the day broke, he vanished in the forests again until his reappearance next New Year's Eve. Therefore, on New Year's Eve, to escape from his mischief,young and old villagers would pack up and leave the town. They would not return until they heard the cocks crowed the daybreak.

Another New Year's Eve was coming. The folks gathered their valuable belongings, livestock and got ready to leave and it was full of chaos and panic. When they were about to go away in a hurry, a child aged 11 or 12 came inthe village. The kid was good-looking. He asked an old womanwhy this village was alarmed so much. The old woman told the kid helplessly that the villagers had to escape from the harmful Monster Xi. The lady advised the kid to go with them immediately. The kid refused with a smile and said, "There's nothing to fear about Xi. Let me stay for a night and I will get rid of it out

Legendary Monster Xi

here."Though the kid talked in a composing way, but the old woman cannot believe that such a boy could drive a beastly monster like Xi. She attempted to persuade the kid to flee with her, but she failed. She had to leave the kid alone in her house and then ran away. After the old woman was gone, the kid began to decorateher house by plastering red paper on the door and setting up a fire at the door gate.He also prepared piles of bamboo.With these things done, the kid dressed himself in a red gown and lit up all the candlesand lamps, awaiting the arrival of Monster Xi.

In the middle night, Xi broke into the village and found that the village this year had something different. He noticed thatthe old lady's house was brightly lit up. Xi trembled before that sight and made a charge with aweird shriek. As Xi drew close,there came out the sound ofexplosive crackling. Xi stopped and hesitated. The kid in the red gown came out at the moment. He picked up the fire-red crackling bamboos and tossed them at Xi. With an odd cry, Xi ran away as fast as possible. Since then, Xi dared not to go into the village any longer. What scared the monster away was red color, flames and burn-

fireworks setting off

ing firecrackers.

The next day, the kid wasfound safe. Folks who returned to the village were surprised. The kid turned himself into a puff of smoke rising up to the sky. A voice was heard in the distance that he was Zi Wei Star in the Heaven. When he saw the villagers suffer from Monster Xi, he decided to drive him away. The villagers by far understood what had happened to them. They saw the red paper posted on the old lady's door, the burning bamboo still crackling in the fire and the lamp being lit inside the house, they knew how to do with the monster. The story spread far among the villagers. Hence, on New Year's Eve, every household needed to post red paper on the door, set off firecrackers and wear bright red clothes. The next morning congratulations would be exchanged among relatives and friends that people were still alive. The kid under the transformation of Zi Wei Star drove away the monster, so the night was named as "Chu Xi", in English, "New Year's Eve". Monster Xiwasdriven out of the villages butthe folks were stillworried that the monster would show up again. Although they needed not toleave their houses, people cooked the dinner ahead of usual time and locked all the cattles safe. They closed the door and had their dinner inside. They burned the bamboo in the yard where they thought the monster was likely to come along. On the whole, on the night, the villagers dared not to fell into sleep. They sat together chatting and waiting for dawn and kept their doors locked until the cocks crowed the daybreak.

This custom has been handed down through generations. At present the firecrackers has taken bamboo's place, and con-

Fireworks Playing, a Fundamental Custom for the Spring Festival

gratulation exchange became a part of New Year celebration; however, the story of driving away the monster never became less popular.

2.5 Spring Festival Couplets

All things take on a new form in spring. The Spring Festival celebration means for folks a new beginning of life. When Chinese New Year is on the way, people are busy with washing, cleaning and shopping. Pasting couplets and door god portraits are among these important New Year activities.

There are various kinds of Spring Festival Couplets. They

Couplets for Chinese Spring Festivals

can be grouped into Men Xin, Kuang Dui, Heng Pi, Chun Tiao and Dou Jin according to the places to which they were stuck. Men Xin, for example, usually means that the couplets are on the top center of the door; Kuang Dui refers to the couplets will be pasted on the door frame. Heng Pi is on the horizontal top bar of the door frame. Dou Jin, is also called "Men Ye", is a kind of diamond-shaped couplet, and is attached to the surface of the furniture and screen walls. Each pair of couplets will match witha horizontal scroll. Besides on the doors, Spring Festival Couplets also go to the piggery and poultry house. That conveys people's wishes for thriving of domestic animals.Generally, the contents are "Chickens and ducks fill, cattle and sheep flock, domestic animals thrive" and so on. Trees in the yard need to be pastedon "May it grow tall and deep-rooted", and the courtyard walls need to be labeled "beautiful spring". Even we can see the red couplets like "being happy and healthy" on the walls inside rooms and "saving is money-making" on the kitchen walls. Red color could be seen everywhere.

Couplet is a unique-styled form of Chinese literature. Chinese people express their good wishes in use of couplets, which are neat and dual, simple but ingenious.

Among the couplets collection by the World Record Association, there is one that says "The sun is rising and the world begins", written by LiuQiuzi in the Kai Yuan 11th, Tang Dynasty. And this one is considered to be the earliest couplet in Chinese history.

Spring Festival couplets areoriginated in the peach wood charms against evil at earlier times. (Rectangle peach wood suspendedat both sides of the gate).However, the couplets were still regarded as "peach wood charm" in the Song Dynasty. On every eve, Chinese people paster new charms written on peach wood on their door faces.

Mountains and Seas, a classic that records Chinese ancient myth, tells us a story about the peach wood charms.

Long time ago, there grew a group of peach trees in the scenic Du Suo Mountain along East China Sea. Among the trees there was a huge one, luxuriant and deep-rooted. And its branches and leaves extended as far as three thousand Li (ancient Chinesemeasurement of distance). It is said that mortals could become immortal if they could eat its peach. There hid a hole down the root, which served as an entrance to the ghost world. Two gods named Shen Tu and Yu Lei guarded the door. Every night the ghosts came out of the entrance to wander around. They had to go back when the golden rooster perched on the huge tree crowed at dawn. Two gods standing at the entrance checked out whether the ghosts had done something harmful during night. Once a ghost was found guilty, he would be tied up tightly with a reed rope by the two gods to feed the tiger.

All the ghosts are afraid of them for this reason. In order to prevent ghosts from entering their houses, folk people hanged on the door the peach wood with two gods' picture inscribed on it. Later, the names of the two ghost-catchers were engraved directly for the same purpose. This peach wood thus served as a kind of spell or charm to drive the ghosts.

After the Song Dynasty, along with the emergence of the Goalkeeper and auspicious red paper, peach wood gradually

Couplets Writing

stepped down from the history. And the name was changed correspondingly to "Spring Festival couplet" or "spring sticker".

'Spring Festival couplets' as a new phrase appeared in the early Ming Dynasty. The custom of couplet sticking also began to prevail at that time. Zhu Yuanzhang(A.D. 1328-1398), founder Emperor of the Ming Dynasty,was fond of the couplets. He not only could compose and write the couplets, but encouraged his ministers to do so. After he selected Jinling (now

Nanjing) as the capital city, he gave an order that all the ministers, officials and commons must paste a pair of couplets which they write by their own on the door. He liked to patrol in casual clothes at the Spring Festival and got pleasure from door to door couplets viewing. The men of letters at that moment were interested in such a composition, so writing couplets soon became social chic fashion.

But couplets nation-wide popularity attributed greatly to the regulations by the Founder Emperor who issued his sacred decree for couplet promotion among every household.

One year just before the Eve, he requested every family in Jinling to stick their red-paper couplets on their doors. On the morning of the first New Year day, he went around in casual clothes and watched the couplets door to door. When he saw some brilliant lines, he burst into laughter and praised profusely. Suddenly a house without couplets came into view. He flied into anger and asked why the family denied his order. His attendants answered immediately, "This is a butcher's house. He was so occupied that he didn't even take time to have the couplets written". The Emperor asked to serve brushes and paper. He wrote down a couplet for this family which says, "Blaze a life and death trail with two hands; Remove fussy and annoying root by a single cut". After finishing his writing, he went on with his tour. A short time later, he passed by the butcher's house when he returned to his palace from his inspection. He saw there was no couplet still on the butcher's door and asked what happened. The butcher answered in a pious manner, "the couplet written by the Emperor is hanged in the central hall. The whole family burn incense every day to show our respect and loyalty". At hearing this, the Emperor was satisfied and ordered to grant the family 30 Liang Silver as a reward.

Many Families Are Pasting New Year Couplets

"Fu" character is a part of the spring couplet. Long time ago, People began to plaster "Fu" character of all sizes on the room door, the wall and top bar of the door. In the past 'Fu' refers to luck and blessing and now is interpreted as happiness, showing people's desire for happy life and wishes for a better future. In order to express good wishes to the full length, folk people like to plaster the "Fu" character upside down. This upside-down sticking means that the happiness has come already. And this practice is relevant to a story in the Ming Dynasty.

Zhu Yuanzhang of the Ming was ready to kill people whose houses were marked with "Fu". While the kind Queen did not want to see the violence by ordering people must paste a "Fu" character on their doors before the daybreak. Every family followed her order except one. This household made some mistakes by plastering the "Fu" upside down as the family members were illiterate. The Emperor sent his soldiers to watch around the street the next morning. These men found that every family got a "Fu" character pasted right on the doors except for that house that put the "Fu" character in the wrong direction. The Emperor became furious at the news and ordered his guards to kill the entire family. The queen stopped him and explained, "They did that intentionally, my Lord, the character upside down does not mean that the blessing is coming?"The Emperor submitted that the queen got the point after thinking. He ordered to set free the family and a cruel execution was thus evaded. Since then, people pasted the character upside down for the purpose of luck, and in memory of that great and gracious Queen too.

The implication of"Fu" Infers Family's Happiness, Safety and Health

Except a single word "Fu" on the red paper, "Fu" character designs feature all sorts of background including the god of longevity, birthday peach, carps jumping, a bumper grain harvest, and dragon and phoenix dance.

2.6 The God of Door

The door god was born after the emergence of peach wood charms. It is said that a charm made of peach wood is usually as wide as an inch and as long as seven to eight inches. Toscare away the evil spirits, people engraved the names of Shen Tu and Yu Lei, the two legendary ghost catchers, on the wood board and hanged it onto their door.

The purpose of sticking door gods to the door is evident. So door gods are usually those who were good at ghost catching or killing such as Zhong Kui. These men looked ferocious

The Door God

with eyes staring red open. They held all sorts of weapons and ready to catch any ghost who risked entering the house. After the Tang Dynasty, two famous founding generals named Qin Shubao and Yuchi Jingde were added to the list of door gods.

This can be traced back to the following legend. Li Shimin, the second emperor of the Tang Dynasty, eliminated the entire family of his brothers Li Jianchen and Li Yuanji after severe power infighting. No one was spared including the old-headed or newly born babies. Li Shimin was succeeded to the throne finally. However, the ghosts he ordered to execute haunted him every night so that he could listen to their screaming cry and their tossing bricks outside of his palace. During night he had nightmares in which his brothers attempted to take revenge on him. The Emperor could not fall into sleep out of fright and his wives were disturbed too. The emperor had to turn to his ministers for help. Qin Shubao went forward and reported that he killed countless enemies in his military career and the dead bodies were piled up like mountains, but he was not afraid of the ghosts at all. At last he expressed the wishes to guard the Emperor's safety in armors with another general Yuchi Jingde during night. The emperor adopted his suggestions. On their first duty night, those ghosts dared not to disturb the Emperor anymore and the Emperor got his peace with him. But another problem arose. The two general fell ill finally because they kept awake long time to be on their guard duty. The Emperor thought it over and over and an idea flashed into his mind. He ordered the court drawers to portray the generals' duty images down and hanged them onto the palace doors. In the pictures Qin and Yuchi were fully armed and holding their weapons in hands, frightening enough to scare away all the evils.

Form that time on, the custom of pasting the picture of Qin Shubao and Yuchi Jingde has been widespread at the Spring Festival.

第二章 春节过程

世界各地的民族节日一般在三五天或一周，加上准备时间，最长也不超过 10 天。而中国的传统春节，始于农历腊月初八，到农历正月十六结束，时间跨度超过一个月。腊月初八又称“腊八节”，民间有吃“腊八粥”的习俗，从这一天开始，各家进入筹备过年的阶段，采办年货、准备新衣、拆洗被褥。随后的每一天几乎都是节日，如腊月二十三是“小年”，人们要祭灶神；腊月三十为“除夕”，家家户户贴对联、吃年夜饭，守岁、包压岁钱；正月初二称“米娘娘日”，出嫁女儿要回娘家；正月初五称“送穷日”，人们要祭财神；正月十五称“元宵节”，人们吃元宵、闹花灯；正月十六作为年节的尾声，民间有“过完十六从头受”的谚语。在这样长的一个时间段内，祭祀、庆祝、娱乐活动充斥其中。

一、腊月二十三“过小年”

小年又被称作“小岁”，因相对于除夕夜的大年而得名。关于小年和大年的关系，有这样的民间故事。

小年是大年的伙伴，曾化身成神龟为大禹敬献“洛书”，其背上神秘的“洛书”图案被称为中国万经之首的《易经》的起源。每年除夕前，大年都会回到它的居住地北斗七星宫，闭关积蓄吉祥能量，直到除夕夜（腊月二十九或三十）。在腊月二十三日的时候，他都会派小年先到人间，看看都有哪些人需要吉祥能量的补充，为他通报情况。小年爱吃灶糖，于是人们为了小年和灶王爷能“上天言好事”，就形成了过小年吃灶糖的民俗。

小年一般是在农历上一年的十二月（腊月）二十三或者是二十四日，南北略有不同。南宋以前，过小年有“官三、民四、船五”的说法，意思是官宦人家过小年是在农历十二月二十三日，平民百姓则是在二十四日，而以打鱼、渡船为业的水上人家则是在二十五日。南宋以前，北方是中国的政治中心，受官气影响较重，因此北方的小年多在二十三日；远离政治中心的南方百姓便在二十四日过小年；居住于鄱阳湖沿岸的居民由于受船家影响较重，则保留了在二十五日过小年的传统。

关于百姓过小年的历史，最早可见东汉文献。在东汉《四民月令》一书中就提到，人们在过小年时有向尊长敬酒、修书祝贺恩师的习俗。清朝姚兴泉的《龙泉杂忆》中描述说，在小年这一天要准备酒水祭品祭祀先祖，大开家中门户，家家户户燃放花炮，灯火通明。小年的到来意味着人们要为春节做准备了，这时人们便开始谢灶、扫尘、备年货，表示新年要有新气象。

1. 谢灶

作为节日的一部分，小年也被称作“祭灶节”“灶王节”或是“谢灶节”。传说在小年这一天，灶王爷要离开凡间，上天向玉皇大帝报告他所住这一家人的善恶，让玉皇大帝决断对这家人的赏罚。对于大错之人要减寿三百日，小错之人也要减寿一百天。因此，在这一天，百姓为了让灶王爷能在玉皇大帝面前为自己美言几句，都要进行一系列礼拜、祭祀活动，以“贿赂”灶王爷，欢送灶王爷上天。贴灶王爷画像就是必不可少的程序。

灶王爷的画像一般是挂在厨房内灶台一面的墙上，画像下横置一块木板放置供品。灶王爷画像两旁是一副对联：“天上耳目神，人间司命主”，横批为“一家之主”。谢灶所用的供品不同于献祭其他神灵的，献给灶王爷的供品一般都为麦芽糖、糖瓜、汤圆等又甜又黏的食品，目的是要塞住灶王爷的嘴巴，让他上天之后说“甜言蜜语”，民间俗语“吃甜甜，说好话”和“好话传上天，坏话丢一边”等就表达了这样的意思。另外，献祭黏黏的供品给灶王爷的目的也是黏住他的嘴巴，以防他说漏了嘴；有的地方则是在灶王爷上天之前用酒糟涂满灶王爷的脸，让灶王爷醉眼昏花、糊里糊涂地上天去，被称作“醉司命”。

供品摆齐后，便要烧香祭拜。在中国流传有“男不拜月，女不祭灶”的习俗，因此祭祀灶王爷只限于男子。祭拜后分三次向灶王爷敬酒，这个过程中要向灶王爷诚心祷告，心中默念“上天言好事，回宫降平安”之类的话。敬酒毕，要将旧的灶王爷画像取下，并用稻草或篾扎成一匹甲马，作为灶王爷上天的坐骑，因为前往天宫的路途遥远，不能让灶王爷徒步而行。之后将旧的画像连同甲马一起烧化，同时还要烧一些元宝纸钱，让灶王爷在路上花；烧一点黄豆和干草，作为灶王爷坐骑路上的干粮。这些东西烧完，就代表已经将灶王爷送上天了，谢灶的仪式也就完成了，民间称为“辞灶”。到了除夕夜，只要在灶台旁贴上一幅新的灶王爷画像便算是将灶王爷从天宫接回家中了。

○腊月二十三，糖瓜粘

2. 扫尘

“腊月二十四，掸尘扫房子”，送走了灶王爷，家家户户都要开始洒扫庭院，清洗用具，干干净净迎接新年的到来。

每年农历十二月二十三日到除夕止，中国民间称作“迎春日”，又被称作“扫尘日”，意思就是在过年前要对家里进行一次大扫除。“扫尘”在中国北方被称作“扫房”“扫年”，而在南方一般叫作“掸尘”“扫扬尘”。不同地区扫尘的日子也会有所差别，大部分家庭都是集中在二十四日将家内家外打扫干净，有的地区则会一直要持续到除夕前一天。《清嘉录》中提到，在腊月快结束的时候，人们都要看历书来挑选吉日打扫房屋，一般定在二十三日、二十四日或者是二十七日进行。民间的俗语也提到：“腊月二十七，里外洗一洗；腊月二十八，用具擦一擦；腊月二十九，脏土都搬走。”

扫尘的传统在中国由来已久。扫尘不仅是中国老百姓讲究卫生的一种表现，也反映了人们对穷去富来、破旧立新的企盼。按照民间的说法，“尘”和“陈”谐音，因此在新年快要来临时打扫家里的尘土就有了“除陈布新”的含义，用意就是将一年来所积攒的“晦气”和“穷运”统统扫出门。所以俗语说，“一扫金，二扫银，三扫扫个聚宝盆。聚宝盆里有个宝，子子孙孙用不了”。

○年前大扫除

扫尘不仅要清洁

家内家外的墙面地面，而且墙角、床下、房屋梁柱等地方的尘埃都要擦拭干净，平日里生活所用的各种用具也都要清洗干净。扫尘时，全家男女老少齐出动，先将家具用被单遮盖好，全家用头巾或毛巾包好头，然后开始用扫帚将墙壁上下、屋中梁柱扫干净，掸拂墙角蛛网，之后扫净屋内庭院地面。扫完之后便擦洗门窗、桌椅，冲洗地面，最后再将环绕房屋四周的明沟暗渠疏浚一番。

3. 贴“花花”

打扫完了房屋，还要为房屋装点一番，才能衬出新年来到时喜气洋洋的气氛，贴花花是最普遍的做法，包括贴春联、门神、年画、窗花等。

○贴窗花

与贴春联一样，贴年画也是必不可少的。年画因一年更换，或张贴后可供一年欣赏之用，故称“年画”。宋代已有关于年画的记载，清代中期，尤为盛行。中华人民共和国成立后，年画在传统的基础上推陈出新，丰富多彩，更为人民群众所喜爱。

贴年画习俗最早源自贴门神的传统。门神最初取其辟邪镇宅之意，随着人们对祈吉纳福心理需求的不断增长，便仿照门神的形式，每年新年将至时在家中各处贴上绘有草木虫鱼以及各种人物形象的图画，以满足人们祈求家中孩童健康成长、长者福寿延年以及年轻人事业兴旺的愿望。

传统的中国年画以木刻水印为主，追求拙朴的风格与热闹的气氛，因而画的线条单纯、色彩鲜明、气氛热烈愉快。内容有花鸟、胖孩、金鸡、春牛、岁朝、戏婴、合家欢、福禄寿三星、花灯以及神话传说、历史故事、戏剧人物等，表达人们祈望丰收的心情和对幸福生活的憧憬，具有浓郁的民族特色与乡土气息。

○杨柳青年画

河南开封的朱仙镇、天津的杨柳青、江苏苏州的桃花坞、山东潍坊的杨家埠在历史上久负盛名，被誉为中国著名的四大“年画之乡”，其中朱仙镇木版年画历史最为悠久，可谓中国木版年画的鼻祖和发源地。

旅游小贴士

天津杨柳青

天津是一座历史文化名城。天津的杨柳青年画，是中国著名的民间木版年画。它继承了宋、元绘画的传统，吸收了明代木刻版画、工艺美术、戏剧舞台的形式，采用木版套印和手工彩绘相结合的方法，创立了鲜明活泼、喜气吉祥、富有感人题材的独特风格。在中国版画史上，杨柳青年画与南方著名的苏州桃花坞年画并称“南桃北柳”。

杨柳青年画题材的一大种类便是娃娃。这些娃娃体态丰腴、活泼可爱。他们或手持莲花；或怀抱鲤鱼，都象征吉祥美好，非常惹人喜爱。中国非常重视非物质文化遗产的保护，2007 年，天津杨柳青被列入国家首批非物质文化遗产名录。

杨柳青古镇旅游很有特色。杨柳青古镇历史沉积久远，文化底蕴深厚。明清时期，是运河漕运重要枢纽，成为中国北方商贸流通和文化交流集散地，商业繁荣，被誉为北国小江南、沽上小扬州。

杨柳青镇注重通过挖掘、整理、弘扬、发展历史文化，使众多的非物质性历史文化遗产得到了复兴发展。连续两年春节期间（从腊月二十三到正月十六），都举办了有民俗文化旅游节，演出花会、鼓舞、戏曲、民间音乐、堂会等20多道节目。连续七年举办夏季文化大舞台，每节历时一个月，节目多表现传统文化，增加古镇历史文化内涵。

地址：天津市西青区杨柳青镇。

为烘托节日气氛，广大农村在春节前会在窗子上张贴剪纸，称为“贴窗花”。窗花是民间剪纸中分布最广、数量最大、最为普及的品种。分为南北风格，南方以精致为美，特点是玲珑剔透；北方以朴实生动为美，特点是天真浑厚。南北各地农村在春节期间都要贴窗花，以此达到装点环境、渲染气氛的目的，并寄托着辞旧迎新、接福纳祥的愿望。

窗花是有各种颜色、各种图案的民间剪纸艺术品，在中国已有上千年的历史。窗花与立春有着密切关系，唐代诗人李商隐曾在诗中写道：“镂金作胜传荆俗，剪彩为人起晋风。”宋、元以后，剪贴窗花迎春的时间便由立春改为春节，人们用剪纸表达自己庆贺春来人间的欢乐心情。窗花的表现题材极其广博，凡是戏剧人物、历史传说、花鸟鱼虫、山水风景、现实生活及吉祥图案均成为窗花的表现内容。但最多的是花卉动物、喜庆吉祥纹样，常以“吉祥喜庆”“龙凤呈祥”“丰年求祥”“五谷丰登”“人畜兴旺”“年年有余”“贵花祥鸟”等为主体。

4. 办年货

一年的辛勤劳碌，到了岁末人们都期盼着过年的时候好好慰劳自己一番。因此，小年才到尾声便掀起了赶街串集、采办年货的高潮。按照旧俗，街市上的商家到了大年三十的中午就要关门打烊回家过年，商户直至正月初七才再开门营业。此时，精明的商家们筹集货物，都赶在除夕前拿到集市上贩卖。此时，货物堆积如山，街市上人头攒动，叫卖声、讨价还价声不绝于耳，处处都洋溢着喜庆的气氛。

家家户户在此时所置办的年货种类多为春节期间敬天祭祖的香烛纸火，自家食用和款待客人的畜肉禽蛋、蔬菜水果、米面烟酒，以及孩童们玩耍的烟花爆竹、灯笼玩偶等。人们都置办一身新衣裳，买一双新鞋袜，光光彩彩地过年。年货采购差不多之后，便要适时做年菜了。将买回的鸡鸭鱼肉腌制成腊肉腊鱼，碾米打年糕，宰年鸡、福年猪。在民间，人们把过年时候宰杀的猪叫作“伏猪”，取“伏”与“福”同音之意。这些都准备好后，便等着大年三十的到来。

○年货市场

二、腊月二十三“辞旧岁”

每年农历腊月的最后一天晚上，称为“除夕”。它与春节（正月初一）首尾相连，是人们辞旧迎新的日子。由于农历大月有三十天、小月只有二十九天，所以除夕的日期也就有二十九、三十的不同了。但是这一天常常不论是二十九还是三十，习惯上都被称为“大年三十”。

到了大年三十，过年的物品都准备得差不多了，桌底墙角也被打扫得一尘不染，这时人们也就渐渐闲下来。到了中午，等到身在他乡的游子返家后，便闭了家中大门，一家人聚在一起闲聊，坐等除夕夜的到来。

1. 年夜饭

下午，各家各户都生起炉灶准备年夜饭。太阳落山后，全家人便齐聚一堂，享用年夜饭了。

吃年夜饭是除夕当天最为惬意的事情。年夜饭要求全体家庭成员都参加，意味着一家人在吃饭时已经团团圆圆，所以被叫作“团圆饭”“合家欢”等。如果家中有家人因远行而不能在除夕夜赶回来，家人也要在桌上给他留一个位子，摆上一副碗筷、一个酒杯，代表他已经回到家中和家人团聚了。

○普通人家的年夜饭

年夜饭的习俗南北各地不同，有饺子、馄饨、长面、元宵等，而且各有讲究。北方人过年习惯吃饺子，取新旧交替“更岁交子”的意思。又因为白面饺子形状像银元宝，一盆盆端上桌象征着“新年大发财，元宝滚进来”之意。有的地方包饺子时，还把几枚沸水消毒后的硬币包进去，说是谁先吃到了，就能发大财。南方人新年吃馄饨，寓意从混沌状态走向新气象。传说世界生成以前是混沌状态，盘古开天辟地才有了宇宙四方。长面，也叫长寿面，新年吃面是预祝寿长百年。此外，年夜饭的菜肴也很有讲究，要求正菜有八碗或十碗。八碗菜要求七荤一素，据说源自于八仙下凡，百姓为了款待他们而准备的八个菜；十碗菜则是为了讨十全大福的彩头。菜里面必须要有一碗肉丸子，象征着一家人的团圆；还要有一碗鱼，寓年年有余之意；还必须要有一只鸡，取“鸡”与“吉”之谐音的口彩。

2. 压岁钱

吃年夜饭时，趁着酒酣耳热，长辈们纷纷掏出事先准备的红包，给晚辈们分发压岁钱。这时候家中的孩童、晚辈都不再打闹嬉戏，纷纷围坐在长辈身旁。待儿孙们一个个都给长辈磕头拜年之后，老人们就笑容满面地将红包分发给孩子们，红包里装的便是压岁钱。压岁钱不仅是长辈对晚辈经济上的一点小小奖励，其中也深含着长辈对小辈新的一年里吉祥平安的祝福。

○压岁包

压岁钱最早源自于“压岁果子”的风俗。过去，大年三十晚上孩子们上床睡觉后，大人们都要在孩子的枕边放上橘子、荔枝等水果，等第二天清晨睡醒后吃掉。到后来，压岁果子逐渐演变成“压岁盘”，在除夕之夜，各家各户的孩童们都用盒子或器皿装上果脯蜜饯、糕点糖果，小伙伴们之间相互赠送。不仅在民间的孩童中存有这种风俗，在宫廷中，每到除夕之夜官员们也要向皇帝进贡精巧的果品盒子。所以,除夕夜散发压岁钱的传统最早是起源于宋朝的互赠压岁盘。明清时期，形成了真正意义上的压岁钱。清代以后，孩童们过年时长辈们都要将铜钱用红绳子串成龙的形状，放到孩子们睡的小床的床脚下，这样的钱也就叫作“压岁钱”了。

民国时，长辈们分发的压岁钱开始用红纸包裹，包裹一百文钱的寓意“长命百岁”，包裹着一块大洋的象征“一本万利”。

压岁钱为何称为“压岁”呢？据说压岁钱和驱邪避祟联系在一起，意思是要压住年岁祈求晚辈们在新的一年里无病无灾。在新旧年交替之时，人们都要熬夜守岁，送走旧的一年，把新的一年迎进家。孩童们往往都熬不过漫漫长夜，早早进入梦乡。而此时家中的诸神都已经上天，没有了神灵的护佑，为了防止小鬼伤害到孩童，长辈们便要悄悄塞一点钱在孩子们的枕头下面。如果真的有小鬼前来，就可以用这些钱贿赂他们，让他们不去伤害孩子，所以压岁钱又被称为“压祟钱”。

3. 守岁

分发压岁钱的喧闹过后，一家人又围坐在火炉边或桌前，吃着苹果、大枣、杏仁、年糕，谈笑畅叙。也有百姓人家打麻将、推牌九、打扑克，喧闹欢笑之声穿街过巷。那些不愿上床睡觉的孩子还三五成群地在庭院中放烟花、点鞭炮，火光映上云霄。除夕夜子时将近，家家户户欢声笑语，灯火辉煌，这就是旧的一年中最后一个活动“除夕守岁”。

传说在上古时候，每到了新旧年交替之时，天门大开，天上就会降下金银珠宝。人们到了这个时候都熬着夜，等待天上降金银珠宝下来。也有自私的人不懂得施舍，而是自己分享这些金银珠宝。后来老天爷一怒之下，决定不再抛撒金银。但是人们到了岁末除夕，依然整夜不睡，希望有一天老天爷回心转意，再次撒下金银。守岁的习俗就这样保留了下来。

○上海话剧中心《守岁》剧照，讲述了一家人除夕夜的故事

4. 迎神祭拜

到了除夕夜子时，也就是凌晨十二点这一刻，新的一年就正式到来了。此时各家各户都在家门口燃起一串串鞭炮，用隆隆的鞭炮声迎接新年的到来，冲天的火光也将条条街道映照得如同火龙一般。

新的一年开始了，上天去汇报工作的诸神大部分也要返回下界，老百姓要将他们接回家中，继续庇佑家人。接神回家要在天地桌前完成仪式。天地桌是一个临时性的供桌，是除夕专门为接神而设的。

天地桌的内容与常年佛堂有所不同，除共有的挂钱、香烛、五供、大供之外，受祀的神像大都是临时性的，有的接神后即焚化，有的则须到破五甚至到灯节才焚烧。摆天地桌的位置也不统一，如堂屋地方宽大，可置于屋中；如屋内摆放不下，就置于院中。

○除夕夜祭祀祖先

大地桌前，须备齐三牲、酒水、水果等物，点烛焚香迎接众神回家。由于众神住在天上的不同地方，因此他们回家时也是从不同地方下界，为此，在接神前家中的长者都会，找准诸神下界的方位，率领全家老小在天地桌前按照不同方位接神，而对于灶神来说还要换上一幅新的灶王爷画像。

除夕夜不仅是家中诸神归位的日子，各个庙宇的神灵也在这个时候返回他们所住的寺庙。这些神灵当然也不能怠慢。迎回了家神之后，人们便带上香烛纸火、瓜果供品匆匆赶往邻近的寺院、土地庙、关圣宫、龙王庙，争取能头一个为神灵敬香，成为最早欢迎他们下界的人，民间称之为“烧头香”。将诸神迎下界后，人们便纷纷返回家中，继续闲话、玩乐至天明。

三、
正月初一“过大年”

正月初一，也称作大年初一，是中国农历新年的第一天。由于大年初一是新年的第一天，又是春季的第一天，还是正月（一月）的第一天，因此大年初一又被称为“三元”或“三朝”。这一天，相关的活动也比较丰富。

○大年初一放鞭炮、焰火

1. 放鞭炮

新年的头一天，只有早上将自家大门打开，百姓才算真正进入了新的一年。由于是新一年的开端，如何开门步入新的一年，民间十分讲究。一年之首，人们都争相早起，以求新的一年每天都能像当天一样早早醒来，不耽误农事、买卖。最早醒来的人一睁眼就要念《五更歌谣》，以求每日起五更的人们都能勤劳致富、身体康健、衣食无忧、子孙多福。

“起五更，拍炕头，银子钱，往家流。起五更，拍炕帮，银子钱，往家装。起五更，摸炕沿，有的是，银子钱。起五更，摸水瓮，喝凉水，不生病。起五更，摸摸锅，吃饱饭，子孙多。”

歌谣念完，就要将家中大门打开了。据说新年的第一次开门开对了便能开门大吉，一般由家中的长辈来完成，不轻易让年轻人和小孩子插手，以防止他们毛手毛脚而走掉了风水。开门还要讲究时辰，不同的年份人们都按照黄历上说的具体时辰打开大门，开门后还要朝大吉大利的方位敬拜那些居住在天上的神灵。

大门打开后，家家户户都将事先准备好的鞭炮用竹竿挑在门边，依次燃放，通过“开门爆竹”达到除旧迎新的目的。

鞭炮是中国特产，至今已有两千多年的历史。放鞭炮可以制造出喜庆热闹的气氛，是节日的一种娱乐活动，可以给人们带来欢愉和吉利。随着时间的推移，鞭炮的应用越来越广泛，品种花色也日见繁多。每逢重大节日及喜事庆典，以及婚嫁、建房、开业等，都要燃放爆竹以示庆贺，图个吉利。

放鞭炮中，谁家的鞭炮声最响、谁家的鞭炮放得最长变成了人们议论的话题。鞭炮声渐渐淡去后，家家门口和街道上被炸碎的鞭炮纸铺满，一地碎红，灿若云锦，民间称为“满堂红”，借着这一地碎红，喜气、瑞气也就进了家。放完鞭炮后，有的人家还将一些零散的炮仗撒在门外，引得各家的孩童们争相捡拾，孩童们口中叫喊着“有呀”“好多呀”，而这户人家也讨得了口彩。

现在，湖南浏阳，广东佛山和东莞，江西的宜春和萍乡、浙江温州等地区是中国著名的花炮之乡，生产的爆竹花色多、品质高，不仅畅销全国，而且还远销世界。

近年来，随着国人环保意识和安全意识的增强，很多城市开始发布节日期间禁止或者限制燃放鞭炮的规定，因为放鞭炮既浪费资源、污染环境、噪音扰民，而且容易引发人身伤害和火灾、爆炸。这项古老的传统，正在不断被一些时尚、环保的新型过节方式所取代。

2. 拜年

放完鞭炮，人们都穿上新衣新裤，踏着碎红走出家门，去给本家的亲戚拜年。拜年又称“走春”或“探春”，是人们在辞旧迎新之时相互表达美好祝愿的一种方式，表达新年大吉大利的愿望。

○初一大拜年

拜年的先后次序在古代中国很有讲究。拜年的对象主要是五代以内的父系亲属，也包括上司及密友。拜年先从家里开始。初一早晨晚辈起床后便要向长辈叩头行礼，祝愿如意吉祥。给长辈行完礼后就要出门给亲友拜年了。晚辈前来拜年时，家中主人不会让其空手而归，都会赠一点糖果，叫作“赐福”。也有大家聚在一起相互祝贺，称为“团拜”。

现在，拜年的方式已经多种多样了，包括当面拜年、红包拜年、短信拜年、电话拜年、贺卡拜年、写信拜年、电子邮件拜年、鲜花快递拜年、立体真人拜年、视频拜年等。

3. 开门吃饺子

春节早晨，开门大吉，先放爆竹，叫做“开门炮仗”。爆竹声后，碎红满地，灿若云锦，称为“满堂红”。这时满街瑞气，喜气洋洋，该开始吃饺子、年糕或者汤圆了。

○中国饺子

除夕、大年初一吃饺子是北方人的习俗，不过现在不少南方人也加入到吃饺子的行列中。在除夕时吃饺子，取“更年交子”（来年交好运）之意，大年初一吃饺子则是为了一年交好运。

大年初一吃年糕也是中国人的传统，寓意着“节节高”。年糕的式样有方块状的黄、白年糕，象征着黄金、白银，寄寓新年发财的意思。

江浙一带流行大年初一吃汤圆。大年初一的早餐汤圆一定更具特殊意义，它的取意是：事事如意，全家团圆美满。大年初一这天，汤圆不叫“汤圆”，叫“元宝”，吃汤圆也不叫“吃汤圆”，叫“得元宝”。

○吃汤圆，寓意“得元宝”

也有些地方流行大年初一“吃斋”。吃过了年三十的大鱼大肉后，初一当天第一顿饭，全家人却要吃素食。“斋”与“灾”同音，而吃斋也意味着“吃灾”，将新的一年中的各种灾难全部“吃掉”，保佑一家人平平安安。初一午饭吃斋，用粉丝、腐竹、发菜、冬菇等煮一锅“罗汉斋”，寓意这年该吃的素菜都在这天吃完，往后就可大鱼大肉，祈求来年顺利，所以有“年初一吃斋，胜过吃一年斋”的说法。

古代还有大年初一饮屠苏酒的习俗。屠苏酒是一种药酒。在古代习俗中，元日全家饮屠苏酒，以祛不正之气。古时饮屠苏酒，方法很别致。一般人饮酒，总是从年长者饮起；但是饮屠苏酒却正好相反，是从最年少的饮起。大概年少者一天天长大，先饮酒以示祝贺，而年长者过一年少一年，后饮以示挽留。

浙江绍兴人有大年初一上茶楼喝“元宝茶”的习俗。所谓“元宝茶”，一方面是这里用的茶叶比往常提高一个档次，并且在家里的茶缸中添加一颗“金橘”或“青橄榄”来指代“元宝”，象征新年“元宝进门，发财致富。”二是因为茶缸上贴有一只红纸剪出的“元宝”，大致意思也不外乎“招财进宝”。

4. 不动扫把来聚财

根据民间传统，正月初一为扫帚的生日。这一天不能动用扫帚，

○大年初一不扫地

否则会扫走运气、破财，而把“扫帚星”引来，招致霉运。“扫帚星”其实就是彗星，它在运动时后面好像有个尾巴，形状像扫把，故得名。中国民间认为，彗星为怪异之星，有首有尾，因而是“灾星”。彗星出现时，会给人间带来战争、饥荒、洪水、瘟疫等灾难。所以在扫帚星的生日当天，不能轻易招惹它。假使非要扫地不可，也必须从外头扫到里边。这一天也不能往外泼水倒垃圾，怕因此破财。

现在，许多地方还保留着这一习俗。大年三十夜扫除干净，年初一不动扫帚，不倒垃圾，准备一个大桶来盛废水，而且当日也不外泼。

四、正月初二“拜年忙”

“回娘家”拜年是大年初二的传统。

正月初二，嫁出去的女儿纷纷带着丈夫、儿女回娘家，给父母拜年，这天也是女婿给岳父岳母拜年的日子，称作“迎婿日”。在中国民间，认为出嫁的女儿在大年初一这天不能回娘家，因为会把娘家吃穷，只有等到初二以后才能夫妻双双拖儿带女回去。实际上，由于嫁出去的女儿已经是夫家的媳妇，大年初一会有很多人前来夫家拜年，作为媳妇便要帮忙招待客人，只有等到初二有了闲暇才能回娘家。

在古代中国的父系家庭中，女儿出嫁后便是夫家的人了，几乎没有机会去探望父母，更别说照顾他们了。然而子女是父母的心头肉，即使成了别人家的媳妇，做父母的何尝不对自己的女儿牵肠挂肚呢?因此每年大年初二女儿回娘家，一是给双亲和家中长辈拜年，二是女儿平平安安地出现在父母面前，也了却了父母的思念牵挂之情。“回娘家”拜年还被认为最早是从“回门”的婚俗演变而来的。回门是指古代女子在新婚后的第二天便要携新郎返回娘家，女婿给岳父岳母行“成婚礼”，并给女方家的长辈亲属行礼请安，而岳父岳母则要盛情款待新郎。之后逐渐演变为夫妻在大年初二携子女前往娘家拜年的习俗。新婚夫妇双双要回娘家，而有了子嗣的老夫老妻，便是妻子带上儿女回家，丈夫就不一定回去了。

○水彩画“回娘家”

女儿回娘家，不仅要穿戴一新，带上鸡鱼、酒肉、水果等礼物，还要准备一大兜饼干和糖果，交由母亲分送给街坊四邻，女婿还要准备好“回门钱”献给岳父母。女儿回到家中，若家中有侄儿，当姑母的必须再掏腰包，尽管在初一日给压岁钱时已经送了，可这一次意义不同。

女儿女婿回娘家，是长辈最为高兴的一件事了，他们早早就准备好了丰盛的宴席款待家中的“稀客”。此时女婿成了岳父母家最为尊贵的客人，入席时女婿要坐在上席，由岳父母家的长辈相陪，好酒好菜都先让女婿享用。“回娘家”这种习俗,潮汕人称为“食日昼”。顾名思义，就是只吃中午饭，女儿必须在晚饭前赶回夫家。女儿在父母家过夜是绝对不允许的，这被认为很不吉利。

此外，中国的北方有在正月初二祭财神的习俗。这天，无论是商贸店铺，还是普通家庭，都要进行祭财神活动。各家把除夕夜接来的财神祭祀一番，祭祀的供品用鱼和羊肉，也有焚烧象征性物品的。这天中午要吃馄饨，俗称“元宝汤”。老北京的大商号这天都会举行祭祀活动，祭品要用“五大供”，即整猪、整羊、整鸡、整鸭、红色活鲤鱼等，祈望今年要发大财。

五、正月初三“困到饱”

从头一年的腊月二十三日开始，为了迎接新年、庆贺新春，人们一直忙个不停，奔波劳碌了十多天，也该好好休息一下，放松放

○大年初三不拜年

松了。因此民间有“初三困到饱”的谚语，就是说到了正月初三这一天，人们就什么都不做了，躲在家里呼呼大睡。正月初三是“赤狗日”。赤狗是掌管南方的神灵，还掌管着烈火，也是夏天的象征，因此人们认为出门遇到赤狗是不祥之兆。赤狗的“赤”字象征着赤贫，所以这天大家都闭门不出，也不宴请宾客，生怕触怒了这位掌管烈火的神灵。同时，正好也借这个机会养精蓄锐、好好休整。

当然，这天除了在家休息，也还有一些必须遵守的习俗。例如，家里或附近有井的人家要祭祀井神，早上在井栏边焚香烧纸、供奉素菜，然后将除夕时贴在井上的红纸条揭去，名为“开井”。晚上，要把年节时的松柏枝及节期所挂门神门笺等一并焚化，叫作“烧门神纸”，以示年已过完，又要开始营生，所以有“烧了门神纸，个人寻生理”的俗谚。这一天也是谷神的生日，为了求得新一年能有一个好收成，人们在这一天都不吃米饭，以防因此而触怒了谷神。这天还是女娲造羊的日子，故称“羊日”。当天，人们不能杀羊，这样羊就会养得很好，养羊的人家会有个好收成。到了晚上，则是老鼠娶亲的日子，人们在家中角落里撒上米、面、食盐，让老鼠好好享用一番。早早熄灯也是希望老鼠们找不到娶亲的路，否则老鼠成家生儿育女，家中就要遭殃了。

在中国南方的一些地方，大年初三的早上有贴“赤口”（禁口）的传统，因为这一天里容易发生口角，不宜拜年。所谓“赤口”，一般是用长七八寸、宽一寸的红纸条，上面写上一些“出入平安”等吉利的话贴在前门和后门的门顶上，另放一张在垃圾上面挑出外面倒掉。这些垃圾是初一初二两天积下来的，一定要到初三才一起清理倒掉，否则，等于是家中的金银财宝全部向外流。

六、正月初四城隍庙

这天是土地神和城隍神返回凡间的日子，人们要早早准备好香烛供品、水果酒菜盛情将他们迎回来。

○土地神

土地神在民间被称为“土地公公”，是民间信仰中最为普遍的神灵。土地神是财神与福神，因为“有土才有财”，因此土地神被奉为地方的守护神。据说，他不仅掌管着土地，还能使五谷丰收。对于以农耕为主要生计模式的中国老百姓，土地及土地上生长的农作物决定着民众的生存和延续，因此人们对土地神都格外敬重。这天，很多人要把土地神迎进家里祭拜。一般家庭的厅堂五神中必有供奉土地神，或是在门前设香案、烛台、供品祭拜。

城隍神也是地方的保护神，他掌管着城池的安宁，包括当地的水旱疾疫及阴司冥籍。安居才能乐业，只有城池牢不可破才能抵御住外敌的入侵，生活在城池中的百姓也才能平安快乐，而这一切都要靠城隍神来维护。最初人们并没有分开对土地神与城隍神的信仰，只祭祀一位掌管土地的神灵。直到唐代城镇的兴起才分别出现了城隍和土地两位神灵，而城市功能和地位的不断上升也使得城隍神地位逐渐上升，土地神反而成了他的下属。春节期间，人们通常是到当地的城隍庙进行祭拜。

○上海城隍庙

旅游小贴士

上海市城隍庙

上海市城隍庙（City God Temple of Shanghai），是一座道教庙宇，位于上海市黄浦区方浜中路。城隍，又称城隍神、城隍爷。是中国宗教文化中普遍崇祀的重要神祇之一，由有功于地方民众的名臣英雄充当，是中国民间和道教信奉守护城池之神。

上海城隍庙传说系三国时吴主孙皓所建，明永乐年间，改建为城隍庙。前殿祭祀金山神汉大将军博陆侯霍光神主，正殿供诰封四品显佑伯城隍神明待制秦裕伯御史，后殿乃寝宫。现门前存有 1535 年所建的牌坊，戏台建于 1865 年。上海城隍庙殿堂建筑属南方大式建筑，红墙泥瓦，现在庙内主体建筑由庙前广场、大殿、元辰殿，财神殿、慈航殿、城隍殿、娘娘殿组成。

上海城隍庙坐落于上海市最为繁华最负盛名的豫园旅游景区，是上海地区重要的道教宫观，始建于明代永乐年间（1403–1424），距今已有近六百年的历史。风雨仓桑，朝代更迭，上海城隍庙也历经兴衰，已成为上海著名的旅游景点，在国内外享有盛名。随着经济的发展，已经成为上海小旅游圈，城隍庙道观、城隍庙小吃、豫园环在周围。

地址：上海市黄浦区方浜中路 249 号。

七、
正月初五“接财神”

正月初五在春节中是一个特别的日子，所有的活动都围绕“接财神、开利市”进行。

每到正月初五零时，人们就要打开大门和窗户，燃香、放爆竹、点烟花，向财神表示欢迎。这一天，人们都必须吃得特别饱，俗称“填穷坑”，表示一年都不为贫穷饥饿所困扰。

○中国的“财神”形象

正月初五是“送穷”的日子，是中国古代民间很有特色的岁时风俗。各家都用纸造妇人，称为“扫晴娘”“五穷妇”“五穷娘”，身背纸袋，将屋内秽土扫到袋内，送到门外燃放鞭炮炸掉。所以这一习俗又称为“送穷土”“送穷媳妇出门”。

正月初五又被称作“破五日”，人们认为从大年三十到正月初五这段时间百事禁忌，人们的很多活动都受到了约束，诸如不准妇女串门、不准动针线等。初五这天也有禁忌，比如这一天不能用生米做饭，必须吃饺子等。但是过了初五，这些禁忌都可以破除了。因为初五过后人们便要开始工作，商店开门营业、学子返回学堂。

初五还是五路财神的生日。所谓五路，指东西南北中，意为出门五路，皆可得财。五路财神即东路招财神、西路进宝神、南路利市神、北路纳珍神和中路玄坦神。传说他们是兄弟五人，生前劫富济贫，死后依然常常显灵，对穷苦者有求必应，而对为富不仁的人则破其财，因此他们兄弟五人被人们供奉为财神。兄弟五人成为财神后分别掌管着东西南北中五条财路，而财货的流通都要从这五条路上通行，因此五路财神尤其被商家所看重。

由于初五日是他们的诞辰，为争利市，人们要提前在初四就迎接，越早越好，最早接到的才是真神，特别灵验，因此叫“抢路头”，又称“接财神”。

凡是接财神，必须供羊头与鲤鱼，供羊头有“吉祥”之意，供鲤鱼是图“鱼”与“余”谐音，讨个吉利。

八、初六开张放鞭炮

农历大年初六，又称为“马日”。这一天都有哪些传统的习俗与禁忌呢？

1. 挹肥

初六是马日，古称挹肥，人们在这一天才真正开始工作或做生意。而自进入正月以来，一直到初五皆不能打扫，厕所中的粪便累积，于是这一天做一个大扫除，并祭拜厕所神明，将平日污秽的厕所清扫干净。所以称为“挹肥”（但现今之人家多使用新式的卫浴设备，故已无此俗）。这一天也表示旧时农民于此日开始下田，准备春耕。

中国民间信仰普遍认为厕神即紫姑神。客家俗称紫姑神为七姐、七姑。正月初六客家人挹肥之后拜祭紫姑有三重寓意：其一，祈祷丰年；其二，感谢神恩；其三，问卜吉凶。清理或清洁完厕所等卫生场所后，客家妇女就会在该场所的门前点亮红蜡烛或茶油灯，焚烧线香敬拜，在门楣或门框上粘贴红纸表示吉庆。

2. 求顺扔穷鬼

初六占马，送穷鬼。传说穷神是姜子牙的妻子，人们为了防止春节期间穷鬼进家，门上挂红挂笺可以防她。不知什么时候，北京的穷神变成了男性，而且成了杠夫供奉之神。这一天，家中主妇要把节日积存的垃圾扔出去，谓之送穷鬼，门上的挂笺也可摘下来同时扔出去，叫做送穷神。

这一天最受欢迎的是当年满 12 岁的男孩，12 是 6 的二倍，可称六六顺。又传说福神刘海是北京人，是个穿红披绿的胖小子，民间流传着“刘海戏金蟾，步步钓金钱”的俗语，这种形象很受市民欢迎。正值本命年的男孩，以刘海打扮，背着 5 个用白纸或彩纸剪成的小人上街，谁抢到就算谁抢到了财神，被抢者叫扔掉穷鬼。

如果两位均值本命年者相遇，谁先抢到对方背后的小人谁吉利。也有用布制小包当穷鬼向外扔的，双方背后均要背个小筐，先把小包投入对方背后筐中者为先扔穷鬼，吉利。今民族传统体育项目“狩猎”即从“扔穷鬼，抢财神”游戏发展而来，惜此活动在辽宁尚有，而北京却很少见到了。该日小贩上街，因是马日，家中应给“扔穷”男孩买“驴打滚”吃。

○初六送穷神

3. 开市大吉

把财神接回了家，人们就不能再待在家中吃喝玩乐，而让财神爷无事可做。因此，到了正月初六，经商做买卖的人们的生活也就恢复了正常。一大早店铺开门前，商家们都要在自家燃放鞭炮，以作开市之兆。商家们所准备的鞭炮数量之多不亚于除夕夜的盛况，鞭炮声长久不歇。开市时燃放鞭炮，一是告诉四邻和路人商家们已经营业了，欢迎光顾；二来鞭炮炸出的一地碎红是商家期望自己的生意能红红火火，也让进门光顾的人们踏着碎红沾上点喜气。

有的人家在初六开市前，找一个“全可人”（丈夫、孩子、公婆都有的妇人）来到各屋转一下，嘴里说吉庆话，如“开市大吉、吉庆有余、事事平安，多赚银子多赚钱，金子银子赚一炕”等。开市前忌讳外姓妇女到家里串门，等到“开市”以后，所有春节禁忌即告结束，一切恢复如常，邻里也可恢复串门交往。

这一天也是农民们开始下田劳作、准备春耕的日子。另外按照“三六九，朝外走”的传统习俗，大年初六也是中国大批农民工新一年进城务工动身的日子，无非是希望在新一年“行大运”、“多挣钱”，讨个好彩头。

○正月初六庆祝开业

九、正月初七“人胜节”

正月初七是中国传统习俗中的“人胜节”，因为这天是人的生日，所以又叫作“人日”。汉朝开始有人日节俗，魏晋后开始重视。唐代之后，更重视这个节日。每至人日，皇帝赐群臣彩缕人胜，又大宴群臣。

人胜节的来历源于女娲捏土造人的传说。相传女娲在世的时候天地一片寂静，女娲闲来无事便掺水和泥想捏些小玩意让天地间多些生气。于是女娲从大年初一便开始捏制，第一天捏出了一只雄鸡，雄鸡一叫天门便开了，日月星辰都跑出了天门留在了天上。第二天女娲捏出了一条狗，这条狗跑到空旷的大地上对着四周一顿狂吠，便出现了东南西北四个方位。从初三到初六女娲分别捏出了猪、羊、牛、马，这六天所捏出来的动物合起来称为“六畜”。六畜东奔西走，散落在大地上，女娲为了看管六畜便在初七捏出了人，因此这天就是人的生日。为了纪念人的出生，就有了戴“人胜”的习俗。人胜是一种头饰，又叫“彩胜”“华胜”。从晋朝开始有剪彩为花、剪彩为人，或镂金箔为人形贴在屏风上，也戴在头上。

正月初七这一天如果天气晴朗，人们就相信这预示着新的一年家中人寿年丰、出入平安。

在人日，要食用七种菜做成的七宝羹，以此来取吉兆，并可以去除邪气、医治百病。各地物产不同，所用果菜不同，取意也有差别。广东潮汕地区是用芥菜、芥蓝、韭菜、春菜、芹菜、蒜、厚瓣菜；客家地区用芹菜、蒜、葱、芫荽、韭菜、鱼、肉；台湾、福建用菠菜、芹菜、葱蒜、韭菜、芥菜、荠菜、白菜。其中芹菜和葱兆聪明，蒜兆精于算计，芥菜令人长寿。

十、正月初八“散灯花”

正月初八晚上要祭星。等到天上星斗出齐后，各家都要举行一个顺星的祭祀仪式。祭星时，要在案头、灶台、门槛、锅台等处各放一盏“金灯”（黄灯花）并点燃，叫“散灯花”，有避除不祥之意。祭星结束后，全家聚在一起吃一顿元宵。

○放生祈福

正月初八还有“放生祈福”活动，就是把家里养的一些鱼、鸟放归野外。放生，不仅体现了人们尊重自然万物、和谐相处的品德，也表达了自新春开始，企盼世间各种生物兴旺发达的美好愿望。

十一、初九之后仍是节

○搭灯棚，准备元宵节赏灯

正月初九是天日，传说这天为天界最高神玉皇大帝的生日，俗称“天公生”。天公就是玉皇大帝，道教称为“元始天尊”，是主宰宇宙最高的神，代表至高无上的“天”。祭天日的主要习俗有祭玉皇、道观斋天等。在有些地方，各家要备清香花烛、斋碗，摆在天井巷口露天地方膜拜苍天，求天公赐福。

“十”的谐音为“石”，因此初十为石头生日。这一天凡磨、碾等石制工具都不能动，甚至要祭祀石头，唯恐它们伤了庄稼，也称“石不动”或“十不动”。在河南，这一天家家向石头焚香致敬。午餐必须吃馍饼，这样一年之内便会财运亨通。在山东郓城等地，有抬石头神的习俗。初九夜，人们将一个瓦罐冻在一块平滑的大石头上，初十日早晨，用绳系在罐鼻上，由十个小伙子轮流抬着瓦罐走。石头不落地，则预示当年丰收。

正月十一是“子婿日”，是岳父宴请女婿的日子。初九庆祝“天公生”时剩下的食物，除了在初十吃一天外，还剩下很多。所以娘家不必再破费，就利用这些剩下的美食招待女婿及女儿，民谚称为“十一请子婿”。

正月十二为搭灯棚日，即日起人们开始准备庆祝元宵佳节，所以要选购灯笼，搭盖灯棚。民间谚语说：“十一嚷喳喳，十二搭灯棚，十三人开灯，十四灯正明，十五行月半，十六人完灯。”

十二、正月十五闹元宵

正月十五是春节的最后一天，也是一个特别的节日——元宵节。

正月又被称作元月，夜晚在古代叫作“宵”。正月十五是新年的第一个月圆之夜，因此被称作“元宵”。元宵节这天最具代表性的习俗便是吃汤圆和赏灯了。这天晚上，家家户户晚饭时都要煮食汤圆，吃完汤圆后家人还要一同携手出门赏灯、观灯。

○元宵节灯会

汤圆是一种用糯米面揉制的圆形食品，有团圆美满的含义。里面包着芝麻、豆沙、玫瑰、枣泥等馅料，不仅可以煮，还可以油煎、上锅蒸，风味各异。到了晚间，家家户户都将扎好的花灯挂在屋檐下，还在彩灯上描绘出传说故事、历史人物、花草、鸟兽等。

灯市、庙会、集市是元宵节中最热闹的地方。

○庙会是春节期间最热闹的地方

正月十六作为年节的尾声，民间有“过完十六从头受”的谚语，过完这一天，春节才算真正过完了，人们的生活又逐渐恢复到平日的状态。

Chapter Two

How to celebrate or spend Chinese New Year

The world-wide folk holidays usually last for three, five days, or even a week. If the preparatory time is included,it will extend to no more than 10 days. But Chinese Spring Festivals span over a month, which begins on the eighth day of lunar month December and ends till the 16th of lunar January. The eighth day of lunar December is also named "La Ba" and enjoys the tradition of eating porridge of La Ba. And from this day on, every family will begin their preparation for the new year including shopping, new clothes making and quilts washing. And in the following days people also enjoy many festivals. For instance, the 23th of lunar December is a small-scaled one on which the Kitchen God is to be worshiped. The eve falls on lunar December 30th when every family post couplets, eat festival dinners and stay up together. Lunar January 2th is the Day for Goddess Rice, and married daughter will return to their parents' home. While on the 5th, people ought to pay respect to the God who is in charge of wealth to "say goodbye to poverty" . And on the 15th , the Lantern Festival comes when people are so happy to eat rice dumplings and watch lanterns show. The celebration of the New Year comes to an end eventually on the 16th, however, people are so unwilling to accept it so that there goes the folk saying that we need a new round of celebration for New Year Festivals at the closing moment. Therefore, as we know now, the festivals celebration is a long–lasting one filled with a variety of worship, celebration and entertainment, if compared to that in other places in the world .

1. The Small Year in Lunar Month December

Small Year, also known as "Small New Year's Eve" or "Small New Year", got its name from its close association with New Year Day. Here is a folk tale about the festivals.

In lengend, Small Year and New Year were good companions. Xiao Nian once transformed into a turtle and presented Luo Shu Book to Da Yu (Yu the Great). The mysteriouspattern of Luo Shu Book on the turtle's back was regarded as the origin of The Book of Changes. Before the Eve, New Year would return to his Big DipperPalace, where he gathered positive energy till the Eve was coming. (29th or 30th of the twelfth lunar month) On the 23rd of the twelfth lunar month, he sent Small Year to the man's world to see who were in need of energy and made himself informed. Small Year loved sugar eating. To meet Small Year the God's satisfaction and make him speak highly of them, people developed the habit of sugar eating on that day.

Small Year falls on 23rd or 24th of the 12th month in Lunar Calendar. The date differs in the North and in the South. Before the Southern Song Dynasty, people of different class celebrated the festival on the given day. Officialsspent it on 23rd of the 12th lunar month; civilians on 24th and fishermen or ferrymen on 25th. The reasons may lie with this. Before the

Southern Song Dynasty, the political center was located in the north and northern people were under political influence. So Small Year in the North was celebrated on 23rd as it was celebrated in the family of officials. While the South was relatively away from such a political impact, so people there spent the day on 24th. The fishermen near the Poyang Lake kept their own tradition that generations had the festival on 25th.The custom of Small Year was first recorded in Si Min Yue Ling (A book on farming and seasons) written in the Eastern Han Dynasty. It said that during the festival, People drank to the elders and sent messages of congratulations to their teachers. Long Quan Za Yi ofQing Dynasty recordedthaton that day people prepared drinks and offerings toancestors. They kept the door wide open and set off firecrackers. After Small Year comes soon New Year, so people are bustling with their preparations. They begin to thankthe Kitchen God, sweep the dust anddo New Year shopping.

1.1 Thanking the Kitchen God

As a part of the Spring Festival, small year (Xiao Nian) is also called by the folksthe festival ofthankingthe Kitchen God. On Small Year Day, according to a legend, the kitchen god will leave the earth to the Heaven reporting to the Jade Emperorright or wrong doings of the family where he has been staying so as to let the Jade Emperor decide to give this family reward or punishment. If a man has made serious mistakes, his life expectancy will be deducted three hundred days. For a man who has made some small mistakes, the punishmentis 100 days' deduction of living days. Therefore, people spare no efforts to offer sacrifice to "bribe"the kitchen god in order to make the kitchen god praise them before the Jade Emperor. Pasting the kitchen god portrait is an indispensable program.

Kneeling to pray to the God of Kitchen

The portrait of the Kitchen God is usually hanged on the kitchen wall with the hearth, and there is a board under the portrait used to place offerings on it. The kitchen god portraits are lined with a pair of couplets which read "the ear and eye of the Heaven, the life Lord of people". And the horizontal scroll is "the head of the family". The sacrifice served to the kitchen god is different from that to other gods. Generally, there are maltose, sweet melon, sweet dumplings and some other sweet and sticky food. All the food is said to please the kitchen god, making him speak "sweet words" instead of "bad ones". And people also intend to use sticky food to stick his big mouth. In some other places people even smear the god' face with white wine pasta so that the god losses his mind when he flies to heaven.

When the sacrifice is offered, people need to burn the incense to worship god. Traditionally, men do not worship the moon while women need not kowtow to kitchen. Thus men folk are responsible for the worship. After pray, they propose

Watermelon-Shaped Sweets and Candies

a toast to the God three times. And they can ask the kitchen god to do them a big favor that the God speaks highly of the family and brings them back peace. After the toast, people will take the old portrait of the god off the wall and put it aside. They are sitting together to make a horse model with straws for the god to ride on. The journey to the heaven is so long and the man is considerate enough not to make their respected god to walk on foot.

Then the old portrait and the horse model are thrown into a firealong with some paper currency for the god to spend on the heaven way. Finally people need to put some soybeans and hays into the fire as food of the god' horse. All of these are burned out and men have done everything they could to send the kitchen god to the heaven. By this time, the ceremony of thanking the kitchen god is completed. The process is also known as "farewell to the kitchen god" among the folks. Interesting enough, putting on a new picture of the kitchen god represents that people welcome the kitchen god home from the heaven temple.

Zhou Qin in the Qing dynasty described vividly the process of thanking the kitchen god in his poem The Kitchen God:

Eating up sweet sacrifice on the spring plate;

Before midnight he is arriving at the Heaven.

Is there any good to tell the Emperor all?

No, he is kind enough only to report good deeds of the human.

1.2 Cleaning

After sending the kitchen god off, households should start to sweep the courtyard and clean house appliances to meet the arrival of the New Year."24thof the last lunar month is the day to clean the house".

It istime to welcome spring from 23rd day of the last lunar month to New Year's Eve. These days are also given a name "cleaning days" during which people have been occupied with washing and cleaning. Before the arrival of the Eve, households need to have a thorough clean inside and outside of their rooms. In the north of china, cleaning literally means house cleaning while in a symbolic sense it could be interpreted as getting rid of old and bad things. For example, the old dust must be swept away for the sake of luck. The days to clean may differ from place to place. And the majority of families did this job on the day of 24th the last lunar month.Oddly enough in some regions cleaning days will last from 24th to the day before the New Year's Eve.The book Qing Jia Record mentioned that when it was near the end of the yearpeople checked almanac to choose a right day to clean the house. The days generally fall on 23rd, 24th, or 27th of the last month of lunar year. The folk saying also goes this way--"Take a wash on 27th, do cleaning on 28th and remove the dirty mud on 29th."

The tradition of "Cleaning" has a long history and it can be traced back as early as to the Yao dynasty. It is generally acknowledged that cleaningderives its originality from religious ceremonies of driving diseases away. LvLan Note has recorded thatat the end of each year people had to beat drums to drive diseases and ghosts away. In the Tang and Song dynasties, this disease driving ritual gradually evolved into an annual family cleaning at the end of a year. According to Dearming-liang Record written by Wu Zimu ofthe Song dynasty, in the last of the month of lunar year, both civilians and officials families cleaned houses and swept dusts and dirty things to pray for safety of all families in a new year. Therefore, people did such a big cleaning not only out of the hope that people could sweep away the old things and have something new, but also out of the need for health and safety. The two Chinese words, "chen(dust)" and "chen(old)" are homophonic. That means that cleaning the dust in the house equals to getting rid of the old evil things out of the house such as poverty and bad luck.So the folk saying is quite popular that people sweep away bad luck and become wealthy enough to have a treasure bowl which is full of gold and silver that all the offspring cannot exhaust.

Thorough cleanup before New Year

People should not pay attention to the walls and floors only when they do cleaning. The other places need to be wiped clear too such as the corners, the top of the pillar and the floor under the bed. The daily used house appliance need a polish too. All family members, men or women of all the ages, participate in the labor when the dust sweeping starts. They cover the furniture first with sheets, and then wear headscarf or towels on their heads. They clean the floor and the wall up and down in use of brooms and sweep the dirt away from pillars and brush spider webs off the corners. After doing these, they need to scrub stains off windows, desks and chairs. The ground also needs to be flushed clear. The last step is to remove unwanted sands from the wells and drains surrounding the building.

1.3 Pasting paper-cut

The next work for people to do is to decorate their houses. This is undoubtedly a creative job for each household.Sticking window flowers or paper cutting is a part of decoration, along with Spring Festival couplets, door god, New Year paintings, etc.

Just as putting up Spring Festival couplets, sticking New Year pictures is also a necessary and pleasant decorating activity at the Spring Festival. The old paper-cut pictures need to be peeled off and the new ones will take their places. Therecord about New Year pictures was found in the Song dynasty. It is in the middle of the Qing dynasty when New Year pictures gained their popularitymore than ever. After the foundingof the People's Republic of China, there have been more New Year pictures tinged with modern color

Pasting Window Paper-cut

and patterns on the basis of tradition. Thesepicturesbroaden people's scope of knowledge and draw more attention.

The custom of pasting New Year Pictures came from the tradition of pasting the Door God at the earliest time. To drive away the evil spirits and guard the house, people attach a door god to the door. So as to meet people' other needs, for instance, that children grow up smoothly and they have a better future, more pictures were made which extend much more wishes. These pictures featured all sorts of subject matters such as grass, tree, insects, fish and men, which demonstrates Chinese people's sincere hope for better life and romantic view on nature and social life.

Pasting "Fu" Character

Traditional New Year pictures are characterized by wood carving and watermark making. The atmosphere created is both simple and happy. The drawing line may not be so complicated while colors are bright and boisterous enough to make a warm and happy air. Everything could be suitable for painting includingflowers and birds, fat boys,golden roosters, cows and cattles, playingbabies, family reunions, the three gods of blessing, wealth and longevity, color lanterns, myths and legends, history stories, drama characters and so on. The subject of these pictures lies with people's wishes for the harvest and happy life. And they are loved by all for their strong local style and national features. The most typical New Year painting is entitled as "five Lucky Things". They are respectively camelliatrees, daylily, ranturf, rock and green bamboo. The camelliatrees and daylily symbolize father and mother while ran turf symbolizes young children of the family. Flat thick rock represents the stability of the family and green bamboo is considered as a plant which is magic to predict safety.Therefore, we can understand the whole implications from the picture that father and mother live vigorous lives and all the children are elegant-mannered and well-educated. The family bond should be strong under a peaceful and safe environment. This picture is usually treated as a symbol of family protection.

Wood-Cut New Year Pictures Made in Green Poplar and Willow Town of Tianjin Province

Zhuxian Town of Henan Province, Yangjia Bu of Shandong Province, Taohu Wu of Jiangsu Province and Yangliu Qing of TianjinProvince are famous for New Year pictures' making and are all on the list of "Towns of New Year Pictures". Among the four, Zhuxian enjoys its reputations for the longest history as the birth place of New Year Pictures.

Wood-Cut New Year Pictures Made in Green Poplar and Willow Town of Tianjin Province

Tips for Tourism

Yangliuqing Town in Tianjin Province (or Green Poplar and Willow Town of Tianjin Province)

Tianjin is a famous city of a long history. And its Yangliuqing New Year Picture is well known among Chinese folks. And it has inherited the tradition of Song and Yuan Dynasties' drawing, and learned from the form of wood-cut curve, fine arts, crafts and drama stage of Ming Dynasty. Its technique is characterized by the combination of wood-cut and hand-drawing, and thus form a unique style with vivid and exciting matters of subject. In the history of wood print, Yangliuqing New Year Picture enjoys great reputation just as that of Tahuawu in Suzhou does. Both of them are reclaimed as the best of the same class products. .

One subject of these New Year Picture involves boys and girls both with a round figure and lively and lovely body gesture. Some of them hold a lotus in hand, some a fish in arms. No matter what kind it is, it is charming and attractive. In 2007, it was on the list of the first intangible cultural heritage and received due attention from local and central governments.

The tour to Yangliuqing Town is special with its long history and rich cultural background. The small town had once been one of the most important junctions, a center for trade and cultural communication, and thus boasted itself as a prosperous northern market as those in the south of China.

The town has been working on tracing back to and reviewing its historical legacy. To revive and enrich it, local people have already organized many related activities. For instance, the past two years saw a special folk-styled tourist holidays where people could enjoy 20 different shows including parades, drum dance, drama performance, and folk music play and talk shows. Another exciting example is that the town has hosted stage performance related to its cultural tradition in seven summers in a row and each lasted for a month. All these will undoubted enhance people, local or abroad, the awareness of this town' s history.

Address: Xiqing District, Yangliuqing Town, Tianjin.

Traffic tips:

No.1: First, you could arrive in Tianjin Binhai Airport by flight. And then you could catch the airport bus to Chanpagne Town then and get off at the stop of Yangliuqing. Or you could take the airport shuttle bus Line No.5 and get off at the stop of Sun City.

No.2: By train. First you need to arrive in Tianjin Station or Tianjin West Station. And then take Bus No. 824 and quit at Shijia Dayuan. Or first you reach Tianjin North Station by train and then get off at North Gate stop by taking Bus No.903 or tranfer to Bus No.824. The last available one is that first arrive in Tianjin South Station and take Bus 707. You will leave the bus at Zhangjiawo Hospital Stop and need to transfer to Line No. 1 of Jinxi Bus and get off finally at Shijia Great Yard Stop.

In order to make festival atmosphere happier, the vast rural areas will post paper-cut on the window before the Spring Festival, which is known as the "window grilles pasting". The window grill is a kind of paper cutting loved by the folk with most varieties and in largest quantity as it has spread widest and farthest. It can be divided into north and south styles. The south style is characterized by delicate and exquisite design and cutting, while the northern grill is marked by its simplicity and lifelikeness. The country folks in the South and the North will post grilles during the Spring Festival to decorate the house, creating the atmosphere to welcome the New Year and receive blessings.

Here is a story about grilles in the folk legend. Chuan Xu(ancient emperor in the legendary), the Emperor Huangand HouYi hada fierce fighting with JinWu, a ferocious evil bird which caused havoc in the realm of earth and heaven. The heroes won and brought heaven and earth back to normal order. To memorize the heroic moment, and to make the posterity cherish the regained light, people named the day New Year 's Day on which the sun rose again (the first day in the first lunar month) in the hope that there would be more new changes every day in future. And at the same time, the paper-cut was employed to note down the battle and was plastered on the window for permanent commemoration. Then the custom of sticking grilles during the Spring Festival was handed down from generation to generation.

The window grill belongs to a kind of paper-cut art with various colors and pictures. It can boast a long history of thousands of years. A window grill is closely related to solar term "Li Chun" (the Beginning of Spring). In one of his poems, Li Shangyin in the Tang dynasty wrote"good custom as engraving the picture on the gold, grilles carving on paper have been popular from the Jin dynasty". After the Song and Yuan dynasty, the best time for cutting and pasting window grilles has been shifted from "Li Chun"to the Spring Festival. People use paper-cut to express their happy feelings towards a new spring. The subjects and characters of grilles are wide-ranging. Drama figures, historical legends, flowers and birds, fish and insects, landscape scenery, life stories and auspicious patterns are all included. Flowers, animalsand festival auspicious patterns are most liked by the folks such as "dragon and phoenix", "a bumper grain harvest", "prosperity of human and livestock", and "elegant flowers and blessing bird" and so on.

The cutting and engraving forms of window grilles are various. One is the monochromatic scissors cutting which is mainly used for red papercutting in many areas. The second is the tinted paper-cut, often used on the large windows of palaces, shops or halls. The third is embossed paper-cut, popular in the areas like Gansu, Qinghai. The style is unique as this kind of paper cut integratescutting and engraving skills and paper-folding into an organic unity. The fourth is color grilles among which dyeing window grilles is most distinguished. The most famous examples could be seen in Fengning and Weixian of Hebei Province. Carving first and dyeing later, the grills are shining with bright color and splendid visual effect. Lining color window grilles in Foshan of Guangdong Province are noted for theri magnificence and elegance. The main body pattern is made first on the gold foil paper and tin foil paper with multicolor paper backing beneath. Shandong's window grille has more vertical straight lines, suitable for the straight Ling window. In the North West, the window grilles are divided into four parts by a character "+". In order to let out more daylight, grilles are often made in a simple cutting way to have more hollow space.

1.4 Shopping

After one year's hard work, people are looking forward to resting and relaxing themselves. Therefore, just at the end of Small Year, people will go shopping and travel around. The merchants usually close their shops at the noon of the day before New Year Day as they need to spend the New Year at home with families. The shops won't be open until seven days later when all the business is restarted. Businessmen know how to seize the best moment to sell off their goods at a good price. On the days before the Eve, the goods are piled up and the streets are crowded. The bargaining sound could be heard everywhere. People are bustling with selling and buying in a happy mood. The scene of purchasewas describedvividly in Qing Jia record written by Gu Tieqing of the Qing dynasty:

When the Eve is approaching, the merchants or vendors have been busy with buying all kinds of groceries to meet the demands of the residents at the end of the year and selling them, which is commonly known as "sixty days of selling and buying". Cooked food shopsserve more goods than usualsuch as swine feet,chickens and ducks.Paper horse and candles shops printmore horses of wealth, paper silver balls and silk, prepare huge candles and pile up incense. Some merchants are singing to sell kitchen curtain, gourd ladle bamboo basket, porcelain and loop brush. Fruit, vegetable and fresh fish are sold everywhere. The workers to grind the sword and knife are noisy with their work. Drinking herbal and medicine shop give constant customersvinasse, rhizoma atractylodis, monarch wen as gift. On the whole, the boisterous and bustling market at this moment is so-called "New Year Fair".

New Year Fair or Market

People have numerous kinds of goods to buy during the Festival. For examples, candles and papers are needed to worship gods and ancestors. Food to eat and to treat the guests are also needed to get ready including rice, wheat powder, meat, poultry, eggs together with fruits and vegetables. Rice wine and tobacco are absolutely necessary. The fireworks, lantern and dolls for children areunalienable part of happiness. Besides, it is decent for people to put on new clothes and new shoes on such a big day. Shopping is finished and then the time comes to cook New Year dishes. Firstly people marinate newly bought pork and fish and turn them into bacon and salty fish. And then grind sticky rice to make pasty food. Last slaughter chickens and pigs. The pig killed at the moment is called 'Fu Pig' for the lucky purpose as we mentioned above "Fu" means "blessing". With all got ready, the whole family is waiting for the arrival of New Year Eve.

2. On New Year's Eve, family reunion

The last night of the last lunar month is New Year's Eve (Old Year's Day). It is time to bid a farewell to the past year as it isfollowed behind by New Year Day or the Spring Festival. (The first day in the first month of lunar year) New Year's Eve falls on 29th or 30th due to a fact that there are 29 or 30 days in the last lunar month. But whether on 29th or on 30th, the day is generally entitled as "the Eve".

On the eve of New Year, everything needed is ready. Every corner is shining as well as the ground under the table. People begin to have a rest after preparation. By the noon, people close the door after other family members return. The whole families sit around chatting and waiting for the arrival of the New Year's Eve with excitement. The poem Thoughts of the New Year's Eve by Du Shenyan ofthe Tang dynasty has described that "singing to send the old festival off, holding the candle to welcome New Year."Few people could be seen in the street and only fireworks'crackling could be heard afar.

2.1 Family Dinner

In the afternoon, every family is ready to cook their family dinner. The sun sets before the whole family gathers together to enjoy the feast.

The most pleasant thing is to have the festival meal at that specialmoment. All members are requested to be present because that is a valuable reunion for all. The dinner is thus called

New Year Dinner of a Family

"Family Reunion Dinner", "Family Programs" and so on.If someone is absent due to a long travel, the family will place a pair of chopsticks in the seat reserved for him to symbolize his participation.

Dinner customs on New Year's Eve are different in the north and the south. Generally people have dumplings, wonton, long noodlesand rice glue balls as main food. The northernerslove eating dumplings as dumplings and 'Jiao Zi" (the transition from the old to the new) are homophonic. Another factor could be put into consideration is that dumplings resemble to silver ingots in appearance. When they are served to the table, silver ingots will be brought in the house in a figurative sense. Sometimes, people like to put several coins into the fillings after the coins are disinfected in the boiling water. The person who is lucky can eat the dumplings with coin, which means that he will make a fortune the next year. The southerners like eating wonton symbolizing that we part with

Delicious and copious New Year Dinner

the chaos to welcome a new orderly world. A hero named Pan Gu cut the chaos into halves with his ox and brought everything into order. People eat long noodle with a hope of having a long living expectancy. In addition to different sorts, how many dishes to serve is also a question. Generally, eight or ten main dishes are demanded. There are seven meat dishes and one vegetarian for aneight-dish dinner, which is said to treat eights gods descending from the heaven. Ten is an auspicious number in Chinese culture because ten implies perfection. To cook ten dishes stands for that people could reach a peak of perfection in career or in life. A meal ball dish and fish are needed. The former symbolizes the reunion of the whole families and the latter means the family is rich enough to have money and food left at the end of a year. A chicken is necessary too for it has the same pronunciation as another character "Ji". (Luck)

The reunion dinner is served, but it is not time to enjoy because they have another important work to do. The whole families come to pay tribute to ancestors. They offer fresh dishes, fruit and cakes as sacrifice and invite these forefathers back home to spend the festival with them. All the food is put on the table which was washed and wiped stainless and spotless. Everyone stands in the line according to their position. The elderslight the candles and then they kowtow to the ancestors one by one. Afterwards, they burn paper money and set off firecrackers. There is a memorial scroll reading "heaven, earth, sovereign andancestors" in the mourning hall to commemorate those heavenly and earthly gods, kings and deceased parents and teachers. The memorialboards in honor of dead families are erected in the halls. The length and breadth of these boards may be different. But one thing in common is to write the names and ranks of the dead on the front and to write their birthday and dead date on the back. All families will bend their heads to show full respect and humility, offer sacrifice in a pious manner to make their genuine and sincere feelings known to the ancestors. When all is done, they need to retreat in an obedient attitude to win the heart and mind of the ancestors. And now people could sit down to enjoy this big and significant dinner.

2.2 Money Gift

In the middle of the dinner, the elders who are eating and drinking happily will take out red envelopes with money and give them to the juniors as a gift. At this time children and younger generation stop playing andsit around the elders. After receiving kowtow of the juniors, the elders will give all the red envelops to children with smiles. The money given to children as New Year gift is not only a kind of economic reward but also means that the elders bring New Year blessing they pray such as luck and peace to children.

New Year's money is derived from the custom of "Ya Sui fruit" (a fruit that could make people become old slowly). In the past, after children fellinto sleep in the evening, adults

Money gift bags

picked up the orange and put them besidechildren's pillow for them to eat them next morning after waking up. And slowly these fruits besides pillow took a form of "Ya Sui" dish full of sweet and confectionerygiven by the elderly. On New Year's Eve, children of all the families filled the boxes with these snack and candies to give each other as exchange gifts. The custom was not only observed in the folk. The court also followed the style to pay tribute to the emperors with delicate fruit boxes. As a matter of fact, the tradition of giving New Year's money on New Year's Eve first originated in the Song dynasty's mutual presents "Ya Sui dish". During the Ming and Qing dynasties, the true sense of New Year's money is formed. After the Qing dynasty, when the children enjoyed their New Year, the old folks put the coppers with a red string to make them the shape of a dragon and put it beside their feet. This money thus can be called as "New Year's money". New Year's money by Wu Manyun of the Qing dynasty described vividly that "100 cuppers is stringed by a long and colorful string; children hide them under the pillow by themselves. Consulting the prices of fire-cracker and sugar, they are busy with spending the money."

In the Republic, the custom began to prevail that the elders had wrapped up New Year's money with a red paper and gave it to children as presents. Parceling one hundred pence means "to live a life for one hundred years" and wrapping in a piece of oceanic symbolizes "one coin makes ten thousand benefit".

Why New Year's money is called as "Ya Sui'? It is said that New Year's money was related to the dispelling disease and disaster for the younger generation to keep healthy and safe. At the turning time between the new and old, people stayedup to send the old year away, which was known as" Sou Sui". People reckoned children were vulnerable at this critical time as all gods left for heaven and there were no gods available to protect their families. The adult could go through by keeping awake while children can't stay up all night long. They went to bed and fell into dreamland. In order to prevent harmful spirits, the elderswill quietly put some money under children's pillow. Once the ghosts came, the money was used to bribe them and kept children unhurt. So, New Year's money is also known as 'Ya Sui(fear) money'.

2.3 Stay up All Night

After distributing New Year's money, the family is to sit around the stove and the edge and table, eating apples, almond and rice cake and chatting. Some people will play mahjong, PaiJiu and cards with noisy sound of laughter through the streets and lanes. The kids who don't want to go to bed still set off fireworks and watch the scene of crackling in the courtyard. New Year's Eve is at hand and every family laughwith lights blazing. This is the last event of the old year — Stay up Late or All Night on New Year's Eve. The Emperor Li Shimin once wrote a poem Stay up Late on New Year's Eve which describes a sleepless scene where people enjoy themselves and stay up late. "An elegant palace is in the twilight; it is beautiful and luxuriant. Cold winter brings the white snow away; Warm breeze of spring blows gently. The fragrant of plum flies far; Flowers blossom like the red light of candle. Welcome the New Year together; See the old year off during a night."

It is said that in ancient age every time when new and old year alternate, the heaven gate would open wide and gold, silver and jewelries fell down from the sky. Peopleboiled the oil of the night to wait for the treasure descending from heaven. Some selfish people didn't know to share this charity with others. Then the god of heaven was in a rage and decided not to scatter gold and silver any longer. But people still preferred to stay upon New Year's Eve and hoped that the god might change their mind to give away gold and silver again. In this way, the custom of Staying up Late on New Year's Eve was kept down.

Stage Photo of Staying-up By Shanghai Drama Center, a story about a family's staying up on the eve of New Year.

2.4 God worship

At mid-night, the clock strikes twelve. New Year is coming. Now all families set off firecrackers at the door of their houses, welcoming New Year with loud and rumbling crackling. And streets are shining like a winding fire dragon under plumes of firelight.

New Year starts. The gods who report their work to the Jade Emperor, as is told above, are to come back to the man's world. They are warmly welcomed to bless people and their family. The ceremony of welcomeis held in front of aHeaven-and-Earth table, which serves as a temporary altar for the gods. The sacrifice on the table is a little different from the counter-part in the Buddhist temples. Besides hanging-money, joss sticks and candles, five sacrifices and greatest sacrifice, there are some temporary portraits of the gods they worship today on the table. Some of the gods' portraits need to be burned away in a fire at once while some will be kept for several days and then put into fire until the fifth day of New Year or the Lantern Festival. Where to put the Heaven-and-Earth desk depends. If

Worship table and sacrifice

the hall is spacious enough, set the table just in the center. If the space is limited, just put the table in the yard.

People also need to prepare wines, fruit and cooked swine, mutton and beef in front of the table. Then light the candle and incense to welcome gods back home. Because these god lives different places of the Heaven, they are back to earth in different direction. The elders of the family need to find out the accurate location where the gods are landing from the heaven first of all. Next to do is that the families led by the elders welcome the gods from certain directions. And , a new portrait of the kitchen god is a must rather than may or may not.

Besides home gods, the deities outside cannot be neglected. New Year's Eve is the time to welcome them back to their temples. People will hurry to pray and burn incense in the nearest monasteries, temples of land gods, Temple of Guan Yu and Temple of the Dragon king with joss sticks and candles, melon and fruit, paper and incense. They compete to be the first one to welcome the temples deities, which is referred to as "burn the first incense" in the folk.After all these ceremonies, people return home one after another and go on with chatting and playing to daybreak.

3. New Year Day

The first day of the first month of lunar year, is also called the first day of New Lunar Year. AsNew Year's Day is the first day of New Year, the first day of spring and the first day of the first lunar month, it is named as the "Three Yuan" (three beginning) or "San Chao". Here are some interesting celebration activities.

3.1 Firecrackers

On the first morning of New Year, people open their doors

to breathe fresh air of a new year. How to open the door at the beginning of New Year needs special care. Toget up early is the first step as people need to get up early every day to do their farming work and run their business. The first person to wake up will sing Lyrics of Three to Five O'Clockwith wishes that people could get rich through hard work andkeep healthy and lucky for ever.

Fireworks and skyrockets playing show

"Get up before dawn, pat the Kangtou, the silver money, it can flow toward home.

Get up before dawn, pat kengbang, the silver money, it can be brought home.

Get up before dawn, touch kangyan, the silver money, there are plenty. Get up before dawn, touched the water urn, drink cold water, do not get sick.

Get up before dawn, touch the pot, and eat enough food,

more children and grandchildren."

The door is to be opened soon after the song is finished. If the door is opened in right way, the whole family will be lucky and prosperous. So the elders are usually to take care of this and young men can not be allowed to intervene in the event. It is said that young men are likely to let go luck and hope out of their carelessness. Time matters too, so people need to check out almanac to decide the specific hour to open the door. After the door is open, people kowtow to the god in favorable and auspicious places or directions.

Then every household sets off the firecrackers which had been placed on the other end of a bamboo pole. Bathed in the deafening sound, a new year is coming while the old year is left behind.

Firecrackers were made in China, also called by folk people as "BaoZhang", "Pao Zhang", "Bao Zhu". Ithas a history of two thousand years. Setting off firecrackers can create a lively festive atmosphere. As a recreation, it can bring people joy and luck.

Fireworks setting off

Firecrackers are used in more fields as time goes by with more elegant design and various colors. People set off firecrackers on every occasion when major holidays come, or wedding ceremonies, house building ceremonies and opening ceremonies are held.

It will be heatedly discussed in which family the sound of fireworks is the loudest and longest. When the sound fades away, pieces of firecrackers' red cover paper are scattered away everywhere on the ground, spectacular as brocade sheet if seen far away. The scene got its folk name "all-around red". Happiness and luck thus are said to enter the house in such a red background. Some families cast some small firecracker outside the door for the neighbor children to pick up. That symbolizes that the family is rich and thus get an auspice when children shout loudly "some more" or "so many".

Now,Liuyang in Hunan province, Foshan and Dongxiao in Guangdong province, Yichun and Pingxiang in Jiangxi province and Wenzhou in Zhejiang province are well known for high-quality fireworks making and various design. The firecrackers made in these places sell well in china and all over the world.

In recent time, with the raise of Chinese people's consciousness of environmental protection, many cities have issued some ban or restrict regulations on fireworks during the festivals. It has been accepted by more people that fireworks playing does more harm than good because it has caused serious air pollution and much noise along with resources wastage. Even worse, it often gives rise to injuries, fire accidents and explosion. It is believed that this old tradition has been gave way to some new, fashionable and environment-friendly ways of celebration.

3.2 New Year's Greetings

After setting off the firecrackers, people put on new clothes and step out of their houses to pay their relatives and friends a New Year's visit. It is also called by some folks "walking in spring" or "looking for spring". Best wishes and greetings to each other are exchanged in this way.

A Picture of New Year's Visit and Greeting

Certain rules were followed to greet Happy New Year in ancient China. Firstly, those relatives people must pay a visit were mainly in the male line. Superiors and close friends could be included too. Secondly, it began from home greetings. On the firstmorning, the young made kowtow salute to the elders of the family and greeted them with best wishes regards after waking up. Then people went out to visit the father-side relatives and their own friends. LuRong said in the fifth volume of Note of the Vegetable Gardenthat on the New Year's Day, both officials or civilians went to and fro on their way to visit each other several days, known as "New Year' Visit". Qing Jia

Record written by GuTieqing in the Qing dynasty described the sight this way. "After god worship in the parents' house, the juniors were led by theirseniors or were sent by themselves instead to visit theirrelatives and friends, known as "New Year'call". The relatives who were not in frequent contact paid a mutual visit at the moment too. The hosts or hostesses would not make their New Year visitors leave with two hands empty. Some sweet and confectionary were taken as gift with symbolic meanings "sending blessing". There was another kind of visit worth some words here. People sit around and exchange the greetings, which is known as "greeting all around"

Chinese patriarchal family wasusually huge, so calling at relatives and friends' house consumed too much time and energy. Gradually, people began to use name cards to deliver congratulations, known as"New Year Cards". This earliestcard was made of wood. And later paper-made cards gained their-popularities. They were about 3 inches in length and 2 inches in width with the greeting man'name, rank, address congratulations lines on its front cover. People usually wrote the contents of New Year cards in person out of respect. And some gifts were taken together with the card. With the advent of New Year cards, people didn't suffer from long and hard travel anymore and only needed to send messengers, so these cards were named by "flying cards". Wealthy families put their cards in a specially-made box and sent the box only, which was called as "flying box". All these cards and boxes are considered original forms of present New Year cards.

There have been numerous means to greet New Year up to now. Besides door to door visits, delivering red paper containing money as gift, sending messages and giving a phone call are all chosen to express New Years' whishes along with writing letters, sending emails or flowers, 3D live greeting and video chatting.

3.3Wealth Guarding

According to traditional legends, New Year Day is the birthday of the broom. So on this day, brooms are forbidden to be used any longer, otherwise they would sweep away good luck and wealth of the family as people think that brooms could bring the ominous"broom star" home. "The broom star"actually is comet, which looks like a broom in its movement with a tail-shaped end. Chinese tradition reckons that the comet is a weird and monstrous star with a head and a tail. It could bring war, famine, floods, and plague disaster to people when it appears. So at its birthday people try all not to annoy and disturb it. If a floor-sweeping is a must, it should be done from outside to inside. People are not allowed to sprinkle water and throw away trash on this day either in order to prevent money drain from the house.

At present, the custom is still observed by some folk people in many places. On the Eve, the floor is swept clean and kept

No Floor Sweeping on the 1st Day of New Year

untouched until the second day of New Year comes. People don't throw away garbage either. They put the trash into a big bucket instead and don't splash water outside of their house.

4. On the 2nd Day, Women return to their parent's home

Ontheday,married womenare expected to visit their parentsand greet to them, and people followed the traditionalpractice till now.

On the morning, married daughters will return homes with their husbands and children paying their parents and relatives New Year visit. A son-in-law is expected to express his best regards to the wife' parents on the day and then he will be regarded as the most distinguished guest. Traditionally, on New Year' Day a married daughter cannot be allowed to return her parents' house as it is said that she would eat out all the food there. As a matter of fact, as a housewife and major laborer, a married woman is too occupied with her reception work in

Watercolor Painting Named by a Woman VisitsHer Parental Home

her own family on New Year Day as there are so many visitors. Only on the second day could she take time to visit her own family.

In the past, women had lower social position than men. After marriage women would not be regarded as family members of their pre-marital family. Few chances were given to see their parents, not alone to take care of them. However, the daughtersloved their parents and the parents missed their daughters. So the tradition offered parents and daughters a precious opportunity to meet each other. On one hand, thesedaughters could greet their parents and the elders in the family. On the other hand, the return of the daughter could relieve parents' long-term care and worry. The custom is said to derive from marriagepractice "Hui Men". According to "Hui Men", the newly-wedded couples need to return the wife's home the next day after theirmarriage. The bridegroom is supposed to salute to his father-in-law, mother-in-law and other elders of the family, who treated him with utmost cordiality. Anywhere, on the second day of New Year, newly-wedded couples must come back together. For the old spouse with children, the picture may be a little different. The wife could return onlywith children's accompany.

Another thing needs some words here. If the couple are determined to return home, they will be dressed new and get all gifts prepared. Besides chicken, meat, fish, wine and fruits, a big packet of cookies and sweet should be got ready beforehand. The son-in-law needs to offer his parents-in-law some "Hui Men" money to thank what they did to raise his wife. As an aunt, the married daughter should give her nephews some money as gifts. And this money has different sense from that money given on New Year Day.

It is the happiest time to have daughters and sons-in-law back home. The parents cook early and get delicious meal ready to entertain these distinguished guests. The sons-in-law sit in the most honorable position and surrounded by the elders of the family. Good wines and delicious food will be served to them first. The custom of "Gui Ning" is nicknamed as "Having daytime meal"by people from Chao Xian of Guangdong Province. As the name suggests, it means that wife and husband could only eat lunch in the house of their parents. They have to get back to the husband's family before supper. The married daughter staying in her parents' house overnight is considered unlucky.

In addition, on the second day of New Year, there is another custom in the north of China—people usually offer the sacrifice to the God of Wealth. On this day, stores, shops and household all have offering ceremony. The family will offer fish and mutton to the God as well as to the others they have welcomed on New Year's Eve. And some households burn several symbolic items and articles. At noon, people need to eat "Hun Dun", commonly known as the "Silver Ingots Soup". The big firms or brands of Peking hold a spectacular ritual with famous "Five Great Offerings", namely, including a cooked pig, acooked sheep, cooked chicken, a whole duck, a red live carp, etc to extend their wishes for wealth acquisition in the coming year.

5. On the 3rd Day, have a good rest

The days from the 23rd of the last lunar month to the second day of New Year see people have been busy with the celebration of the Spring Festival. Up to the third day, people feel exhausted just like the folk proverb says that "people are

A Good Rest on the 3rd Day

consumed to the full length". It is time to have a good rest and refreshments after nearly ten-day heavy work. So people will do nothing but sleep for a day at home. The third day is the so-called "Red-Stricken Dog Day" in legend. "Red-Stricken Dog" is said to be a southern god in charge of fire and summer, who is famous for its fiery and violent nature. And moreover, the word "red-stricken" is similar to the word "poverty-stricken", a taboo term at so big a moment. Due to these factors listed above, people try not to get out on the day when the fierce god travels around. They decline all invitations and close the door in order to leave the fire god alone. And meanwhile take the chance to relax their bodies and souls.

Though people rest on the day, there are still some customs to be followed. For example, people need topay respect to the well god at home and nearby their houses. On the morning, people burn the incense and paper-money on the well curb side and offer the vegetarian dishes. Then they will uncover the red note posted on the well before New Year's Eve to "open" the well. On the evening, what they should do is to burn the pine branches and the printings of the door god and the threshold off to show that the festival is over and life will go on. That corresponds to the folk saying that "the day to earn a living will begin after that the door-god paper has been set to fire". The day also serves as the birthday of the grain god. To have a big harvest, people choose not to eat rice to please the grain god. In legend, it is on this day when the sheep was made by NuWa, who created the living things in the world. Therefore on sheep's birthday, people are forbidden to kill sheep so that sheep could be bred well in the nest year. The evening is big moment for rats to get married. People go to bed early in the hope that male rats could not find the way to welcome rat bribes in the darkness. Or the whole family suffers from their disturbance and molestation when they breed groups of children after their marriage. Despite that, people are kind enough to sprinkle at the corners rice, wheat powder, and salt for rats to enjoy.

In some parts of southern China, there is a tradition of attaching a red-paper scroll with some "well-connoted words" on it to the top of the front-door and back-door on the third morning. It is believed that it is easy to argue on this day and thus not suitable to have a New Year's visit. The "well-intentional words" such as safe trip and good luck are written on a piece of red paper 7 or 8 inches long and one inch wide. The trash left two days ago needs to be thrown away on the third day of New Year with a scroll of "well-intentional words". That is said to prevent money drain from home.

6. On the 4th Day, visit city god

On this day the land god and the town's god are said to return to earth from heaven, people need to prepare the offerings like joss sticks and candles, fruit and dishes to bid them a heartfelt welcome.

The land god was nicknamed as "the grand-father of land" and worshipped most frequently and widely in the folk culture. He is considered to be a combination of the god of wealth and the god of blessing because he possesses a huge amount of land.

Land God

He is always regarded as the patron saint of the local place. In legend, he is not only the lord of land, but also is entrusted with the important task of harvest. In the agricultural times, most Chinese made their living by working in the fields and land meant everything. Thus, the land god was especiallypopular among gods and deities and he was on the list of five gods who enjoyed people's frequent worship in the hall of average household. On the fourth day of New Year, people hold an offering to meet the land god and pay him their great respect. They set an offering table on which the candles and incense are kept burning and the sacrifice is served ready.

The guardian godof towns, closely related to the land god, takes charge of the peace of their places. Specifically, he prevents flood, draught and epidemic from happening in the towns and cities. And he is also one of the rulers of the underworld. Only in a peaceful place can people live and work happily. The cities and towns under his protection are safe enough to resist any invasion of foreign enemies and people are obliged to him for their peaceful and happy life. At first, people did not separate the land god from the town's god until they worshiped them respectively in the Tang Dynasty. With the growing development of cities and towns, the guardian god had attracted more worshippers and the land god thus became his subordinate. So at present people often have their worship ritual in the temples of town's gods rather than in the temples of land god.

City God Temple of Shanghai

Tips for Tourism

City God Temple of Shanghai

City God Temple of Shanghai, a Taoist temple, is located in the Middle Road of Fangbin, Huangpu District. The City God or Lord is among one of Gods most widely worshipped in Chinese context of religious culture and tradition, and the heroes and ministers contributing greatly to local people play the role of the God. He is always regarded as the god to defend cities and towns.

The Temple had been built in legend by Song Hao, the King of Kingdom Wu in Three Kingdoms Period and rebuilt during Yongle Years of Ming Dynasty. Its front hall is for Huang Guang, a general knighted Sir Bolu in Han Dynasty while its main hall for Qin Yubo, who was a well-known minister and later titled grade 4 Count Xianyou in the Ming Dynasty. Its back hall is a the resting place. And in front of the temple lie a memorial gateway completed in1535 and a performance stage built in 1865. On the whole, the building is dominantly in southern temple style with red walls and earthen tiles. At present the main buildings are composed of the square before the temple, main halls, Yuanchen Hall, Wealth God Hall, Cihang Hall, City God Hall and Queen Hall.

City God Temple of Shanghai,now an important Taoist Palace, is located in the tourist attractions of Yu Garden, which has been well known for its prosperity. Contrary to the legend mentioned above, it actually enjoys a history of 600 years after it was finished at the period of Yongle reign. (1403-1424) Things changed over time and so did the Temple. But fortunately, it survived every twist and turn to be a famous historic and tourist spot in Shanghai. With the development of economy, it has formed a mini tourist circle by itself including the temple, the snack around the temple and Yu Garden.

Address:Middle Road of Fanbin No.249,Hupu District

Traffic lines： take Bus NO.11、66、126、926

7. On the 5th Day, welcome “wealth” home

The fifth day in lunar January is a special day characterized by the events of “receiving the god of wealth and openbeneficial business”

When the day is approaching, people burn incense and set off fireworks to welcome the god of wealth with doors and windows kept wide open. People must eat much more usual, which is known "fill the hungry holes", to stand for that they will not be consumed by poverty and starvation.

One Image of the God of wealth in China

Sending the poverty away was a typical and interesting custom observed by the ancient Chinese folks on the fifth day of New Year. Every household made a paper woman model with a bag on her back. She was also named as "woman sweeper", "poor woman" and "poor female". Later people swept the dirty dust and gathered it into the woman's bag. And then the model was taken outside and blasted into piece by the firecracker having been buried into the dust. The event is also called as "sending the dirt" or "sending the poor woman away".

The fifth day is also well known for another name "Rule-breaking Day". There are many rules for people to follow on the days from New Year's Eve to the fifth day of New Year. Take this as an example, women are not allowed to visit the neighbors and to do their needling work during these days. Another instance is also awkward that people cannot cook rare rice and must eat dumplings on New Year's fifth day. People can break these rules when the fifth day is over. By then, people begin to work and study while the merchants start to run their business, the New Year rules no longer works.

The Taoists set the fifth day of New Year as the birthday of five Taoism gods which are named by the five gods of treasure

Welcome the God of Wealth home

from five directions—the east, the west, the south, the north and the central part of the world. That reveals people's wishes that they will be faced with treasurewherever they go. In Taoist' teaching, the gods from the east and west can bring wealth and jewelry; the gods from the south and north can benefit the businessmen and antique collectors. And the god from the middle can bless people everything goes well. In folk stories, they were five brothers who often took away the property of the malevolent rich and give it to the poor. They robbed the rich and assisted the poor when they were alive and they often made their presence to help the poverty-stricken people after death. So they were worshipped as the gods of treasure. They are said to be in charge of five directions in which goods and money is transported to and fro. Thus the five gods are attached more importance by the dealers and investors.

In order to please the gods, people are to make their preparation in advance and wait to begin their reception on the earliest morning of the fourth day with the basic principle "the sooner, the better". The first to meet the god could invite the god Himself to be with him, which is alluded to as "compete for the gods of treasure" or "meet the gods of treasure as early as possible".

CaiYun in the Qing dynasty describes the picture in a realistic way in his prose poem. "On the fifth day people pray to five gods of treasure that all their wishes may come true at the moment under their blessing. To meet the gods earlier than others do, they have to be in a hurry at the previous night".

The sacrifices offered to the gods of treasure must include the head of sheep and fish. The former is well-connoted with "luck" while the latter "fish" is pronounced same with another Chinese word "Yu" which means that there is always enough food and clothing in one's house.

With the gods of treasure home, people cannot stay at home idling around. Therefore, they are back to work on the sixth day of New Year. The business is restored. Before the shops open, the businessmen set off fireworks as profit-making sign. The noisy and uproarious situation is no second to the spectacles on the Eve with large quantity of firecrackers are

Cooked Sheep Head and Fish as Sacrifice for the God of Wealth

blasting loud and long. The fireworks announce the opening of shops and stores to the customers and neighborhood. And furthermore, pieces of red paper scrapes all over the ground could predict a promising and prosperous trend of trade and the customer could have good luck stepping on them. On this day, the farmers resume their work in the fields and prepare for the spring plowing.

8. On the 6th day, start business again

This day is also known as Horse Day. Here is where this name is derived as follows.

8.1 Toilet cleaning

As is stated above,people are not allowed to clean their rooms from the first day to the fifth of new calendar year. And on the 6th,people need to begin their work and business, they have to clean all rooms including toilet and stable. And in ancient times, they would gather man's excretion and horse manure and turn these into fertilizers. (the tradition has been ruled out of many modern men's life as they have used new sanitary appliance in daily life) Meanwhile, farmers were started to get ready for field plowing.

8.2 Keep the Ghost of Poverty out of door

It is also the day to keep the Ghost of Poverty away from home. In a tale, the Ghost is the wife of Jiang Ziya. To prevent her form entering their house, every family need to hang red paper on the door head. But surprisingly enough in Beijing, we even fail to know from what time, the Poverty Ghost became a male and he was worshiped by porters. The housewives would throw away all the cabbage left during the holiday, and this in literary meaning, saying goodbye to the Ghost of poverty. And sometimes the red paper on the door head would be abandoned.

On the day the most popular person is a little boy of 12 years. 12 is double 6, which implies that everything goes smooth. In another tale,Liuhai, God of happiness, is actually a fat boy in red and green from Beijing. There is a folk talethat Liuhai wins a beautiful wife who has been transformed into a golden toad, and more interesting, the toad wife can produce gold coins. Chinese people buy this story and the image of Liuhai. When a 12-year-old boy like this carries 5 mini white or colored paper-cut man on his back walks on the street, his paper-cut figures will be grabbed by others. A man who get it is considered to be lucky to have the blessing of the God of Fortune.

If two boys comes across each other, one who first takes the other's paper figure will feel more lucky and better. People also enjoy themselves by throwing away cloth bags, which symbolize the Poverty Ghost of course. One needs to have a basket on his or her back, and then try to throw the cloth bag into the others' basket. The person who goals first, according to the traditional belief, is lucky enough to part with poverty. And this game later evolve into a traditional sport "hunting", which we could enjoy watching in Liaoning Province, while pitifully, it is rarely seen in Beijing. On the day street vendors are everywhere, parents

Farewell to the God of Poverty

should buy their boys a traditional food soybean-flour cake because its Chinese name is related to horse.

Some families would look for a woman with families members all alive and ask her to go around their rooms while speaking something auspicious and happy related to a good business for the next year. Have a good start to open the market door, and earn more money till gold and silver fill in the room and so on. There is a taboo to watch that women without family names are not welcome to their homes before the market opening, while after that the taboo will be put aside. Everything will return to its usual routine and neighbors can visit each other at their will.

This 6th day also serves as the time for farmers to begin their labor and plow their fields. Besides, it is on this day when many a Chinese Migrant worker leaves their land and find jobs in cities as traditional belief tells them that it is better to travel abroad on the 3rd, 6th and 9th day every month. All that they want is just to make more money and get good luck in the next year. They anchor their hope for a new tomorrow on their departure on the 6th day.

Fireworks play to celebrate to start business again

9. On the 7th Day, man's birthday in Legend

The seventh day of the first lunar month is entitled as "man's day" as it is considered on this day man was made. The day is also called as "man's festival", "man's birthday", "seven beginning day" and "man's seventh day". The daygained some attention in the Wei and Jin Dynasties and attracted more care in the Tang Dynasty. When Man's Day came, the emperors gave his ministers man-shaped gold foils as gifts and then held a big feast in his palace. The poet LiShi of the Tang dynasty recorded the situation for us.

"The red-painted city (the emperor's palace)is waiting for New Year;

The green glazed tilt palace is immersed in happy mood with dragon and phoenix dancing;

Flower-and-bird gold foils have been newly carved;

They are shining bright on the tents or the screen walls.

The scent of the trees fills the spring garden;

Green mountains far way toast long life of the universe;

The evening landscape is so wonderful when seen from the pitch;

All is bathed in a glory and peace."

The originality of Man's Day could be traced back to the legend that the Goddess Nuwa made human beings and other animals in the world. And now let's see what happened in the story. There was a dead silence between heaven and earth at the times when Nuwa was present. She felt lonely and made some living beings to accompany her out of the mixture of mud and water. Just similar to Genesis where God made everything in the world, Nuwa created seven living beings in seven days, which made the world full of vigor and vitality. On the first day of the lunar year, she shaped a rooster. As soon as the rooster crowed, the gate of heaven was opened with the sun, the moon and all the stars getting out and scattering away. Since then they have been glittering and sparking under the canopy of the sky. On the second day, Nuwa made a dog which ran to the wildness at once. The door barked fiercely and four directions like east, south, west and north emerged immediately. On the next three days, pigs, sheep, cows and horses were created one after another. Then these six animals spread over the ground and ran here and there. To keep them under watch, the Goddess decided to shape a man as their keeper on the seventh day. Therefore the seventh day was remembered as man's birthday. Ancient people developed a custom to wear "Ren Sheng" to celebrate the birth of the human race. Ren Sheng is a kind of man-shaped headpins made of gold foils, called also as "Color Sheng" or "Hua Sheng". (Colored headpins) In the Jin Dynasty, people began cutting the ribbons into certain flower patterns or carving gold foils into man shape. These cutting clips or carved gold foils could be attached to the screen walls for decoration or were put on in women's hair for sake of beauty.

The fine weatherof the seventh day is believed to predict that people could have a big harvest in this new year and thus live happily and safe.

OnMan's birthday, the food is a little different from at usual time as people need to eat a soup named "Seven Bao Geng". It is made from seven kinds of vegetable which could dispel pathogenic virus and bacteria and heal all illnesses. The vegetables vary from place to place thoughtheirconnotation conveyed may be quite similar. In Chaoshan of Guangdong Province, people choose mustard, broccoli, leek, Chun cai, celery, garlic, thick valve dish. Hakka people prefer celery, garlic, onion, coriander, leek, fishand meat. While in Taiwan folks would like to have spinach, celery, onion garlic, leeks, mustard, shepherd's purse and Chinese cabbage.In a symbolic sense, eating celery and onion represent that people can become clever; eatingmore garlic could make a businessman who is good at calculating; shepherd's purse could make a man live longer.

10. On the 8th Day, burn the light against evils

People still need to hold a ceremony for the stars on the evening of the 8th day when the night falls and the sky was glorious. When the sacrifice begins, people need to put lamps with yellow flame burning on the hearth, stove, threshold and cooking bench. That is called as "scattering yellow flame away" or "scatteringvillains away" for luck's purpose. The offering is ended and the family get together to eat sweet dumplings.

Another interesting activity is to set captive animals or birds free. According to folk tales, people could get the blessing of gods if they put some domestic fish back into the sea or send some caged birds back to nature. LiuDongof the Ming dynasty describes the scene in his Empire Sceneas follows. "On the eighth day, releasing of the captives began

Set captive animals free

down ShiDeng Lane. There were cages of birds, bowls of fish and baskets of clams or shrimps in front of the Buddhist temple. The monks were chanting Sanskrit together when people opened the cages and set thousands of birds flying in opposite directions. Some landed on the roof and soared away in a moment. The aquatic animals were put alive into the water of the Golden River around the Imperial Palace where nets and baits to catch fish could hardly be seen."The event of Releasing not only manifests that people respect nature and expect to live harmoniously with it, but also conveys their best wishes for all kinds of prosperous living beings at the beginning of spring.

11. On the 9th to 14th Day, celebration goes on

The 9th day of the first lunar month is the day of the sun. It is said that it is the birthday of the gods' king—the Jade Emperor of Heaven, which is commonly known as "the birth of the Heaven Lord" or "the birth of the Lord of Sun". "The Heaven Lord" or the Jade Emperor is also referred to as "the most respected Buddha at the beginning of world" in Taoist. He is believed to rule the universe including the realm of god, of man and of the dead. His power was bestowed by the heaven and did his governess on behalf of the 'supreme' heaven. To worship "the Heaven Lord" and to worship the most respected Buddha in Taoist's temples are two major customs practiced in some places. Each family prepares the fragrant candles and the bowls contain vegetarian food. They offer their sacrifices in the open air and kneel down to the Heaven to pray for His blessing for ever.

"Shi" or ten in Chinese is homophonic with "stone", so the tenth day is considered to be the birthday of the stone. On the day grinding stones and stone tools making are forbidden.

Besides that, people need to worship the stone god to avoid his harm to the corps, which is clear in the folk saying that "we keep the stones still on the tenth day; they will be kept still in the other days". In Henan province, the custom to worship the stone with the incense burning has been still kept. On the tenth day people must have pancakes for lunch as this represents that they will make more money.

There has been a custom of carrying the god of stone in Yucheng, Shandong Province. On the night of the ninth day, people put a pottery jar on a flat big stone. And then they watered the jar till it was frozen and stuck to the stone's surface tight and firm. The next morning, 10 young men carried the jar in turn by its nose with the big stone glued under. If the stone didn't fall down, a big harvest of the year would be guaranteed.

The 11thday is the time for the parents to entertain their sons-n-laws again after a reunion party on the second day, which is thus named by "Son-in-law Day". But the reception is more casual than the second day's formal party. As there is a lot of food still left after the "Heaven Lord"sacrifice which is held two days earlier, the parents need not to be bustled and hustled with cooking. Therefore they have more time available to enjoy the time staying with their children.

On the twelfth day people will set up the tents of lamps and lanterns, that is, from this day on, people need to do preparations for the Lantern Festival. Lanterns or lamps need to be purchased or made by hand two or three days earlier before the festival. And at the same time building a shelter (usually a tent) for the coming lantern show need to be put into consideration. Just as folk proverbs tell us, "the noisy and happy chatting is heard on the 11th day and men are putting up a lantern tent

Build a framework for the coming lantern shows

a day later; The lights are flaring up on the 13th day and 14th day; Up to the 15th half month is passing by and the festival is over on the 16th day.

12. On the 15th Day, enjoy Lantern shows

The 15th day is the last day of New Year and serves as another special traditional holiday, the Lantern Festival.

The first lunar month is also known as "Yuan month" while the night is known as "Xiao" in ancient or present times. "Yuan Xiao" is another well-known name for the 15th night of

The Lantern Festival

New Year. Only at that night of lunar January can we have a full moon in sight. The most beloved and popular customs are to eat sweet dumplings and to enjoy all kinds of lanterns. Every household cooks sweet dumplings as dinner before they walk out hand in hand to watch the beautiful scenery made by numerous illuminating lamps and lanterns.

Sweet dumplings taste well and are round-shaped with an implication of reunion and completion. The sweet dumpling is made of sticky rice with sesame, bean soup, rose and mashed data fillings inside. The flavors differ when it is cooked in the boiling water, fried in a pan or steamed in a hot pot. People not only watch the lanterns in fairs, they also hang their hand-made ones under the eaves for the others to enjoy. The historical stories and famous figures in the stories painted on the paper cover are shining and glittering alive together with flowers, grass, birds and animals, which has created eye-catching fairy world for people to wander along.

The Most Crowded Temple Fair during the Spring Festivals

As the last day of the Festivals, the 15th day is tinged with a complicated mood that the Spring Festivals will come to an end after it. Willingly or not, we will back to our usual life mode again. A new year starts.

第三章 全国性的春节习俗

春节是中华民族迎春祈福、合家团聚的节日，期间所呈现的各种习俗，是中华民族多元文化的集中展示。

一、
春节的饮食习俗

1. 年糕

年糕，是一种用大米和米粉等黏性粮食蒸制出来的食品。汉代扬雄的《方言》一书中就已有“糕”的称谓，魏晋南北朝时已流行。明清时，年糕已发展成市面上一种常年供应的小食，并有南北风味之别。

○特色年糕，做成了鲤鱼和元宝的模型

年糕最早是在大年三十夜晚用来祭祀神灵和供奉祖先的，由于年糕具有多样的口味，加之年糕“年年高升”的谐音意喻家人的收入、孩童学业一年比一年高，而年糕黄、白的颜色也象征着金银满堂，使得年糕逐渐成为新年里老少咸宜的应景食品。有的地方则直接把年糕叫作“年年糕”，与“年年高”同音，更体现了人们在新的一年步步高升的愿望。

虽然年糕都是由大米等粮食为主料制成，但是人们根据地方的特产和喜好，在年糕中加入各种辅料，并用各具特色的烹饪技艺加工而使得年糕口味多样、各具特色。例如，北京、河北等地的年糕用黄米或江米、小麦磨粉蒸制而成，在年糕中放有大枣、红豆、花生、瓜子等干果，形成了枣年糕、豆年糕、白果年糕等品种。而在山西、内蒙古等地，人们则喜爱将年糕包上枣泥、豆沙等馅料油煎食用。与北方以甜年糕为主不同，南方的年糕则是甜咸都有。北方年糕有蒸、炸二种，南方年糕除蒸、炸外，还有片炒、汤煮等方法。

2. 饺子

饺子是北方民间的一种主食和小吃，还是过年时必吃的一种食品。北方流传着一句民谣：“大寒小寒，吃饺子过年。”

“交子”，即新年与旧年相交的时刻，饺子就意味着更岁交子。在新旧两年交替之时吃“交子”正应和了时景。而且，做饺子首先要和面，和面的“和”字就是“合”的意思，饺子的“饺”又与“交”谐音，“合”字与“交”字都含有相聚之意，因此春节吃饺子便象征着全家人团聚合欢。另外，饺子形状像元宝，包饺子就带有了“招财进宝”之意，象征包住福运、大吉大利。

在传统中，除夕之夜叫作“团圆夜”，全家围坐在一起吃的是团圆饭，而团圆饭的主食便是饺子。

○饺子是中国最具特色的食品之一

饺子是用小麦面粉和水擀皮，里面包上馅，用水煮或上锅蒸制而成。饺子的馅可荤可素，甜咸皆可。较为常见的馅料有猪肉、牛肉、羊肉、鸡肉、虾仁、海参等，配上白菜、韭菜、粉丝等菜蔬。饺子皮薄馅大、劲道爽口，人们百食不厌，因此在民间有“好吃不过饺子”的俗语。大年三十这天，主妇们在包饺子时，都会在其中的一个饺子里放上一枚硬币，待饺子煮熟上桌，谁要是吃到了这个包着硬币的饺子便会一年大吉大利。

各地吃饺子的习俗有所差异。有的地方在除夕之夜吃饺子，有的地方在初一吃饺子，北方一些山区还有初一到初五每天早上吃饺子的习俗。

3. 腊八粥

“腊八粥”又叫“七宝粥”“五味粥”，不仅清香甜美，而且能畅胃气，生津液，因而颇受人们喜食。

腊八，是腊月初八的简称，本身是个传统节日，又是年节的前奏。“小孩小孩你别馋，过了腊八儿就是年”，“吃了腊八饭，就把年来办”。腊八节后，春节将至，人们便开始购置年货、打扫卫生、布置居室，以崭新的面貌迎接新年的到来。

○腊八粥

中国民间喝腊八粥的习俗已有千年历史。因为临近岁末，农作物已收晒完毕，人们便到野外猎取禽兽，用来祭祖先、敬百神，以祈福求寿、避灾迎祥，称为“腊祭”。南北朝时，农历十二月初八才被正式固定为“腊八节”。在这一天要祭祀祖先和神灵，祈求丰收和吉祥。据说，佛教创始人释迦牟尼的成道之日也在十二月初八，因此腊八也是佛教徒的节日，称为“佛成道节”。因此，腊月初八这天，中国各地都有喝腊八粥的习俗。

最早的腊八粥是用红小豆来煮，后经演变，加之地方特色，逐渐丰富多彩起来。

4. 年年有“鱼”

年夜饭中，有一道必不可少的菜——鱼。年夜饭里的鱼与人们平时吃的鱼又有些区别，它是年夜饭里的最后一道菜，要等年夜饭吃到酒酣饭饱之后才端上桌。人们基本也不吃这道菜，只是随便意思下便放下了筷子。

鱼是中国民间的吉祥物，是富贵的象征，表示生活的美满幸福。因为“鱼”与“余”同音，年夜饭里的这道鱼人们不吃，而是留到大年初一才吃掉，便有了“年年有余”的意味，象征着人们新一年里粮食满仓、金银遍地。

○年年有“鱼”，寓意是年年有余

年夜饭里鱼的做法没有太多讲究，但人们多选用鲤鱼、鲢鱼、鳜鱼做菜，因为鲤鱼象征着“得利有余”，鲢鱼象征“连年有余”，鳜鱼则有“富贵有余”的含义。年夜饭的鱼上桌之后如何摆放也是很有讲究的，鱼头要对着家中的长辈，以示尊敬；鱼肚要对着家中读书的孩子，期盼满腹文章；鱼的脊背要对着家中的壮年男子，因为他们都是顶梁柱。鱼上桌后，鱼头所对的长者要与鱼尾所对的人对饮一杯，意为为这道菜“剪彩”。

5. 屠苏酒

屠苏酒是用一种叫作“屠苏”的中药配制而成的药酒，相传由唐代“药王”孙思邈（581—682）所配制。“屠苏”是一种阔叶的草药，最早被古人用来装饰房屋，称作“屠苏屋”，孙思邈便住在这样的屠苏屋内。为了预防瘟疫，孙思邈在每年腊月时都要向乡亲邻里分送他所配制的草药一包，告诉人们用草药泡酒在年末的时候服下，便可保一年不被瘟疫恶疾所害。之后经过历代相传，在除夕夜饮屠苏酒就成了一个过年的风俗。

在过去，饮屠苏酒的方法很特别。一般人饮酒，都是从年长者饮起，而饮屠苏酒则要从最年少者开始。因为年少者过了这一年后便又长大一岁，便要先饮以表庆贺；而年长者过了一年少一年，因此心中忧愁，便要后饮，以示挽留。宋朝文学家苏辙的《除日》诗写道“年年最后饮屠苏，不觉年来七十余”，说的就是这种风俗。

二、
春节的娱乐活动

1. 舞龙

舞龙，也叫“耍龙灯”“龙灯舞”，是中国独具特色的民间娱乐活动。从春节一直到元宵节，在中国城乡都有舞龙的习俗。

舞龙与人们对龙的信仰密切相关。龙是中国的四灵（龙、凤、麒麟、龟）之首，既是祥瑞的灵物、和风化雨的主宰，能消灾降福，也是狂涛骇浪的破坏者，能行云布雨。数千年来，华夏民族将龙作为世代崇拜的图腾，认为自己是龙的后代。

舞龙，是起源于中国的传统舞蹈。在古代，如果遇到了天灾人祸，人们便用舞龙的方式来祈祷，企望获得龙的保佑，求得一年风调雨顺、五谷丰登。经过长期发展，舞龙逐渐从一种祭祀仪式演变为形式欢快活泼、表演动感优美的民间舞蹈。春节期间，舞龙是最受欢迎的表演节目之一。舞龙能在民间受到人们的喜爱，不仅与它的娱乐性有密切联系，而且还和群众性分不开。舞龙简单易学，上至六旬老太，下至七岁孩童都能舞得有声有色。民间就有俗语说：“七八岁玩草龙，十五六岁耍小龙，青年壮年舞大龙。”

舞龙所用的道具是“龙”。龙头、龙身一般用竹篾、木条扎制而成，外面糊上棉纸或布，再用不同颜色颜料为龙头、龙尾上色，龙身则绘上金光闪闪的龙鳞，最后由人们公认最有威望的长者为龙点上双眼，为龙赋予灵气，即“画龙点睛”。有的龙还会在中空的龙身内放上蜡烛或油灯，晚间舞动起来更是壮观，舞动中的龙犹如活了一般。

○准备由德高望重者为这条龙“点睛”

龙身分为数节，以单数较为吉利，常见的有九节龙、十一节龙、十三节龙等，最多的可长达二十九节。龙身超过了十五节便较为笨重了，这样的龙不适宜舞动，只能抬着游街串巷供人观赏，但这样的龙则更注重装饰、色彩艳丽，具有很高的观赏价值。

用来舞动的龙，每节龙身之间都用布相连，龙头、龙身和龙尾下面都有一根竹竿支撑，舞龙者每人持住一根，由头至尾十数丈长。龙头前还有一人手持一杆，杆顶置有龙珠一颗，引导龙头。舞动时，手持龙珠的人左右摆动龙珠，而龙头跟随龙珠作抢珠状，龙身龙尾跟随龙头左右游动、上下翻飞，只见一条巨龙时而腾起钻入云雾，时而俯冲潜入深渊，变化万千，看得人们眼花缭乱。一颗龙珠还能同时引导两条或三条龙，被称为“二龙戏珠”“三龙戏珠”。

中国舞龙的风格有南北之分，以长江为界，以北的舞龙形式叫作“北龙”。从外观上看，北龙龙头小巧，龙身龙尾细小精巧，多为竹篾扎制龙头龙身框架，用纸糊出龙的形状。轻巧的龙身不仅扩大了参与舞龙者的范围，男女老少皆可，而且也为舞龙者动作的创新留下了更大空间。因此，北龙的动作范围和花样都较南龙为多。南龙是在江南一带发展起来的舞龙风格，更注重龙的气势及外观，因此龙头龙身都做得较为庞大，也更为沉重。由于重量的原因，舞南龙的多为青壮年男子，动作也没有北龙那样花样繁多。由于不追求灵活，人们都把心思花在龙的外观和体积上，龙身上的装饰和彩绘较北龙更为艳丽，而且龙身长度一般都在二十米以上，甚至有超过百米、长达千米的龙。

在浙江、福建等地，春节时人们还有舞板凳龙的习俗。这种龙只制作龙头和龙尾，龙身则是每家各拿出一条条凳连接而成，有多少户人家就有多少节龙身。舞板凳龙时，各家板凳首尾相连，每家派出一名青壮年男子举着自家板凳，在龙头的带领下游村走街，场面蔚为壮观。龙的动作，通常有盘圈、S 弯、龙头越过龙身等。

从种类上看，湖北仙桃市沔阳的高跷龙、四川济州龙溪一带羌族的麻龙、浙江衢州市开化县苏庄镇的稻草龙、湖南汝城县的香火龙、湖南湘西土家族的泼水龙、浙江长兴的百叶龙、广东丰顺县的烧火龙等各具特色。

2. 舞狮

在人们心中，狮子是瑞兽，有驱邪的能力，象征着吉祥如意。人们对狮子的喜爱，不仅表现在门墩、屋檐、石栏、印章和年画上随处可见的狮子形象，而且还让狮子活了起来，就是模仿狮子的舞蹈。

○中国北方的舞狮

舞狮，又叫作“狮灯”“狮子舞”。在春节期间舞狮，寄托着人们纳吉纳福、消灾辟邪的愿望。舞狮在中国的历史长远，南北朝时期便已流行，唐代起已形成了百人共舞的集体性表演。不仅在民间，在宫廷中舞狮也十分受欢迎，称为“太平乐”或“五方狮子舞”。

舞狮所用狮子的外观形象以及舞狮的步法也有南北之分，被称作“北狮”和“南狮”。

北狮所用的狮子道具外形酷似真狮子，全身覆有金黄色狮毛，怒目圆睁、龇牙咧嘴。舞狮者的裤子鞋子上也会披上狮毛，二人相互配合，一人手持狮头，一人弯腰在后扮作狮身，舞动起来惟妙惟肖如同真狮一般。舞北狮时候一般是雌狮、雄狮成对出现，雄狮狮头上有红结，雌狮狮头上则为绿结。舞狮时多以扑、跌、翻、滚等较为灵活的动作出现，还会有一人手持绣球在场中引导两只狮子，叫作“狮子抢绣球”。有的时候，表演中还会配上一对小狮子，大小狮子互相嬉戏玩耍，妙趣横生。

南狮又被称作“醒狮”，造型较北狮更为威猛和抽象。南狮也是二人共舞。狮头一般以戏曲脸谱为蓝本，色彩艳丽、做工考究，狮子的眼睑和嘴都可以活动。南狮主要分三种，分别根据三国时期刘备、关羽、张飞的形象制作。三种狮子不仅外观不同，舞狮的人还要根据狮子所代表的人物形象以不同的步法表演。如红色狮子代表关羽，是忠义和胜利的象征，因此在舞动时步法沉稳有力；黄色狮子代表刘备，象征仁义和皇家气息，舞动时步法便要大气和雍容华贵；黑色狮子代表的是张飞，步法霸气、勇猛，张飞狮因为多暴戾之气，在节日喜庆之时一般不使用，多见于比赛和挑战时。

3. 打麻将

红火热闹的春节中，人们不仅可以看到舞狮、舞龙这些公共娱乐性的表演，在家中也能玩得开心愉快，其中最有代表性的便是有“国粹”之称的麻将了。

麻将是一种四人玩骨牌类型的游戏，娱乐性就在于要通过骨牌的排列组合来赌输赢、决胜负。麻将主要流行于华人文化圈内，不仅在中国城乡十分普及，即使到了海外的华人圈中也依然盛行，是中国最具规模和影响力的博弈游戏，亦被称作“国玩”。

传说麻将是明朝时期一位叫万秉迢（万、饼、条）的人所发明的。由于他十分仰慕《水浒传》中梁山泊的一百单八位好汉，便想制作一种娱乐工具来纪念他们，让人们在娱乐的同时也能时时缅怀这些英雄好汉。经过多年的冥思苦想，他终于创制出了麻将牌。他将麻将牌设计为 108 张，与《水浒传》中的一百单八位好汉一一暗喻，如麻将牌中的二条是“双鞭呼延灼”，而九条则暗指“九纹龙史进”等。万秉迢还考虑到这一百单八位好汉来自天南海北，因而又设计了东、西、南、北、中各四张牌，说明这些好汉来自东、西、南、北、中各个方向。梁山好汉中有的出身富贵，有的出身赤贫，为此又设计了“白”和“发”各四张分别暗喻出身贫寒和出身富贵的好汉。到最后，整副麻将牌共计 136 张。万秉迢还考虑到梁山泊的领袖宋江一心想与朝廷求和，为朝廷所招安，所以打麻将时赢牌要说“和”（音 hu），而不说“赢”或“胜”。

○打麻将

麻将游戏最初只流传于民间，人们往往在一天劳作之后用于放松消遣，代表了劳苦民众在朝廷高压下对梁山好汉“大碗喝酒、大块吃肉”的自由生活的向往。发展到后来，麻将的娱乐功能逐渐代替了其他功能，这一游戏也逐渐走进宫廷，为王公大臣们所接受。

○打麻将已经成为中国人流行的娱乐方式

麻将牌大多以骨面竹背嵌合而成，骨面上雕刻有从一到九的“饼”“条”“万”等字样。与其他骨牌相比，麻将集趣味性、益智性和博弈性为一体，玩法简单、易于上手，其中的变化又繁复无比，各种搭配组合令人眼花缭乱、乐趣无穷。麻将不仅独具魅力，且蕴涵着丰富悠长的东方文化底蕴，不仅有中国古代的文化思想，其中的中国古代数学思维和理论也独具东方情趣，是中华传统文化的重要组成部分。由于麻将游戏方法的变化多样，因而在不同地区人们为了增强趣味性而制定了不同的游戏规则，由此造就了具有地方特色的麻将玩法。具有代表性的有古代的洛书麻将以及现代的四川麻将、广东麻将、长沙麻将等。

三、春节逛庙会

庙会，又称“庙市”或“节场”，指在寺庙内或附近聚会，进行祭神、娱乐和购物等活动，流行于全国广大地区，是中华文化传统的节日风俗。

庙会在中国有久远的历史。在古代，“日中为市”，进行集市贸易。秦代庙会的内容仍然单一而稳定，即祭祀祖先与神灵。西汉时期，道教初步形成。庙会受到宗教信仰的影响，内容开始出现多元化色彩。东汉时期，佛教传入中国，道教也已逐渐成形，两教之间展开了激烈的竞争并相互影响。两晋时期，社会动荡，原本较为兴盛的儒教开始衰落，饱经战乱和欺压的百姓纷纷皈依佛教或道教。六朝以后，佛教寺院、道教宫观日渐增多，于是附于佛寺、道观的庙会逐渐兴盛起来。唐宋时期，两教均达到了全盛时期，特别是佛教文化影响空前巨大，无论南方还是北方，佛教庙寺林立，崇佛成为民间信仰的主流，佛事渗入庙会，使庙会文化呈现出更大的宗教特征。明代，许多庙会开始向市集性质转变，游玩观光或购买商品称为主流，真正进行祭祀或拜谒的人并不多。到了清代，庙会已分为所谓的“多内涵型庙会”与“迎神赛会”。前者在宗教、娱神的同时有游乐等活动，而后者则是把神像抬出庙外巡行，是没有集市但有表演的庙会，如北京妙峰山庙会。同时也有部分地方无庙有市也称庙会，如北京著名的厂甸庙会。

○北京地坛公园的庙会

早期的庙会仅是一种宗庙社郊制度——祭祀。远古时期，人们为了求得祖先及神灵的保佑，选择在宫殿或房舍里通过供奉与祭祀的方式，与之进行对话。在祭祀祖先神和自然神的过程中，人们聚集在一起，集体开展一些活动，如进献供品、演奏音乐、举行仪式等，这种为祭祀神灵而产生的集会可以看作是后世民间庙会的雏形。庙会起源于寺庙周围，所以叫“庙”；又由于小商小贩们看到烧香拜佛者多，在庙外摆起各式小摊赚钱，渐渐地成为定期活动，所以叫“会”。久而久之，庙会演变成了如今人们在节日期间，特别是春节期间的娱乐活动。

民间的庙会有自己的核心特征，即在经济技术方面是百货交易，在社会组织方面是“社”或“会”，在意识形成方面是礼神娱神。这便是我国庙会能够长期传承的经济基础和民俗惯制。

庙会一开，八方来拜，敬神上香，祈愿还家。这是围绕“庙”和所祭之神而展开的活动，是传统庙会的主题。这方面比较典型的庙会有河南淮阳的人祖庙会、天津的妈祖（天后宫）庙会、山西平遥的双林寺庙会、北京的妙峰山和白云观庙会等。

庙会的时间最初是在举行各种宗教节日（佛道二教为主）庆典时，后来发展为某些固定日期，现代举办时间则多为春节、元宵节等节日。

在当代中国，春节期间的庙会遍布各地，各具特色。庙会既然在春节期间举行，主要内容少不了各色小吃、各种小商品和游乐项目，为逛庙会的人们提供了方便。庙会中的文化娱乐包括各类民间艺人进行的表演，如地方戏、木偶戏、曲艺、魔术、耍中幡、旱船、秧歌、舞龙舞狮、高跷等。庙会中的民间玩具种类繁多，制作精巧，包括假面、戏剧木人、小车、刀矛、竹龙、空竹、扑扑登、走马灯、鬃人、吹糖人、画糖人、塑糖人、面塑、九连环、拨浪鼓等工艺品。

在各种庙会的小吃中，最值得一提的是历史悠久的北京小吃，如茶汤、杏仁茶、油茶、面茶、江米粥、豌豆黄、老豆腐、炸丸子、豆汁、灌肠、炸肠、凉粉、糖瓜、糖饼、吊炉烧饼、艾窝窝、扒糕、豌豆糕、煎饼等。

庙会贸易活动体现了集市的特征，包括农副产品市场（农具、家禽家畜、鱼肉、蔬菜、水果、鲜花等）、饮食市场（饭馆、酒馆、茶馆、布棚、席棚）、商品市场（服装、鞋帽、箱包、日用品、文具、书画、电器等）、古玩市场等。

旅游小贴士

北京庙会："闹"中过大年

"庙会是老北京人心里的一个念想儿，它包含了对家人的回忆、对北京的一种怀旧。"这是北京人对庙会的概括。在北京过春节，无法想象没有庙会会怎么样。那是北京年味儿的集中展示，也是过年必备的一种仪式。

每年春节，北京都有数十场上规模的庙会，天坛、地坛、北海、厂甸、龙潭湖、莲花池公园……但凡有名一点的去处，都有热闹的民俗庙会上演。如果在春节期间去北京旅游，最值得推荐的游玩项目也是庙会。

这种最大众化也是最嘈杂的场所是体验北京数百年民俗的最佳选择。尽管现在的庙会早已商业味道浓厚，但游人们仍然可以吃到最正宗的北京小吃，买到最地道的老北京工艺品，感受到最原始的买卖场景，也就足以慰藉向往古都文明的人们了。

对于一名外来者，最饶有兴致的是欣赏庙会上的花会表演。民间的艺术团体在庙会期间一下子蜂拥而出，聚集在那一小块区域，展示着高跷、太平鼓、秧歌、皮影戏、练把式、吹糖人、泥人制作、老北京木雕门楼等传统的民俗艺术，赢来一阵阵喝彩。

1. 北京地坛公园春节庙会

时间：每年正月初一至正月初五

地址：北京市安定门外大街地坛公园

票价：10 元

乘车线路：乘地铁 2 号线到雍和宫或安定门站，地铁 5 号线雍和宫或和平里北街站，乘公交车 13、特 2 路汽车到地坛南门，104、108、124 路电车或 27、104 快、643、430 到地坛西门，125、117 到地坛东门。

2. 龙潭公园春节庙会

时间：每年正月初一至正月初五)

地址：北京市东城区龙潭路 8 号龙潭公园

3. 北京八大处新春祈福庙会

时间：每年春节前后一周时间

地址：北京八大处公园

4. 北京龙潭湖龙潭庙会

时间：每年正月初一至正月初五

地址：北京龙潭公园

四、元宵节赏灯

正月十五元宵节，又叫灯节、上元节，届时家家挂灯，人人赏灯。关于元宵赏灯的来历，这里有个十分曲折动人的传说。

汉武帝时，有个足智多谋、诙谐滑稽的东方朔，武帝十分信任他。宫门森严，他却可以随便出入，以随时取悦皇上。他外表随便，内心善良，常为宫中彩女向武帝求情。

○元宵节赏花灯

这年腊月，一连下了几天大雪，东方朔去御花园给武帝折几枝梅花，忽见一个宫女哭着向玩月池中跳去，慌忙上前拉住。细细一问，她叫元宵，家住长安城外山上，家里还有父母、妹妹，进宫之后再没见过他们。每逢佳节倍思亲，近几日风雪交加，愁闷不堪，想与家人见见面，又怕武帝不允。思来想去，还不如一死了之，黄泉之下再与父母相会。

东方朔安慰了她一番，答应设法让她与家人团聚。他出皇宫，离长安，到元宵家里如此这般地安排了一下，然后就回到长安，在大街上卖起卦来。人们久仰东方朔的大名，争着前来求签问卜，得到的都是“正月十六火焚身”的卦语。众人大惊，纷纷求教解脱的方法。东方朔郑重地说：“正月十三日，火神君会来长安察看地形，你们可到城西北十里的大路口等候。中午过后，会过来一个骑红色毛驴的红衣姑娘，她就是奉旨焚烧长安的火神君。你们前去拦路哭求，或许有救。”

人们听了，互相串联，相约多邀一些人，去十里铺大道口等候。正月十三中午一过，果见从西北方向过来一个骑着红色毛驴的红衣女子，众人连忙上前苦苦哀求。姑娘道：“我是领旨火烧长安的，玉帝到时候要亲自站在南天门察看的。你们既然求情，我把抄录的偈语给你们，可让皇上想想办法。”

人们拿了火神君赐给的红贴，回到长安跪在午门前，要把贴子献给皇上。汉武帝接过侍卫们传进来的红贴，见上面写着四句偈语：“长安在劫，火焚帝阙，十六天火，焰红宵夜。”武帝看了吓得魂飞魄散，忙请东方朔商量应付的办法。东方朔禀道：“听说火神君最爱吃汤圆，宫里的元宵做得一手好汤圆，火神君也会知道的。皇上可在十五晚上，让元宵做汤圆祭献天神，再传谕全城百姓家家做汤圆，一齐敬奉驾临长安上空的火神君，想来她会心软下来不再放火的。同时，您再下旨让京城臣民一齐动手做花灯，于十五、十六晚上在大街小巷、内屋外院一齐挂上红灯，从天上看起来就好像满城大火，这样，便能骗过在南天门察看的玉帝。此外，再令城外臣民届时进城观灯，皇上与皇后、妃子、宫女，分散在人群中去街上赏灯，驱灾解难。”

武帝大喜，依言而行。正月十五，太阳刚向西天斜挂下去，人们已纷纷张灯结彩准备起来。武帝带了皇后、妃子，皆穿便服，在几个也穿着便服的亲近大臣和侍卫的保护下，混在人群中去街上观灯。宫女、太监们也三三两两上街而去。华灯初上，万灯争辉，各种火伞、火马、转子莲、花筒、炮打四门、火龙摆尾等花灯呈奇争彩，颇为壮观。元宵的妹妹领着父母也来长安观灯，当她看到写有“元宵”字样的大宫灯时，忙叫姐姐的名字。元宵早在这里等候，见父母妹妹果然赶来，忙扑到母亲身上。亲上团聚，互叙衷肠。

十五夜平安过去了，十六夜也平安过去了，元宵与亲人团聚了两个晚上，心情十分欣慰。由于东方朔的努力，以后每到正月十五，人们就过灯节，并逐渐流传到各地。这一节日因元宵而起，故称“元宵节”。又因元宵节要吃汤圆，汤圆以元宵做得最好，所以也称“元宵”。

赏灯也是春节期间不可缺少的娱乐活动，一般指从腊月三十到元宵节期间人们观赏悬挂在家中、庙会、集市、街道等地方的彩灯或由政府举办的大型灯展，俗称“灯会”或“灯市”，并常常附带有一些民俗活动，极具传统性和地方特色。

按中国民间的传统，正月十五皓月高悬，人们要点起彩灯万盏，以示庆贺。出门赏月、燃灯放焰、喜猜灯谜、共吃元宵，合家团聚、同庆佳节，其乐融融。

五、春节的现代习俗

随着时代的变迁，传统的节日民俗也在发生变化。当代中国的春节，一方面执着地延续着传统，另一方面又时时透射出现代的节奏与气息。

1. 回家过年

中国经济的飞速发展，使城市化和人口流动成为现实，越来越多的中国农民离开家乡，到经济发展迅猛的东南沿海地区打工，更有一部分中国人远渡重洋去海外谋生。但中国人浓重的思乡情结永远都解不开，从而形成了如今每年春节的“人口大迁移”。为了买到一张回家的车票，很多农民工在火车站要排几天几夜队。春节回家与亲人团聚，是中国人一年中最大的牵挂。1980 年，“春运”这个词语，第一次出现在官方的报道上。春运被誉为人类历史上规模最大、周期性最长的人类大迁徙。直到现在，“春运”仍是让人心绪复杂的一个词语。年年此时，无数人一定要在谋生的城市和故土家园之间，完成一次次充满幸福和心酸的辗转旅程，因为回家过年就是中国人的“朝圣路”。

○每年春运都将引来中国最大规模的人口迁移

每年春节，“有钱没钱，回家过年”。在中国传统文化里，过年就是要和家人在一起。没有亲人的地方，即使年夜饭吃的是山珍海味，也只是食而无味的一餐饭，而不是和家人团圆的年夜饭；即使住的地方奢华富丽，也只是栖息的房屋而不是有归属感的家。和父母亲人一起过年，纵然辛苦，也很幸福。

2. 春节黄金周

1999 年 9 月 18 日，中国国务院修订发布《全国年节及纪念日放假办法》，决定增加公众法定休假日。中国人在春节时的闲暇时间增多，越来越多的人不再满足于过节的时候待在家里，而走亲访友、打牌聚会也被认为是不健康的过节方式。于是，离开常住地方出门远行便成了很多人过春节的新方式。黄金周是出游的好机会，但是现在人们出游已经趋于理性和成熟，很多人不会选择热门的景点，而是选择观光式旅游，目的在于能彻底放松身心，追求旅途中的宁静。

近几年，政府加大铁路、公路、航空等基础设施建设，地方政府积极发展旅游产业，开拓各类旅游项目，为春节黄金周提供支持。

○春节黄金周

临近春节的时候，各大旅行社的业务量飞涨，许多人早在过年前两个月就预定了行程。据有关统计，第一个黄金周全国出游人数 7 天内达到 2800 万人次，旅游综合收入实现 131 亿元。黄金周旅游的势头始终保持了快速增长的趋势，游客的大规模出行，极大地刺激了餐饮业和商业的发展。

3. 除夕看春晚

享誉中国大地的春节联欢晚会，通常简称为“央视春晚”，或直接称为“春晚”，是中国中央电视台在每年农历除夕晚上为庆祝农历新年而举办的综艺性文艺晚会。春晚在演出规模、演员阵容、播出时长和海内外观众收视率上，共创下中国世界纪录协会世界综艺晚会评选的世界收视率最高、世界上播出时间最长、世界上演员最多的三项综艺晚会世界之最。2012 年 4 月，中国春节联欢晚会获得了吉尼斯世界纪录证书。

广义上的春节联欢晚会可以追溯到 1956 年。当时由张骏祥任总执导，谢晋、林农、岑范、王映东任导演，中央新闻纪录电影制片厂出品了《春节大联欢》。根据影片内容显示，当时的中央人民广播电台向全国现场直播了演出。很多大师都曾经出镜，如越剧演员徐玉兰、王文娟，评剧演员新凤霞，京剧演员梅兰芳、相声演员侯宝林以及老舍、巴金、赵丹等人。

央视具有春晚性质的“迎新春文艺晚会”自 1979 年除夕开始播出。1983 年，央视首次举办了春节联欢晚会，到现在已经成为中国人的“新民俗，新文化”，是千家万户每年除夕夜必看的电视大餐。现在，全国大大小小的地方电视台频频效法并力求创新，推出了各自的地方春节晚会。

○除夕夜全家欢笑看春晚（来源：央视网）

央视春晚在每年的除夕之夜 20:00 都会通过 CCTV–1、4、7、NEWS（英语新闻）、西班牙语、法语、阿拉伯语、俄语、高清频道进行现场并机直播，中国网络电视台（CNTV）也在网络上直播。随着科技的发展，CCTV 手机电视、CCTVip 电视也在直播，直到凌晨 1:00 左右，全长达约 5 小时。全国数亿观众都会守在电视机前，迎接新的一年的到来。

从春晚 30 年的发展历程看，经历了 20 世纪 80 年代启动期的火爆，20 世纪 90 年代成长期的壮大，直到 21 世纪成熟期的稳定。无论如何变化，央视春晚这个诞生在改革开放初期的电视综合文艺形式，已经成为家喻户晓、闻名海内外的春节期间节日文艺大餐，成为所有炎黄子孙追求和谐、进步、吉祥的民俗盛典。

过去，中国人过春节的习俗怕只限于吃团圆饭、放鞭炮、走亲访友和朋友聚会等。随着改革开放，经济条件逐渐好转，很多中国家庭都有了电视机，为收看中央电视台春节联欢晚会提供了可能。年长的一辈喜欢在除夕夜守着电视收看春晚，年轻一代则更热衷于网络娱乐，在网上与广大网友一起迎接春节的到来。

2002 年，网易首推“虚拟春晚”，极大改变了传统的节庆方式。“网络守岁”，就是在网络的虚拟空间和平台上度过除夕。“守岁”一族大多是年轻人，除夕之夜就守在电脑前迎接新年，因为在网上过除夕互动性比较强，选择空间比较大，可以听歌、看电影，在网上聊天。上网过年、虚拟空间里的喜庆，凸现出的是另一种“春节模式”，并没有使传统的年味减少，只是给过年的习俗增添了一种新的承载方式。

Chapter Three

National Custom of the Spring Festival

The Spring Festival is a holiday for Chinese people to celebrate the spring, to pray to the heaven, and to reunion with family members. And the customs that people observe reveal the diversity of Chinese culture to a great degree.

1. Food and Drink Tradition

1.1 Nian Gao

Nian Gao is a steamed pastry made of rice and sticky flour. The food was recorded earlyin Dialects, written by Yang Xiong of Han Dynasty. Nian Gaohad been quite popular during the Wei and Jin Period and the Northern and Southern Dynasties.In the Dynasties of Ming and Qing, itbecame an ordinary snack that people could afford to enjoy as they wished.

Steamed sticky rice Niao GAO

Nian Gao at first was used as a sacrifice to the Heaven and ancestors on the Eve of the Spring Festival. Later it has gradually been loved by people of all the ages for it has a variety of flavor to select. Chinese eat it even for its cultural connotation—Niao Gao is often referred to the rise of family income and the growth of children year by year because the pastry is like gold and silver with golden and silver color. In some places of China people intentionally speak out Niao Gao loudly (年

Special-designed Nian GAO shaped by Fish and Ingot

年高 pinyin: Nian Nian Gao--- life is better year by year) for luck's saketo express their wishes for the new year.

Nian Gao is mainly made of rice. People can put inside different fillings made by local specialties, and cook it detestable with their own cuisine skills and preference. For instance, local residents in Beijing and Heibei Province usually like to fill in dates, cooked beans, peanuts and sunflower seeds inside the

Fried Niao GAO

pastry; while people choose smashed dates and beans fillings in Shanxi and Inner Mongolia, and they fry it rather than steam it. In the south of China, Nian Gao tastes both sweet and salty. And the southerners have moreways to cook, for example, to cut it into slices and fry the slices in a pan or put them into boiling water.

1.2 Dumpling

Dumpling is both a main dish and a snack in the north. At the Spring Festival people must eat dumplings as a famous folk goes "major cold minor cold, eating dumplings makes a new year."

Jiaozi, Chinese name for dumplings, means literally a transitional periodfrom the old year and the newly-coming year. Eating 'Jiaozi'at the moment coincides perfectly with time changing. People need to mix the flour and water as first step to make dumplings.

And interestingly, the first step to is to which is pronounced in Chinese 'huo'. Both 'jiao'and 'huo' connotes peaceful and

Dumpling, a kind of food with Chinese style

Dumpling making

pleasant gathering in harmony, so dumplings eating symbolize reunion for family and friends. Besides, dumplings look like a kind of silver ingots and dumplings making thus represent that people would make more money and have good luck in the next year.

Traditionally, on the eve of the Spring Festival, families sit around and enjoy delicious food and Jiaozi is certainly served as the main dish.

How to make dumplings? First of all, combine the flour and water into a mixture and then make thin dough coverings by rolling a small ball of mixture with a stick. Put the fillings inside the dough and cook them by steaming or boiling. They may have different ingredients like pork, beef, mutton, chicken and vegetables. The fillings could be sweet and salty. Thin covering and delicious contents makes it one of the enduringfavorite foods in china, just as some believe that nothing is more palatable than Dumplings. On the eve, the housewife always hides a coin inside one of the dumplings. The person who gets it is believed to have a good fortune in the next year.

The time of dumpling eating varies in different areas. Some may eat it on the eve; while some others enjoy it on the first day of the Spring Festival. In some mountainous areas of the north, people take it as breakfast every morning from the first day to the fifth day.

1.3 Laba Rice Porridge

Laba Rice Porridge, renamed by Qibao Porridge and Wuwei Porridge, gains its popularity not because it tastes fresh and delicious but also it can help expel waste air out of stomach and produce more digestive juice.

Laba, a short term for the eighth day of the twelfth lunar month, is another traditional festive and a prelude to the Spring Festival. 'child, child, don't make your mouth water, after Laba the big festival is coming,' as some Chinese ballades sing, 'finish eating Laba Porridge and a big feast is awaiting'. When the Laba Festival is over, people begin to prepare themselves for the New Year by doing shopping, cleaning and tiding.

Porridge drinking at Laba can be traced back to thousands of years ago. At the end of each year, people had finished their

Laba Rice Porridge

farm work and went out for animal chasing. The animals hunted would be cooked and served as a sacrifice to the gods and ancestors for bliss, longevity and disaster evasion. The eighth day of the twelfth lunar month didn't become a formal festival until in the Southern and Northern Period and a worship ceremony was to be held to God and ancestors. It is said that the Buddha, the founder of Buddhism, achieved his enlightenment on that day too, so Laba became a Buddhist festival and has been remembered and celebrated heretofore as Bodhi Day by Chinese Buddhism followers. Chinese like to drink porridge as common practice on that day.

The earliest Laba Porridge was made of red beans and was cooked by boiling. And later more ingredients were added to it, which surely made it lookingattractive and tasting more delicious.

1.4 Fish

The big dinner on the eve cannot make it without fish. The fish we have at the Festival is a little different from the fish we have for ordinary time. Cooked fish is usually served at the last moment when all the other dishes are finished on that big dinner evening. People actually cannot any eat more, just have small bitesymbolically and put down their chopsticks. In some places, people will keep fish head and tail untouched and intact to the next day, which means that life should have a beginning and an end.

Fish is the mascot of Chinese folk culture as its Chinese pronunciation is same with another Chinese word 'yu(余)', which means that life is wealthy and well-off. That is the reason why people don't eat fish off and keep it to the next morning. Fish left stands for more crops and more money saved in the next year.

Eating fish at the Festivals means a surplus for every family

There is no much greater difference in cooking way and fish selecting. People usually pick up carp, catfish and mandarin fish as materials for as these threekinds all sound homophonic with wealth and richness. Carp sounds similar to good profit and wealth, and catfish and mandarin fish sound respectively being well-off all the time and wealthy enough or affluent. How to set fish on the table also matters. Fish head should be put towards the elders in regard to respect. The belly needs to be towards the children who are supposed to be full of learning. The back to the male adults may suggest that they are the backbone of the family. After fish is served, the man towards the head and tail will toast to each other, like ribbon-cutting, to start fish eating.

1.5 Tu Su Wine

This is a medicinal wine made of Chinese medicine, and in legend, by an ancient medicine expert, Sun Simiao by name, (A.D.,581--682) who is well known for his splendid research on Chinese medicine. 'Tu Su' is a broad-leaved herb, and was used to decorate the house in the ancient time. Mr. Sun Simiao lived in such a "Tu Su" room to prevent epidemics invasion.

Hegave every folk man a pack of medicine made by him in the twelfth lunar month and told them to pourthe medicine into wine. At the end of the year they could drink the soaked medicine up and later the epidemics cannot do these men any harm a year around. And this recipe was passed down through generations and Tu Su wine drinking slowly became a custom.

Generally, the elders should drink wine first; Tu Su drinking is different and begins from the youngest of the family. Young men will be one year older when the new year comes, to celebrate growth, they are expected to drink first;While the elders will grow old and feel worried and frustrated, hence, they should be left behind to drink and hoped to forget their ages. 'The last one to drink Tu Su wine, I hardly remember how old I am', says Su Che, a famous literary figure in Song Dynasty. Another poet, Gu Kuang of Tang Dynasty also describes the situation in his poem. 'The spring comes with my old age, so sad to see old friends pass away; living in seclusion and loneliness, I am even reluctant to see into the mirror, let the young drink Tu Su first.

2. Entertainment

2.1 Dragon Dance

Dragon dance, renamed dragon lantern dance, is an important part of Chinese specific folklore celebration. From the Spring Festival to the Lantern Festival, dragon dance shows could be seen everywhere in towns and cities.

Dragon dance is closely associated with the tradition that Chinese worship dragons, which are considered the top of one of four spirits. The other three include phoenix, unicorn and fish. Chinese dragons traditionally symbolize potent and auspicious powers, particularly control over water, rainfall, hurricane, and floods. The dragon is also a symbol of power, strength, and good luck.Thousands of years, dragon has been the totem of Chinese people who regard themselves as the descendents of dragons.

The dragon dance derives its originality from Chinese traditional dance. In the past, when natural disasters and accidents occurred, people would pray to god to bless them by dancing a dragon puppet. And with time passing by, the dance evolved from the original pray into a rhythmic, jolly and vigorous dance performance. Dragon dance is beloved so much that no other entertainment could be the highlight of spring celebration. Dragon dancing makes people happier also because it is so easy to participate. Everyone including the old and children can learn it well if they wish. There goes a folk saying, 'children of seven or eight play with grass dragon, teenagers love smaller dragon, while young men favor the big one.'

Dragon puppet is made in hand. The head and body are stapled with bamboo skin and wood piece, the surface will be plastered with tissue paper or cloth. Paint different colors for every part. The body needs to be painted golden-scale pattern. Finally the most respectable senior will draw the eyes for the dragon with a brush, bringing the dragon to life with his finishing touch. Some even put candles or oil lamps inside the dragon puppet and the play is spectacular and more exciting with an illuminating movement.

The body can be divided into several sections. Chinese prefer odd numbers, so the puppet is usually composed of nine, eleven sections and thirteen, at most twenty-nine sections, which is rarely seen sometimes. Dragon models of more than fifteen is heavier to play with but more suitable for patrol and watch. They seem to have more value in artistic appreciation

The dragon model is ready for eye drawing

than performance as their makers pay more attentions to decoration and painting.

The dragon for dance has bamboo sticks attached to its head, body and tail below and every dancer takes hold of one stick. When the performance begins, a man holding a longer pole with a pearl ball on top will stand in front of the dragon head. He will swing the pearl ball left to right in musical tune and the dragon will move forward to get it. The audience may feel bewildered and dazzled when they seem to see a dragon soaring to the sky this moment and diving into deep sea next second. Sometimes two or three dragons fight for one pearl, so is called 'Er Long Xi Zhu' and 'San Long Qiang Zhu' in Chinese.

The dance style in the north is different from that in the south bordered by the Yangtze River. The northern dragon is lighter and smaller in head, and thinner and more delicate in body and tail, which enable more people could participate in the dance whether they are old or young, men or women. Lightness and small size also leave more room for the performers to improve their moving skills and patterns. In comparison, the southern dragon is characterized by its strength and manners due to its heavy body and large size. Most of the dancers are men. With big load, they just act relatively simple and they are more proud of the dragon's volume. The body is usually twenty meters long and some is even as long as hundreds of meters. More decoration and brighter color painting feature the appearance of the southern dragon.

The northern dragon usually has a lighter and smaller head, a thinner and more complicated body and tail compared to the equivalent of the south

InZhejiang, Fujian Province, the custom of bench dragon dance has been practiced till today. People only make the head and tail for dragon model. The body is made up of the benches from the folks and each house is expected to offer one bench. When the dance commences, the representative man chosen by his family will lift his bench high under the lead of the head man and patrol in the street around near villages. Bench against bench, it is indeed extraordinary. The dragon moves in circles or a's' pattern or head over body.

There are still other special categories in the south such as dragon dancing on stilts in Gaiyang, Xiantao of Hubei Province, Qiang Minority's hemp-fiber dragon in Qizhou of Sichuan Province, Suzhuang' s straw dragon in Kaihua, Zhejiang Province, incense-sparkling dragon in Ruyang and Tujia Minority' water-splashing dragon in the west part of Hunan Province. The leave-flower dragon in Zhejiang and fire-works dragon in Guangdong are distinguished too.

2.2 Lion dance

Chinese view the lion as potent animal that has magic power to drive out evil spirits. The lion could be seen anywhere in Chinese culture, not only in the design of the roof, the stone railing, gate pier, but also inscribed in the seals and on the paintings. They imitate the dance of lion to express their adoration.

The lion dance, or 'lion lantern' or 'lion dancing' as it is called, has a long history. People entertain themselves by dancing the lion models to express their hopes of luck and auspicious omen and warding off evil spirits. The dance was very popular in the Southern and Northern Period. And there were already 100 participants in the collective performance. In court, the lion dance was admired by the nobility, too, was called by its noble name 'Tai Ping Lion Dance' or 'Wu Fang Lion Dance'. Bai Juyi, a well-known poet of Tang Dynasty once writes down the spectacular show in his peom The Ambassador of Xiliang as follows, masked Hu Minority dancers are playing with a masked lion with a wooden head and silk thread tail.

The lion dance in the North of China

With its golden-gilded eyes and silver teeth, the lion is shaking its woolen body and ears with all efforts.

The dance of lion could be divided into northern style and southern style in terms of dancing steps and the lion's appearance.

The northern lions resemble their real equivalents. They are covered with golden wool with eyes staring big and mouth wide open. Two dancers will wear the shoes and trousers made of lion-hair-like fibers. One is holding the head in front and the other is in charge of the rear behind. They work together to get it move as the real lion walks in the forest. Male lion with green stripes dance with female lion with red stripes. And they leap, swoop, roll over to attack and play. A man with an embroider ball will tease at the two lions to fight for it. And sometimes, a pair of child lion will join the show and play with their bigger fellows.

The southern is called awakening lion with aggressive and violent appearance design. Two dances are need too. The head is designed based on the face of Chinese opera, striking color

The lion dance in the South of China

and well-made. The eyelids can bat frequently and the mouth can open to devour vividly. There are three kinds of the southern lions on the basis of three characters in Three Kingdm Period. Liu Bei, emperor of Han, led Guang Yu and Zhang Fei to fight for their empire. The dancers should follow different steps in the show to represent different characters. Guang Yu's actor will dance the red lion ad move in a steady and powerful way to show his loyalty and his calmness. And yellow color is reserved for the kings and emperors prohibited in the commons, so Liu Bei will have the yellow lion in a royal and majestic manner. The black lion by Zhang Fei actually seldom appears in the festivals for its brutality and black fury. However, it features determination and aggression in tournaments and competitions.

2.3 Mahjong Playing

When all the outdoors shows are enough, people begin to seek more pleasure at home. And one of the nationalfavoriteactivities is mah-jong.

Mahjong is a game that originated in China, commonly played by four players. They arrange tile cards by drawing and discarding. The person who first forms certain groups can win the game according to the rules. Mahjong is popular in China home and abroad. Nearly everyone is good at its playing, so it is widespread as the most influential competition game.

In legend, a man called Wan Bingtiao (Character suits, Circle suits, Bamboo suits) invented mah-jong. He admired 108 heroes in Water Margin so much that he decided to make a set of play equipment as remembrance. After many years' meditation, he ended up in the creation of mah-jong, with which people can play for fun and pay their respect to these heroes at the same time. He set 108 cards, each of which alluded to a Chinese Robin Hood in Water Margin. Take these for examples, bamboo 2 stands for Hu Yanzhuo who is noted for his two iron chains while dragon 9 refers to Shi Jin who has dragon tattooed onto his back. Besides these simple tiles, Mr. Wan also made four winds tiles North, South, West and East to represent that

Mahjong Playing

the heroes are from every part of China. Another two tiles '白 bai' and '发 fa' was added finally to tell that some heroes are rich enough while some poor-stricken. At last, the number of tiles amounted to 136. Song Jiang, the leader of these heroes, pursued to make a compromise with the government all the time and at last was enlisted into the army of the government. So, the winners or losers cannot utter victory or lose at the last moment. They are expected to say 'hu 和 ' that means Song Jiang's determination to make peace with the court.

Mahjong Playing, a popular entertainment in China

First the folks play with the game as a pastime after a day' heavy work out of their jealousy of the heroes who can eat and drink freely under the pressure of the government. Later, the entertainment function of mahjong prevailed over other roles and the game became known and accepted by the court.

General speaking, most of mahjong tiles are made of bamboo and wood. And there are some Chinese characterslike "wan", "bing"and "tiao"inscribed into the surface. In comparison with other card games, mahjong is more inductive, interesting and challenging. It is easy to learn and it is life-time to master in terms of numerous rearrangements and match. Mahjong is special on the basis of Chinese culture. We can find out Chinese philosophical thought in it and unique oriental characteristics of ancientChinesemathematical theory. Indeed, mahjong is an important part of Chinese traditional culture. Due to mahjong game play's variations, different people in different areas set down different rules and thus mahjong is tinged with local color. And ancient Lushu Mahjong, Sichuan Mahjong, Guangdong Mahjong and Changsha Mahjong are some representative versions.

3. Temple Fair

Temple fair, or fair, means that people gathertogether to pray, go shopping and amuse themselves near the temple on some given days. The tradition ofgoing around the temple fairs is widespread in China and it is an important part of festival

The temple fair at the Earth Temple

celebration.

The temple fairhas a long history. Thousands of years ago, people who lived in some remote places chose to trade their goods at noon, which has been recorded in documents as "Ri Zhong Hu Shi". In the Qin Dynasty, the worship ceremonies to god and ancestors were held regularly in the temples and around them. This tradition remained long time until Taoist teachings came into being in the Western Han Dynasty. UnderTaoism's influence, the fair began to take its cultural and religious functions rather than served as a marketing place only. When Buddhism was introduced to china in the Western Han Dynasty, Taoist had been forming. There came fierce arguments from the followers of both sides, which eventually led to, to some degree, some understanding and communication of two religions. During the time of Two-Jin Period, wars and conflicts took their places. The Confucianism began to lose its momentum; the homeless and helpless countrymen went through difficult martial time and began to convert to the Buddhism and Taoism for spiritual escape. The temples and mosques increased gradually after the Six-Dynasty Period and the fairs around them began to gain their popularities. The Tang Dynasty witnessed the prime time of these two beliefs of which the Buddhism especially spread wide and far and imposed unprecedented impact upon social life in every respect. More temples were built and Buddhism worship prevailed among folks and became a heated vogue. The fair therefore became a place for trade, and more importantly, for religious service. Ming Dynasty seemed to be a turning point for the fairs to be more secular and to reduce themselves to markets mainly for travelling and shopping because there were much fewer religious followers at that time than in the former dynasties. The fairs could be categories into a multi-function fair and a solemn procession of god. Accompanied by people's travelling and playing, religious ceremony and pray would be held in the multi-function kind while in the procession the statute of gods would be carried to patrol out of the temple. For example, Miao Fengshan Fair in Beijing features such a patrol performance without any trade market. Sometimes, a big shopping gathering in some place is also considered to be a fair though there is not any temple around or in sight and Changdian Fair in Beijing is a good example.

In early fairs of ancient times, only certain ceremonies were made for people to worship the heaven and earth in ancestral temples. In remote antiquity, in order to acquire bless and divine protection from the god and their ancestors, people chose to communion with them in the palace or in the house by offering sacrifices or having certain ritual services. People gathered together to offer sacrifice, to play music and perform rituals, which, is thought to be the earliest fair. Temple fairs

Many people go to temple fairs

are usually held near the temples and hence 'temple' becomes a reasonable prefix to fair when we talks about the derivation of this name 'temple fair'. Manydealers and traders found out that they could make a good profit by selling worshipers and travelers incense and souvenirs. They ran all kinds of stalls nearby the temple at regular times, and this phenomena is named "gathering" or "hui" in Chinese. When the time went on, the temple fair or gathering turned into an entertainment at festivals, especially at the Spring Festival.

The folk fair has its own characteristics. It features market and trade of goods in economic respect and it highlights gathering in terms of social life. It is related to god worship in the sphere of ideology. All these elements contribute to the fact that the legacy and tradition of temple fair could be passed down in a long term.

The temple fair begins and people gather around to pray and make wishes. God worship is the main event in the traditional fairs. Ren Zu Fair in Huaiyang of Heinan Province, Ma Zu Fair in Tianjing, Shuanglin Si Fair in Pingyao of Shanxi Province, Miaofeng Shan Fair and Baiyu Guan Fair of Beijing are among the typical examples.

In the mythology, Ren Zu Fair is the place where the skull of Fu Tsi was buried. Fu Tsi, renamed Tai Hao, was one of the kings as early as in the Neolithic Age and Ren Zu Fair thus got another Tai Hao Tomb. Fu Tsi instituted marriage and united men and women. People usually hold a one-mother Fair in the lunar month of February every year. They kowtow to Fu Tsi and pray for more offspring. Childless married women especially need to touch a divine hole in a stone brick that the vulva is implied. In order to have children soon, they may buy some dolls of clay to worship at home. There is a variety of selections including monkey dolls with man face, called by locals'man-faced monkeys', strangle-looking and funny sparrow dolls with monkey faces entitled Hedgehog yan, bellybanded monkeys, cows, pigs, horses and goats. And the interesting designed dolls also could be used as children' play things.

The temple fair was held initiallyon the day when people celebrated religious festivals, Taoist and Buddhism days mainly. Later it was agreed upon certain dates when the fair should be open. In modern times it is usually held at the Spring Festivals and the Lantern Festivals.

The temple fairs could be seen everywhere in china during the Spring Festival and are famous for their local characters. Take several examples here, the fair features storytelling in Baofeng of Henan; Shanxi' Baiyun Mountains Fair and Yan'an Fair attracts many young men to date and be engaged. The others are on the list including Zhou Gong Fair, Jiangyin Fair, Chuandian Fair, The Summer Palace Fair, Huangjue Temple Fair and even those fairs in Hongkong, Macau and Taiwan.

The events in a fair could be snack eating, small wares and souvenirs buying and performances and shows watching, which brings the travelers a lot of fun and convenience.

These performances are interesting and exciting enough as the folk artists from all social walks are masterful and creative. You can enjoy yourself while watching the programs such as local operas, puppet operas, juggling, talk show, flag pole performing, land boat dancing, rural folk dances, lion and dragon dance and stilts walking.

People could have a variety of toys selection in the fair too. These toys are both designed and made well. It is not hard for you to find out your desirable among masks, wooden puppets, handcarts, knives and spears, bamboo dragons, diabolo, Pupu

Deng trumpets, revolving scenic lamps, sugar and dough sculpture, painted and plastic sugar figures, nine interlocking rings and rattle drums.

Beijing Snack is worth some words here. There are so many kinds and we can name several such as tea soup, fried flour, almond tea,traditional porridge, Firm Tofu, bean juice, deep-fried meatballs, bean juice, sausages, fried sausages, stir-fried glutinous rice flour cake, melon-shaped sweets, sweet pancake, pea cake, pancakes and so on. ..

Fair trade attracts many dealers and businessmen. They sell agricultural and sideline products that range over agricultural equipments, poultry, fish, vegetables, flowers and fruits. Beverage and food industry is also prosperous. Many contemporary restaurants and teahouse are set up to offer travelers catering service. Commodity market is crowded and bustling with buying and selling of clothes, hats and shoes, bags and suitcases, daily use, stationery, books and drawing and electric appliances. And so is the antique market.

Tips for Tourism

Beijing Fair: a crowded fair filled with happiness

"Beijing Fair has been remembered all the time by Beijing elders as it conveys a loving memory of family member and the past times of Beijing ", as is summarized by most Beijing citizens. It is hard to imagine what the Spring Festivals would be like without Beijing fairs. And it is a compre–hensive and indispensable representation of Beijing' s local color.

On every Spring Festivals, Beijing will host at least ten large–scaled fairs at parks like the Temple of Heaven, the Temple of Earth, Beihai, Changdian, Longtan Lake, Lotus Pool and so on.And people can always enjoy a lot of folk performance at these parks. It a traveler would like to have a general idea of Beijing, then the best choice is to go around those fairs during the Spring Festivals.

To know Beijing' s 100–year–old folk culturebetter, we need get to the most noisy and popular fairs, where we could experience something unique. Despite its commercial elements, we could still taste original Bei–jing snacks, buy local art crafts and feel the prosperity of the markets of hundred years ago. All this could undoubtedly satisfy our curiosity and de–sires for this old but highly–civilized city.

The most exciting performance for a new–comer would be folk art shows, such as stilt walking, drums playing, yangko dance, shadow puppet play, martial art, sugar–man blowing, clay figurine making and mini– wood–building curving. These will burst into applause and cheers.

No.1 Fairs at the Park of Earth

Time : lunar Januray 1st to 5th

Address: Temple of Heaven, Andingmen Road, Beijing

Ticket fare: RMB 10

Traffic line: take subway Line 2 and get off at the station of Yonghe Pal–ace or Andingmen; or take Line 5 and quit at Yonghe Palace or Hepingli North street; take bus No.13, or T2 and get off at the stop of South Gate of the Earth Temple, or electrical bus No.104、108 or No.27、104(fast–speed) to the west gate; No.125、No.117 to the east gate.

No.2 fairs at Longtan Lake

Time : lunar Januray 1st to 5th

Address: Lngtan Lake Park, Longtan Road No. 8, Dongcheng District , Beijing

Ticket fare: RMB 10

Traffic line: take bus No.34、35、36、743、957、943、822、705 or 41 and get off at the stop of Guangming Lou, or take bus No.6、8、60、607、958、116、750、12、352 or No.807 to Beijing Amusement Parks.

No.3 Pray Fairs at Badachu Park

Time : a week before and after the Spring Festivals

Address: Badachu Park

Ticket fare: RMB 10

Traffic line: take bus No.347、389、598、972 to Badachu Park Stop, which is only 100 meters away. There are three car parking squares having the capacity of 1200 cars altogether.

4. Lantern Fair

Lantern watching is another interesting activity at the Spring Festival. Generally, people enjoy the illuminating colorful-lighted lanterns hung at home, in the street or in the fair at night from New YearDay to the fifteenth day ofthe first month in the lunisolar year. They may go to lantern exhibitions to have more fun, which is funded by the government. This traditional lantern fair as it is usually called has its local characters.

At the night of bright moon, people will light thousands of lanterns to celebrate according to the tradition. They will go out to watch brilliance of lights, to solve the riddles, to set off fireworks and eat sweet dumplings. It brings them a lot of happiness and luck.

The festival has a long history too. The celebration began in the Han Dynasty, throve in the Tang Dynasty and gained wide popularity in the Song Dynasty. From the Ming Dynasty, the lantern fair

A beautiful dragon lantern

became a vendor place for selling or buying. On the tenth day to the fifteenth day of the New Year, light dealers or craftsmanswarmed into the capital city and carried the well-made lanterns just out of Dong'anmen Gate to display and sell. The trade contest is not only related to lanterns' design and making techniques, but also is a matter of financial strategy and ability competition. Every year these days when the fair was to open, the rental price of the shopping malls and houses nearby would double. Jiang Yikui, A man of letters in the Ming Dynasty, told us in The Documentary of Yaoshan House the following story. At the Lantern Festival, a craftsman in Beijing made a glazed light with the juice of sticky rice. The light can be used as a fish tank. When lit, it was crystal-clear. A man named Wang Guzhi spent a lot of money in it. He was so fond of it and unwilling to part with it even a minute. However, one day because of unexpected carelessness, he knocked it over. The light fell to the ground and broke into pieces. He moaned with great pain, 'the asset of my house is gone'. It is easy to see from the story that how ingenious the Ming's lights were and how valuable they were.

The categories of the light, its form, design, names, materials, even making techniques, usage and the moral it convey differs from place to place.

Sincethe PRC was founded, greater program has been made in the art of lights. Modern light-making technology is integrated with traditional ways. A series of new and advanced technology relevant to electronics, architecture, machinery, remote control, acoustics and optical fabric has been applied to the lights' design and making. With form, color, light, sound and motion into consideration, people turn the lights into works of art that convey their thought, ideas, interest and artis-

The lantern show of Yu Garden in Shanghai

tic taste.

At the Spring Festival, the tradition of lantern watching is observed nationally though the practice varies from place to place. And here are some examples.

4.1 Zigong Lantern Fair

Early in the Tang and Song Dynasty, Zigongers went out to enjoy themselves by watching lanterns during the Spring Festivals. And all kinds of lantern fairs had been formed during the dynasties of Ming and Q   ing. For example, in the middle of Qing, the Lion Lantern Fair and Light Pole Fair were held, together with the other activities. In the 20th century, hand lanterns became popular. Every folk travelled around the street with one lantern in hand at night on the tenth day of the first lunar month, which is known as "Hand Lantern Fair". Besides, Floating River Lanterns and magnificent Royal Lanterns boasted their intense indigenous and local flavor.

In 1964, Zigong government hosted the first official fair. Since then, the fair has become larger in scale with great improvement of making techniques. Individuals united together into an organization in which lantern development was planed effectively. By far, the fair united known as the Dinosaur Lanterns has been quite famous internationally and has been invited to give performances home and abroad many times. Spectacular shows win them intense applause and praise. The former president of Singapore, Mr. Huang Jinhui, looked at the beautiful lanterns with great interests when he showed up at the opening ceremony of Chinese Zigong Lantern Show that was held in his country. Li Guangyao, the former prime minister of Singapore wrote down the following when he finished his tour, "lovely to enjoy and deserve its name".

Zigong Lantern Fair is distinguished by its good design and making of lanterns, blending and labyrinthine light scenery, large scaleand magnificence. There are dozens of groups of large and medium-sized lanterns and thousands of craftwork lights displayed in every show, which makes up a sea of fluid light and fairy land.

Everyone cannot help but marvel at the beautiful pictures made by the large lantern groups such as "mermaids teasing dragons", "pearl fairies", "dragon volume fireworks", "the Babel Tower". Anything could be a matter of subject for creation including birds and animals, figures and fruits, painted opera faces and dragon heads, mountains and lakes, pavilions and towers. Sparkling lights and glittering things make such a dreamy picture that the experts from China and abroad pay a great compliments upon the creators'innovative spirits. Look at the following examples, an eye-catching light is actually made by china tableware; a glaring peacock and a bouncing deer are manufactured by used medicine bottles. Silkworm cocoon, coated glass, bamboo skin, dyed cloth could also be used as materials, together with silk, tissue and fabric. The folk artists always use the staff handy and ready to make somethingnew, we have to say, they truly live up their fame.

The lanterns can tell folk story too. These well-known stories and legends can be drawn or inscribed onto the light cover for people to see, some even to participate.

4.2 Qianjiang Lantern Fair

The fair is held on the Lantern Day and particular local. It is said that the earliest Lantern Day was begun in Dalong village of Qinxi, the birth place of the Longding Tea. On the eve, the villagers finished their dinner and they burned a red candle in a rice container. After the cracking of fireworks, the head of every household got out of the house and joined cheerfully the patrol team around the village. New Year Day was the Lantern Day too since the villagers were busy with sweeping away the past and starting afresh. The outsiders seldom joined such a patrol, so married daughters cannot see the candles of her mother's house. After New Year Day, neighbor villages' the Lantern Day came one after another. The streets and roads were full of people, more crowded and noisy even than some markets.

The celebration of the Lantern Day will be held in different time in Majin, an old town of centuries. In Yaoyi Village, it takes place on the eighth day of the first lunar month. While in Xiashan, it lasts until the 22th day, the last Lantern Day in this region and the longest.

When the Lantern day begins, all relatives and friends are invited to a party. A big feast will be served when all the gusts are present. In a small village of Qixi the villagers will turn over the benches and line up one after another. They make up a patrol teamwith red candles lit in front and behind. The team move through the village like a dragon with a deafening sound of trumpets and drums, which is known as "dragon hornet light". Dacun village, however, has another picture. When the day breaks, people beat percussions and drums to announce the opening ceremony. They will meet dragon lanterns after breakfast. Most of villages can make their own dragon lantern. Wooden boards are connected end to head by the poles in the round holes dug at both ends, this way the long dragon can move and circle easily. There are three or four lights on every board, with a cover outside and a red candle inside. Two banners are waving in the air with embroidered dragon and phoenix, or poem lines or riddles on it. The dragon head and tail sculpture are coated with gold. The whole dragon make threatening gestures and powerful.

Yaojiang fair is the most exciting lantern show as the celebration lasts longer and there are so many categoriesincluding shoulder lamps, cloth dragon lamps and board lamps and auspicious animal lamps.

4.3 Qinghuai Lantern Festival

This folk festival has been widespread in the region of Nanjing, formerly known as Jinling so it is also named Jinling Lantern Festival. Jinling Lantern Festival is mainly held between the Spring Festival to the Lantenr Festival. Visitors go to and fro in a great number with thousands of lamps illuminating at night.

The festival can trace its history back to The Wei and Jin Dynasties and the Southern and Northern Period when nearly no other events could equal its spectacles as recorded. The Tang Dynasty witnessed its rapid development and the reputation reached its peak in the Ming when it had gradually enjoyed the fame that "Qinghuai Lanterns ranked the finest all over the china" as most commented. And the Lantern Boat on Qinhuai River thereupon had been widely known to the country. Here is some description from the men of letters in all ages. "All flowers bloom together; vigorous lights bring the spring back.""The light descends from heaven illuminating the sky; the coral comes over the sea with thousands of sail."And "the red light is shining bright beyond the green water on both banks, just as a blue oar rowing in the Milk River."After the 2oth century, the lantern fair has made more progress with the improvement of binding and mounting techniques. Besides its entertainment function and cultural influence, the event also pushes other folk art forms to the further development, for instance, Nanjing paper cut, diabolo, sculpture, pi ying, animal dances, yang ge, stilts walking and so on.

Historically, the lantern festival was held mainly on the Qinhuai River and later transferred to Fuzimiao district after 20th century. Now the location has been extended to 5km east to the Qinhuai River and concentrates on Fuzimiao, Zanyuan, Bailuzhou Park, Wu Jingzi's House, Jiangnan Gong Yuan Museum, and Zhonghua Road, Pingjiangfu Road and Pingpa Road. Among them, Fuzimiao is distinguished for its folk flavor and magnificent and spectacular scenery made by colorful lanterns and sleepless night. A folk sayingcan justify this,'how can you spend your new year festival without lantern watching in Fuzimiao? Buying a lantern there could make a happy holiday".

The folk men in Nanjing are active in lamp and lantern making, displaying, watching, and show and performance participating. In these ways they create cheerful festival atmosphere and thus express their good wishes and dreams for the future life.

The district of Qinhuai is granted in 1996 "home of Jiangsu Folk art" by Cultural Administration Office of Jiangsu Province, together with some other awarded cities. In 2000, it enjoyed another honor as "home of Chinese Folk art" from the Ministry of culture and was entitled "home of Chinese Scenic Lamps" by Chinese Literature Federation in 2007.

The beautiful scene of Yu Garden's Lantern Show

5. Modern ways of Celebration

As time changes,the traditional festival folklore is also updated. The Spring Festival in Modern China not only goes on with its tradition, but takes on a new look with some modern style and rhyme.

5.1 Journey Home

The radical development of Chinese economy speeds up urbanization and population movement. And thus a growing number of farmers leave their hometown to be workers in southeast coastal area. Some Chinese even sail acrossthe sea to earn their living. The intense home-sickness complex of migrant workers causes a present 'large-scaled transportation' of home-return. To buy a ticket home, manywait in line for a couple of nights. It seems to worry every Chinese not to reunion with family in the Spring Festivals Holiday. In 1980, the term ,'Spring Transportation', first came out in the official news. It is considered to be the largestand longest human movementrecorded ever in scale and in time as nearly 3 billion people, half of the world population, have been transported in 40 days. Till now, 'Spring Transportation' has remained a word conveying Chinese people's complicated emotions. During the Spring Festival, a great number of people have to travel a long road between the city where they work and the hometown where they were born. The hard journey full of bitter and sweet is nothing but a pilgrim.

Rich or poor, you'll be home for the Spring Festival. It is a traditional festival for family member to get together. If not, the delicious food would be tasteless. And the luxuriousand

The biggest population migration in the Spring Festival

brilliant palace would not cheer people up without family members, relatives and friends. Spending a simplefestival with family is a bliss, though sometimes full of hardship.

5.2 Golden Week for Tourism

On September 18th, 1999, the State Council of China issued a regulation that the nation adds more days to some lawful holidays, Chinese hence have more time to be relaxed. More and more people are not willing to stay home or to eat all the time while visiting friends and relatives. Card party and mahjong playing are not healthy ways to spend holidays too. Travelling became a new holiday selection and golden weeks offer people more chances to enjoy a trip. Crowded enough, present tourists tend to be rational and mature enough to avoid heated historical and scenic spots and pick up a quiet sightseeing travel, which can rest both bodies and souls to the full length.

In recent years, the government has reinforced the infrastructure construction. Taking the advantage, the local governments have been active in tourism industry and open new

The golden week

travel projects.

Every time when the spring is approaching, the travel agencies will be occupied with soaring business. Many even make reservations two months in advance. The statistics indicates that there were 28 million travelers nationwide in the first golden week and the avenue amounted to 13.1 billion RMB. By far the tourism in golden weeks has gone up steadily, which stimulate the development of catering and business to a great extent.

5.3 Gala enjoying on the Eve

The well--known Spring Festival Gala or CCTV, or simply called the Gala, is a the biggest-scale show hosted by CCTV to celebrate Chinese Lunar New Year Day on the Eve of the Spring Festival. The Gala has set up three records in terms of scale, show time and audience number. It is recognized by the World Records Academy as the longestshow with the largest number of audience and performers.In April, 2012, CCTV was granted the certificate from the Guinness book of records.

Broadly speaking, the Gala could find its roots in a program Spring Festival Get-together produced by China Central News and Documentary Film Workshop in 1956 and directed by Zhang Junxiang, Xie Jin and other famous directors. Central People's Broadcasting Station then gave a live broadcast and many splendid artists and masters performed in the show including Xu Yulan, Wang Wenjuan, Xin Fengxia and Mei Lanfang, famous actors and actresses of the Yue Opera, Ping Opera and Peking Opera.

The show began in 1979 to celebrate the Spring Festivalnationally. Since in 1983 CCTV hosted the Gala successfully for the first time, Gala Watching has become Chinesenew custom and culture. Asthe most popular show, the Gala ranked top

The Gala, a TV program watched by every Chinese, home or abroad

among all the show programs and further its success helped produce a series of new programs. Zhengda Variety Show, the Opera Gala and the Singing and Dancing Gala were among them, together with the National Day Gala, the Labor Day Gala, The Mid-Autumn Festival Gala and international New Year Day Festival Gala. The province-based TV stations and the stations of all levels followed CCTV's example and blazed new trails.

The Gala commences at eight o'clock pm in time and is broadcasted live on CCTV—1, CCTV—4, CCTV—7, NEWS, Spanish Channel, French Channel, Arabic Channel, Russian Channel and some high-definition Channels. People can enjoy the live show given by CNTV through internet or even on mobile TV and CCTV ip. The Gala lasts five hours and it won't finish until one o'clock of the next morning. Billions of people sit in front of the TV to watch the great show while waiting for the coming of a new year.

The Gala has gone through 30-year trial, inspiration and

hope. It initiated with warm applause in the 80s and developed more quickly in the 90s and has ended in keeping pace with the times. Whatever the changes are, the Gala has been, no doubt, a spiritual feast for Chinese all, domestic and overseas and a symbol for them to pursue harmony, better life and happiness.

Gala Watching on the Eve (source: CCTV)

In the past, for most Chinese, the customs for the Spring Festival are only characterized by eating, visiting and fireworks cracking. With the reform and open-up policy, life has been getting better. At present many families could afford TV sets and gather to watch CCTV Spring Festival Gala in front of TV. Many young men prefer to spend the joyful night with theirnet friends and partners rather than with family members as the internet service is accessible at present, and more exciting.

In 2002, Wang Yi, a network company, initiated a program called 'virtual television gala', which changed greatly traditional ways of celebrating Chinese New Year. Cyber stay-up takes the place of the traditional stay-up and has attracted more netizens. An increasingly growing number of young people would like to spend the Eve's night in front of their computer. They entertain themselves by listening to songs, watching movies or chatting with friends. The network offers them more selections and seems more interactive in term of communication than TV is. This undoubtedly will be a new and trendy practice of celebration in the near future.

第四章 少数民族的春节习俗

在当代中国，作为已被各民族广泛认同的一种节庆方式，民族文化的多元性孕育出了诸多庆贺新春的“趣风异俗”。

在中国，居住于不同地区不同民族，在春节期间的过年习俗也各有不同，以下是几个具有代表性的少数民族春节习俗。

一、满族的春节习俗

满族将春节古称为“元旦”，是满族传统的盛大节日。每年农历正月初一举行，节期一般为 3 ~ 5 天，旧时有的地区可以一直过到正月十五。

满族春节源于汉族习俗。努尔哈赤建立后金政权后，天命三年（1618）起兵进入辽阳、沈阳地区，在汉族文化影响下，满族社会发生了很大变化。皇太极即位后，顺治元年（1644）清军入山海关定都北京，大批满族居民迁移关内，与汉族杂居共处，经济文化彼此交流，互相影响，关系密切。

长期的文化影响，使满族的春节习俗已基本上与汉族相一致，但满族的春节也有它的特殊风情。

春节前要做满族传统糕点——沙琪玛，张贴对联、窗花、挂笺（按旗属分别贴红、黄、蓝、白色）、福字。满族人还喜欢戴荷包。古时春节前宫廷要例行赏赐王公大臣“岁岁平安”的荷包，民间也互相赠送。除夕要接神，接神后在大门口放一条横木阻挡鬼魅。除夕这天，也挂门神，用来驱邪避鬼，门神分为“将军门神”“福禄门神”“判子门神”“娃娃门神”等。现在沈阳故宫里还藏有宫廷门神的图样。

节日期间，家家都要挂上红色的大灯笼，由除夕至初六，夜夜不熄。

○红灯笼透着节日的气息

除夕夜要分发“神纸”，然后晚辈男子到族内各家“辞岁”。吃年夜饭前，全家都要换上新装，一起祭祖。依尊卑长幼，向宗亲三代神主叩首，表示辞岁。随后，举行家宴，长辈们坐在上首，晚辈们团团而坐，取“阖第团圆”之意。饭果非常丰富，预示来年丰衣足食、事业兴旺。这顿饭是对年菜的首次品尝，可以荤素一齐上，通常必要有红烧肉、炖羊肉、米粉肉、红焖肘条、元宝肉、南煎丸子、四喜丸子、鸡冻、鱼冻、猪肉冻、豆酱、豆豉豆腐、芥末墩、辣芥菜、炒酱瓜等。饭后，孩子们将芝麻秸遍撒庭院，人走在上面，嘎吱作响，称之为“踩岁”。

满族也有守岁习俗。当天晚上，男女老少都要彻夜不眠，进行不同的娱乐活动，包括抖空竹，抽陀螺，捻升官图，掷骰子，玩牛牌，吹琉璃喇叭、口琴，耍影戏人，点走马灯，放“滴滴金儿”、“耗子屎”。老太太们则坐在一起斗纸牌、打麻将、打十胡，边玩还边吃鲜果、糖果、干果杂拌、“温朴”、炒红果、蜜饯海棠等，直至“接神”。午夜，鞭炮声响彻夜空。家家齐聚天地桌前焚香叩拜，供上素馅水饺，迎接诸神下界。仪式结束后，就意味着旧岁已去，新年来临。由于正是“五更分二年”的庄严时刻，全家要互道“春节快乐”。晚辈们要到堂上给长辈们叩首拜年，长辈们则给未成年的小孩“压岁钱”。最后，全家吃一顿素馅饺子，叫作“五更饺子”或“团圆饺子”。在百十个饺子里，只有一个放有硬币，吃到这个饺子的人，一年都会很顺利，叫作“终岁大吉”。

○晚辈拜年之后可以得到压岁钱

初一凌晨，家家户户都要放鞭炮，辞旧迎新。同时，在自家西墙祖宗板下放置供品、点燃香烛，叩拜祖宗，祈求神灵保佑全家大小在新的一年中平安无事，万事如意。然后全家团聚在一起吃团圆饺子，俗称“揣元宝”。煮饺子时，家中主人要大声吆喝：“小日子起来了吗？”其他人同时回答：“起来了！”他们把饺子从锅底浮起来比作日子起来了。然后让小孩爬上柜子上蹦三下，表示新日子节节高。

大年初一，所有的人都要早起，穿新衣，互相恭贺新春，去亲属家里拜年。晚辈向长辈叩头拜年，家长要给小孩压岁钱。宗族近亲也要互相拜年，亲朋好友则互相邀请至家中做客，一起聊聊家常。

初一至初五，人们都相聚一处，唱歌、跳舞、踩高跷，尽情娱乐。有的地方，年轻人还自发组织演出队，走村串屯进行表演，祝贺新年。

二、蒙古族的春节习俗

关于蒙古族春节的来历有多种说法。据五世达赖《黑白算答问》一书所说：“成吉思汗于公元 1227 年，取西夏国都，盛筵庆功，并以此为蒙历岁首，星宿月遂以正月见称。”星宿月是农历十二月十六日到一月十五日，这与农历前后相差一个月。而鄂尔多斯地区延续下来的蒙古历是以白月、五月、六月等序数记月。这样看来，蒙古历岁首当是农历四月。据史书记载，自元朝起，蒙古族接受了汉族历算法，因此，蒙古族白月与汉族春节正月相符。这就是蒙古族过春节的由来。

过春节，蒙古族叫作“大年”。古时候，蒙古族崇尚白色，为纯洁、吉祥之色，据说与日常饮用洁白的奶食有关，所以将农历正月称为“白月”，把过年节称为“白节”，亦称“奶酪节”“席尼吉勒”，意为新年、春节。

白节在正月初一，是从古代沿袭下来的习俗。元世祖忽必烈在位时，就非常重视过白节。现在蒙古族亦把白节作为最隆重的节日。

接近年底，无论农区还是牧区，家家户户都要立起灯笼竿。

腊月二十三，要清扫庭院，搞好室内卫生。傍晚，有“祭火”的仪式。蒙古族很早就有以祭火迎接春节的习俗，因为燃旺的火焰象征着一年里一切幸运吉祥。祭火是从萨满教传入的，蒙古族信仰喇嘛教后有所改变。蒙民把羊胸脯肉连同白哈达、肉米粥、黄油、酒等做祭品，然后由长辈点燃九个小灯，并将祭品投入旺火里烧，口里诵赞词，祝福家人幸福。祭火的时辰为傍晚黄昏时，上祭品时，男人在前，女人在后叩拜。烧完祭品后，全家进餐。有的把祭品的剩余送给附近亲戚吃。祭火在过去比较盛行，每家祭火的日期和方式也不同。贫民家庭一般在腊月二十三日祭火，而贵族家庭在腊月二十四日祭火。有的牧户把系有五色彩绸的五小捆芦苇插在门外树上，将劈成细条的柞树放在燃旺的火撑子上方的四条腿上，户主穿好礼服跪在正门处的垫子上，把用油网包好的羊胸骨奉献给圣火。妇女们则将美酒、黄油洒进圣火，并按顺序站立、叩头。富裕的牧户则搞大型祭火，祭祀时用整羊，并将左邻右舍请来喝茶吃酒。有的将圣火点燃后三天不熄，三天中不许迁场，不许在圣火上烤脚。目前，传统的祭火在新一代牧民中已很少举行了，但是在草原旅游点和庆祝的喜庆日子，人们还是点一堆篝火助兴。

腊月二十三以后，就准备过春节了。家家户户都备下当年生的公羊和各种奶制品。做件好看的蒙古袍，加上几坛上好的美酒，然后开始“调马”。

年三十是最热闹的一天，全家穿上节日盛装，欢聚一堂，拜贺新年。上午，要上供祭佛，在佛柜供台上摆上各种奶食、油食，摆成小塔形，上边插上特制的金银花。还要用十二个小铜盅倒满白水，一天换一次水，然后点上长明灯。同时，开始贴对联（与汉族一样，只是写的是蒙文）。晚上，备好饭菜后，铺好新毡，摆上酒、菜、肉，开始祭祖先。长辈嘴里念着高祖、曾祖的名字，把酒一盅又一盅地撒在地上，撒向天空。祭完祖先后，全家上席，晚辈向家长献哈达、敬酒、礼拜。午夜，开始饮酒进餐，围坐吃饺子，俗称“黄馍馍”或“扁食”，按常规要多吃多喝，酒肉剩得越多越好，象征着新的一年酒肉不尽，吃喝不愁。

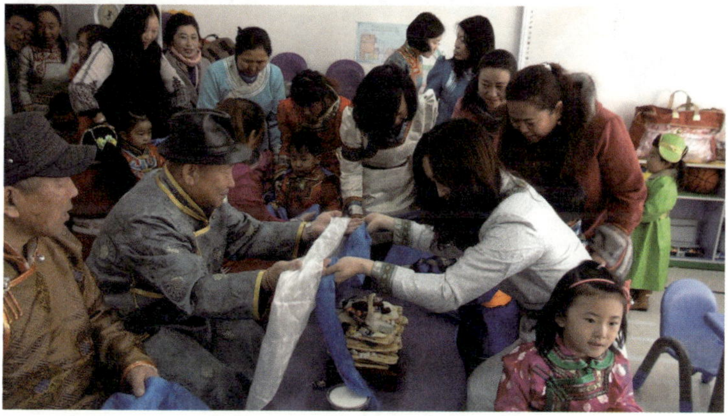

○向长辈献哈达是蒙古族过年的习俗

除夕夜，牧民们还要相互拜访喝茶，然后人们扶老携幼聚集在年长者的家里，进行除夕“乃日”（宴会）或家人聚集在一起看电视节目。接着牧人们要到邀请自己的每家去做客，有时因户多，宴会往往通宵达旦。除夕时，牧民家家都要摆放“花盘”，即将点心、奶食、糖果等整齐地摆放在一个大盘子里，摆放的形式大部分呈圆柱体，也有方形的，每层一种，很有规则。这一习俗，不仅在牧民家中一直保留，而且在城市的蒙古族家中，也沿袭着这传统。

○丰盛的蒙古族美食

拜年是草原上最隆重的活动，在正月初一晨曦微露时候开始，直到正月十五才结束。

初一，牧民们先祭敖包，然后在家庭内部拜年，先是晚辈向长者问安跪拜，敬酒时要跪拜，男人双膝下跪，头往下低，双手上下摆动。未婚女子与男人一样叩拜，而已婚女人则右膝下跪，左膝半跪，右手在面额右侧上下摆动。新媳妇则须唱歌。长者受礼之后，要向弟、侄、儿孙们表示祝福。祝福完毕，要给孩子们一些礼物和压岁钱。然后，家族亲友间就开始互相拜年，相见第一句话是“新年好”“过年好”。一大早身着各色服装的男女，跨上早已备好的骏马，三五成群奔向“浩特”（城镇），挨个地串蒙古包。串包中，先要给长辈叩头祝愿，接着主人家的女婿为前来串包的客人敬酒，习惯上这种敬酒每敬必喝，有的还边歌边舞。给亲戚拜年时，每人带蓝色哈达和酒，先到佛堂或者供佛像之处，给佛像叩头，然后用自备的酒敬长辈。如今拜年时，已改为握手等新习俗了。

拜年时，一般要献上一两首颂词或颂歌。对出色的歌手，户主会捧起放有哈达的奶食盘颂祝词。在边远农牧区，正月十六黎明前，常在一起嬉闹的人还有“哈巴德”（打黑墨）的习俗。就是在对方熟睡时，偷偷在他前额上抹黑，涂物多为锅底灰。

春节期间牧民活动的主要内容之一还有祝寿。祝寿的对象为“本年”长者。祝寿开始时，先为年满 73、85 岁高龄者祝寿，时间一般在腊月二十五或二十六日；腊月二十七至除夕的几天里，则为年满 49、61 岁的“本年”者祝寿。给长者祝寿时，晚辈除要行礼祝贺外，还要赠送寿礼以示尊敬。祝寿礼的轻重多寡，一般视祝寿对象的年龄大小而定。

草原上的春节活动主要有拜年等，并且从农历腊月二十三开始，到正月（查干萨日）达到高潮。串包男女还利用拜年的机会，尤其是青年男女各不相让。大都以“浩特”之间距离为比赛距离，男女互相追逐。

近些年来，蒙古族春节虽与汉族大体一致，并吸收了一些汉族习俗，如吃饺子、放鞭炮等，但仍保留许多蒙古族的传统习俗，如除夕吃“手抓肉”、祭火、祝寿、赛马等。

三、朝鲜族的春节习俗

在朝鲜族中，春节是仅次于中秋节（朝鲜族称为“秋夕节”）的第二大节日。

过年之前，朝鲜族也要办年货，一般由女主人操办，通常是采购日常用品和特色食品，更主要的是图吉利。朝鲜族特色年货有很多种，食品类有打糕、面片、冷面、米肠、紫菜、辣白菜等，供品类有苹果、柿饼、大枣、栗子、鱼、肉等，礼品类有参茸、蜂蜜、钱包、钢笔、袜子等。水酒、牛肉在节日的餐桌上必不可少。没有民族服装的人一定要备上传统的朝鲜族服装。过年前，家中的晚辈要组织起来先打扫屋子。

除夕吃过团圆饭，孩子们要跟大人一起通宵守岁。晚上睡觉时，要把鞋拿进屋里，因为放在外面会被“夜光鬼”偷走，象征着不吉利。这天男人不允许进厨房，由女人准备祭祖食品。现在，朝鲜族年夜饭也吃饺子。另外也有专门的食品，统称为“岁餐”。流传至今最具代表性的春节料理是米糕片汤。此外，年糕汤、朝鲜八宝饭和江米条是朝鲜族过春节的传统美食，一定不可缺。年糕汤是把年糕切成柳叶状，放入各种作料，用肉汤煮成。大人们问孩子吃了几碗年糕汤，就是问他几岁了。此外，每个家庭还会准备蜜糯油果、桂皮汤、八宝饭和肉片米糖等食品接待前来拜年的亲朋好友。

大年初一，街道和村庄都焕然一新，家家户户都很干净。这一天，妇女都穿上漂亮的民族盛装，从早到晚都要在厨房里忙活。嫁到朝鲜族家里的外族姑娘也要同朝鲜妇女一样从早忙到晚。

○朝鲜族春节习俗

大年初一，向祖先贡献饮食、行大礼是最隆重的，意味着新一年的开始。祭祖很严格，供桌上摆法就有“鱼东肉西”“头东尾西”“红东白西”“枣栗梨柿”“生东熟西”“左饭右羹”等规则。每个家庭都有一个祭祀用的小饭桌作供桌。祭祖先由长辈开始，敬酒跪拜。仪式结束后，大家分享供品。民间说法是吃了供桌上东西便会运气好，求心安，同时也是为了不浪费。

接下来，晚辈要给长辈拜年，叫作“岁拜”，大人需要还礼祝愿，发糖、压岁钱，并教导几句。如果是多年不见的贵客或结婚不久的新人，要穿上传统服装，晚辈向长辈行跪拜大礼。男孩要理岁头；女孩要梳岁妆，简单的就扎个五彩头绳。

随后，亲戚们聚在一起玩掷骰、跳跳板等游戏，并把福笊篱（有“装福”的意思）送给别人或挂在家里，孩子们则放风筝、玩陀螺、踢毽子、玩冰车。

朝鲜族过春节有一些禁忌，正月头三天不能扫地、倒垃圾、剪指甲；不生气、不吵架；不戴帽子吃饭；不能坑蒙拐骗；正月里不吃狗肉；传统上也不写对联、不放鞭炮、不贴年画、不烧纸钱。

旅游小贴士

延边朝鲜族自治州

延边朝鲜族自治州位于吉林省东部，东与俄罗斯滨海边疆区毗邻，南与朝鲜咸境北道、两江道隔图们江相望，是一个有山皆绿、有水皆清的美丽地方。

长白山脉蜿蜒起伏，长白林海绵延千里，图们江、第二松花江、牡丹江、绥芬河，宛如彩练玉带，纵横流淌在青山绿野之间。地貌呈山地、丘陵、盆地三个梯度，基本上是“八山一水半草半分田”。山峦迭嶂，森林茂密。

延边朝鲜族自治州是朝鲜族最大的聚居地区，也是我国最早实行民族区域自治州的地方之一。境内居住朝鲜族、汉族、满族、回族、蒙古族、壮族、苗族等 19 个民族。其中少数民族占全州总人口的 43.9%。这里的有一眼看三国的奇景，依偎在长白山脚下，人民的生活像这里的景色一样简单而淳朴。

最佳季节：3 月 –11 月。春天可以看金达莱开遍的草原，秋天去林间拾起金色的梦野，夏天则是适合避暑的时候。这里的冬季虽然寒冷，却也是别有北国风情。这里有着日本海和长白山的庇佑，所以延吉的冬季其实也没那么严酷，去长白山泡个温泉更是潇洒极了。

建议游玩：2 天

交通方案：

1. 航空：延吉机场位于延吉西南，是国际型中型机场，可直航首尔，清州等国际航线，国内航线可直航北京、上海、沈阳、长春、广州、天津。

2. 公路：高速路直达延吉市，从西南往东北方向的两条主干道与长春和哈尔滨连接。新建的长珲高速公路，从延吉到长春只需要四个小时。

3. 铁路：延边有几条主要铁路与内地和俄罗斯、朝鲜相通。一条干线向南通过辽宁沈阳到达大连和北京；往北通往哈尔滨。

四、彝族的春节习俗

彝族称过年为“库史”。彝族语言中，“库”是年或岁之意，“史”即是“新”，“库史”就是过新年。每当深山初雪，秋山红叶，太阳回归时，谷黄米熟，庄稼收进粮仓，便到了彝族过年的时候。有些彝族跟周边的汉族一起在农历腊月开始过年节，而大部分彝族一年一度的年节是在农历十月底，有的地方是把过年日固定在农历十月三十日为除夕之日，冬月初一为新一年的开始。在凉山大部分地区是按区域选择吉日过年，但都在农历十月之内。

“库史”是彝族民间传统节日中最受重视的一个节日。过新年的前一个月，就在做准备工作了。

春节前几天，孩子们除了整天玩鞭炮之外，一项重要工作就是上山砍一棵小松树和采集松针。成年男子的主要精力用于修理陀螺、平整陀螺场地、跳歌场、架设各种式样的秋千设施，女主人则忙于准备家人的服装、打扫卫生。

除夕这天，每户人家的门前都要立起一棵青松，表示除旧迎新、免祸消灾。堂屋的地上铺着一层厚厚的松针，以便坐在上面吃年饭。除夕夜，男子必须通宵达旦守夜。守夜时，几位男子聚在一起，边饮酒边谈论家族往事等，现在也有玩扑克和进行其他娱乐活动的。守夜的目的首先是表达对祖先的敬意，同时也是为了凌晨挑回第一担水，赶在天亮之前做好饭菜。

按照习俗，大年初一妇女要休息，所有的家务活都由家里其他人承担，表示对妇女在过去一年中的辛劳的感激。

春节期间的娱乐活动很多，女子玩各种类型的秋千，男子则打陀螺，两个场所挨得很近。其中，打陀螺是最热闹的。陀螺场一般宽度为 10 多米，长度为 50 米左右。比赛通常在两个村庄之间进行，每方都有 20 人以上，多者达 40 人。一方放置陀螺，另一方打，间距为 15 米左右。届时，男女老少都集于场边观看，热闹至极。整场比赛的胜负，以每一方获得“打”的次数的多少来定。比赛的后期，举办者就已经安排人准备酒、菜、饭，费用由败方出。席间，双方热烈地谈论，也会相互敬酒，胜方自然得意，但败方的脸上也看不出失意，气氛非常和谐。

○彝族民众“跳歌”过春节

晚上，还有另一项隆重的活动，那就是“跳歌”。男女老少都会兴致勃勃地围在燃着篝火的空地上跳歌。跳歌时，入场的男女相间，手拉着手，自然地围着篝火，随着音乐的节奏，向逆时针方向转动。伴奏的乐器是三弦、芦笙和二胡，场内外的人们则唱着彝族民间曲调。舞步是“跺脚”。入场者从数十人到上百人不等，通常是“一寨跳歌，八方相聚”。跳歌的时间一般延续到凌晨两三点，也有通宵达旦跳舞的。

五、壮族的春节习俗

壮族称春节为“新年节”。待农历腊月二十三“送灶”一过，壮家便处处洋溢着喜迎新春的气氛，每户人家都要扫房梁，制作肉粽、糍粑、米花糖、糯米饼等新年食品。其中，过年是一定要包粽粑的。除夕夜放在供台上祭祖，正月初三或初八日再烧热后全家共食。打开粽粑时有一种清香扑鼻而来，令人食欲大振。在广西邕宁县的壮族村寨，过去在有人中举后，全村要筹集糯米、猪脚等物，包扎巨型粽粑。

壮族春节从正月初一前两天开始，第一天称大年，第二天为小年。

除夕夜，壮家户户贴春联、放鞭炮，合家欢聚，喜庆团圆。还要做好“压年饭”，以求有余有剩，吉祥如意。入夜，姑娘描花绣朵、孩童盼放烟火、老人传授着新歌，人们等待着子时的到来。各家在堂屋祖先牌位前设供桌，桌前挂一张美丽的壮锦或者刺绣的桌围，桌上摆有大粽粑、年糕、米花糖及鸡、鸭、鱼、肉等供品。同时，在家中火塘内燃烧一根耐烧的大硬木，直到第二天都不会熄灭，以示子孙绵延久长、烟火不断。大家围坐在一起聆听老人讲故事，守岁到天亮。

正月初一，是新春第一天。天还没亮，壮族妇女就到了山间清泉、村旁小河挑新水。这一天喝的用的，都不能是前一天的存水。过去，有些地区，取回新水后立即过秤，和同量旧水比，如果新水重，就预示有丰收年景。回到家里，将新水倒入锅里，与红糖、竹叶、葱花、生姜一同煮开，让全家喝用新水煮的新年茶。据说新年茶会使人事事顺利。老人喝了健康长寿，小孩喝了聪明能干，夫妻喝了会和和睦睦。同时，还要捡几块与家畜相像的石头回家，并且一路走一路模仿六畜的叫声。回到家，要把这些石头放进猪圈、牛栏，保佑六畜兴旺。

这一天，人们出门无论遇到谁都要相互祝贺，认为这样一年才能吉祥。

节日期间，青年男女聚集在村处路旁或山坡上对唱山歌，有时要连唱三昼夜。在有的地区，青年男女在节日期间还喜欢分队举行抛绣球活动。“春堂舞”是青年男女喜爱的庆祝新年、预祝丰收的舞蹈。他们或背米杆或挑扁担，围绕着米槽边舞边打，希望粮谷满仓。

初一至十五，丰盛的菜肴，无尽温暖，全靠灶膛里的火。因此，春节期间壮家的火是不能熄灭的，火旺象征着家旺，子孙绵延。

民间还有过晚年的习惯，壮族称作“吃立节”，时间在正月三十日。相传在 100 多年前的正月三十日，壮族的一支农民武装抗击外来侵略者后凯旋，但是这时春节已过。壮族群众为了欢迎他们，就在这天为他们重过春节。大年和晚年两个节日同样隆重。

春节的传统文娱活动除与壮族传统的三月三歌圩相同外，舞狮、舞鸡、舞春牛也吸引了不少青年人。狮子队的锣鼓一敲，搭起高台，狮子旋回而上，在十几张八仙桌搭就的高台上行走自如，引来阵阵喝彩。

桂西一些地区，世代流传的舞鸡、舞春牛活动，增添了春节的喜庆气氛。舞鸡的年轻人提着用木头、木瓜做成的两只“斗鸡”，打着锣到村中各家各户去贺年。“舞鸡歌”吉庆幽默，使主家喜笑颜开，不仅会送给贺年的舞鸡者红包，还会从“斗鸡”身上拔几根鸡毛插在自家的鸡笼上，以祈求六畜兴旺。舞春牛更有趣。“春牛”用竹片巧妙编织而成，牛头、牛角糊上绵纸，画上牛眼，牛身是一块黑布或灰布。舞牛人敲锣打鼓在村中表演，钻进布底的两人，一人在前撑牛头，一人在后弯腰拱背甩尾巴，后面跟着的是一个手拿犁架的汉子。此外，还有敲锣打鼓的，领唱“春牛歌”的，他们走到哪里，哪里就有歌声笑声。舞罢上村又到下村，从初一闹到元宵节。舞春牛为家家户户带来了节日的欢乐，同时，也寄托了对丰收、祥和的祝愿。

Chapter Four

National Custom of the Spring Festival

In modern China, the cultural diversity of the ethnicmi-norities gives rise to many exotic and interesting customs of Spring Festival celebration. The minority groups who inhabit different area have different customs too. And here are only some examples.

1. Manchu

The Spring Festival was referred to as "New Year Festival". The celebration is begun annually on the first day of the Chinese year. It usually lasts 3 to 5 days, and in the past it would continue for half a mouth in some places.

Manchu Spring Festival began from Han's custom. Nuerhaci, the leader of a Manchu branch, united many tribes and established the later Jin Daynasty in 1616. Two years later his army invaded Liaoyang and Shenyang regions. Manchu society had been changed greatly in many respects under the influence of Chinese culture. when Hong Taiji, the son of Nuerhaci, took the throne, his army conquered China in 1644 and made Beijing the capital. A large number of Manchu people moved into Shanhai Pass and lived together with Han people (or, narrowly, Chinese). Since then a close relationship grew up between the two ethnic groups due to frequent exchange of economy and culture.

Long term communication leads to many similarities and the Manchu People has been gradually absorbed in Han's culture. However, Manchu has its own style that is still worth mentioning.

Before the Festival, people usually make traditional cakes named Sha qi Ma. Every household paste the couplet and Fu Character, stick paper cut and hang colorful banners according to their branch. People like to exchange mall bags as present. In the past festival, the ministers had bags as rewards from the court which conveyed the wishes for luck ad safety. On the eve, people receive god in the house and will bar the gate with a long pole to drive out of the spirits. The picture of door-god is also needed to be on walls to scare away these evils who want to

Red lanterns are raised

enter. There are several door-gods like 'General door-god', 'Fu Lu door-god'. 'Ghost Catcher door-god' and 'Child door-gate' and those royal pictures of door-gods now have been preserved in the Museum of Shenyang.

The red lanterns hung around the house will be illuminating from the eve to the sixth day during the Festival.

On the eve, the nephews visit elder members of family to bid farewell to the old year. Before the big dinner, everyone puts on new clothes and then pray. They kowtow to the ancestors three times to pay their homage in hierarchical order. When the dinner is ready, the elders are expected to sit first at the head of the table. Young men sit around to enjoy the feast. A variety of food is served at the time to foretell the next year they will be well-fed and lucky. Meat and vegetables are served at the same time. There are though so many delicious foods like stewed pork, mutton, fried meat balls, meat and chicken jelly, people are still looking for new kinds. After diner, children scatter hemp stalks around in the yard to trip over and make a creaky sound, which is known as 'Cai Sui'.

People stay up on the eve night. To be sleepless,they will entertain themselves by playing cards, hand organ, spinning top or dices. The old women prefer to play mahjong and other card games. They eat fruits, sweets and nuts while playing till the moment comes when they should meet god. At midnight, the sound of fireworks erupts from all sides. All the families gather in front of the shrine table to burn incense and worship while the vegetable dumplings is offered to receive the advent of god. After this ritual, the old year is gone already and the New Year comes. At the solemn moment, every one greets with'happy Spring Festival' to each other. The juniors pay the elders a New Year call and kowtow to them while the elders give children pocket money as gifts. Just before dawn, the family get together again and eats vegetable dumplings together, which is known as 'Wu Geng Dumplings' or 'Tuan Yuan Dumplings'. Someone who eats the dumpling with a coin hidden inside will be lucky in the next year.

Money gift bags for the young after they express their New Year greetings to the elders

On the next morning, every household sets off fireworks to celebrate. The sacrifice is offered to the ancestors with burning incense on the shrine board set on the west wall. All kowtow to their forefathers to pray for their protection and bliss that everything goes well in the coming year. After the ceremony, they get together to eat dumplings again, which is named 'Chuai Yuan Bao'. When dumplings are boiled in the water, the household yells out to ask, 'is the happy day going up'. The others need to answer with one voice, 'up, up', an auspicious prediction of their better life. The child will climb up onto a box and jump up three times, which symbolizes that the life is up and better every day.

On New Year Day, everyone needs to get up early including those who stay up all night and take a snap only at dawn. It is the time to pay relatives, friends and even clan members a New Year visit. The juniors kowtow to aunts, uncles and grandparents and the elders give children money as present. Guests or hosts, chatting or eating, they will spend the first day of the New Year full of boisterous joy and happiness.

On the following days, people play hard by singing, dancing and stilt walking. The young volunteers work together as a team to perform for neighborhood villages.

2. Mongols

There are many different versions for the originality of Mongolian Spring Festival. According to the book Hei Bai Suan Da Wen by Dalai Lama the Fifth, Kublai Khan took over the capital of Xi Xia in 1227. He held a big feast and set the conquest month as the first month of Mongolia New Year, which is dated from 16thDecember to 15thJanuary in Chinese lunar calendar. While we can see different opinions in OrdosMongolian calendar which had been passed through generations. White month is followed by the fifth and sixth lunar month on its calendar and therefore white month should be the beginning of its New Year. The Mongols has followed Chinese calendar since Yuan Dynasty. Therefore white month is the counterpart of January on Chinese lunar calendar.

The Spring Festival is called 'Big Year'. At ancient ages, the Mongols were fond of white color as it symbolized purity and luck. The likeness is said to be associatedwith white food the nomadic people enjoyed every day. White month is thus named and the Big Year festival is called 'White Festival' for the same reason.

Traditionally, the White Festival is celebrated on the first day of Mongolian New year. Kublai Khan, the first emperor of Yuan Dynasty, attached great importance to the Festival. Marco Polo proved the point in his book The Travels of Marco Polo. He said that the New Year began in February and Kublai Khan would celebrate the festival in a solemn way with all his subjects. Khan was wearing white clothes and so did the countrymen. People exchanged white objects as gifts and kissed and embraced each other. Every one enjoyed the Festival. By far the White Festival has become the grandest festival of all.

At the end of the old year, every household set up the lantern pole.

On the 23th of the last month, people swept the yard and cleaned the house. A fire party was to be held in the evening as burning fire was a sign of luck and prosperity in Mongolian traditional culture. This fire party derived from the Creed of Shaman and it had undergone some changes since most of the Mongolian people converted to Lama Religion. Here are some details. First, people prepared a white 'khada' and some food as sacrifice such as meat, cheese, porridge and wine. The elders lit nine lamps and then put the sacrifice into the fire while singing some blissful prayer words. Men usually stood in front to offer the sacrifice while women followed to kowtow behind. After this, family's dinner time was coming. According to historical record, the party had been popular for a while and people of different social position would celebrate it on different dates, the commons (Ha Ri Chu, in Mongolian pronunciation), for instance, usually on 23th while the noble (Tai Ji) on the next day.

Some herdsmen celebrated the festival this way. First, put five bundles of reed decorated with colorful ribbons in the tree. And then put wood pieces into fire. The father of the family put on ceremonial clothes before he knelt to his feet on the mat. He offered the packed sheep bone to the sacred fire while the women poured in wine and cheese. Then all stood up in a line to kowtow. While the rich men liked to have a large-scale party. They used the whole sheep as sacrifice and invited all the neighbors to drink and eat. Some fire burned for three days and people were not allowed to warn their feet on it. By far, the traditional fire ritual has seldom been held among new generational. A bonfire is still needed to add pleasure on some tourists' days and festivals.

The New Year is coming. Every household needs to get one-year male sheep and all kinds of dairy products ready, together with new robes and some good wines.

The eve is the busiest day. The whole family put on new clothes and get together. On the morning, sacrifice is offered to the Buddha. On the shrine table are served all kinds of dairy and creamy foods, tower-shaped and decorated with gold and silver flowers on top. There are a dozen of bronze cups filled with water which should be changed daily and ever-burning lamps are being lit. At the same time, people paste the couplets on their doorway. On the evening, the dishes are served and new felted mattress is unfolded before the ancestor worship begins when the elders speak out their fathers' names loudly and splash out one cup of wine after another to the sky and the earth. And then the family members get together to enjoy the dinner. The young should dedicate the Khada to the elders and drink to them. At midnight, they sit around to eat dumplings, as known 'Huang Mo Mo' or 'Bian Shi'. Though people are encouraged to eat more, more food and wine left at the big dinner mean that the next year they need not worry about drinking and eating.

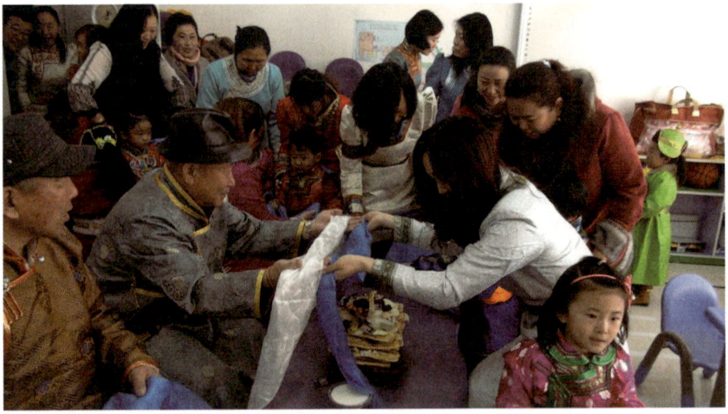

Presenting a Hada to the family seniors is the tradition of Mongolian people

Besides, the herdsmen pay each other a visit and enjoy tea together. And some even gather in the elders' house to have a feast or watch TV. The feast lasts a whole night often as the host has many fellow herdsmen to receive.

To entertain the gusts, the herdsmen need to put cakes, dairy and sweets on a big plate in volume-shaped or rectangle–shaped pattern. It looks so nice with one food on the same level. Even now, the herdsman observes the custom, and the Mongols in the cities also follow it.

Rich and diversified Mongolian food

New Year Visits, the most interesting event in the pasture, start from the dawn of New Year day and will last nearly half a month.

On New Year Day, firstly, the herdsmen worship 'Obo', and then families greet each other with best wishes. The juniors need to drink a toast to the elders while kneeling down on feet. They lower their heads with hands swinging up and down. Unmarried women should do the same. While a married woman falls on her right knee and her half-left knee with the right hand swinging up and down. Newly-wedded women must sing songs. The elders convey their bliss to the young and give children some gifts like pocket money. Neighbors, relatives and friends need to exchange their wishes by saying 'happy New Year' at first sight of each othersoon after family greeting. They put on new clothes and ride horses in groups to visit bigger villages or towns. There they enter every yurt and pay their respect to the elders by kowtowing. The hospitable hosts offer good wines and sometime they can watch dance and singing performances. While when they pay relatives a visit, they need to take blue Khat and wine with them. They are led the Buddhist pray room to worship first and after that they toast the elder's health. And now people need not to kowtow anymore and hand-shaking has been widely accepted.

Generally speaking, visitors usually sing one or two hymns. The host will pick up the plate of dairy food to sing his praise to excellent singers. In some remote pasture, before the dawn comes people will paint the faces of their playmates with some black ink or pot ashes for fun.

Offering birthday congratulation is another important event during the Spring Festival. The elder who is in his animal year will be sent good messages. On the 25th or 26th, people usually celebrate the birthday for old men or women aged 85 or 73. While on the next few days a birthday party is held for those of 61 or 49. The young will bow to the elders and they need to send them some birthday gifts according to their ages.

The celebration reaches its climax on the Day of Cha Gan Sha when the young men and women have a horse race. The race is heated and excited when the young try hard to chase after each other on horsebacks between villages and towns.

In a word, the Mongols celebrate the Spring Festival in a quite similar way to those Hans. Some traditional Chinese customs has been incorporated into Mongolian culture such as dumpling eating and firework cracking. However, they still stick to many Mongolian traditional customs such as eating meat with hands, fire worship ceremony, birthday party and horse race as we mentioned above.

3. Koreans

For the Koreans, the Spring Festival is one of the largest

festivals, only second to the Mid-Autumn Festival.

Before the festival, Korean people need to prepare festival goods. The hostesses usually buysome daily use and specialties. There are many kinds including rice cakes, noodle patches, cold noodles, sausages, laver and spicy cabbages. Fruits and all kinds of meat are also on the list. The gifts to buy comprise ginsengs, honey, purses, pens and stockings. Wine and beef are indispensable on the festival. Traditional costumes needed to be made before hand.

The young members are called to clean the room.

On the eve a big dinner is to be cooked and children are expected to stay up with their parents. If they sleep for a while, they must take their shoes into their rooms to prevent them being stolen by outside ghosts. Men are forbidden to enter the kitchen that day and women are in charge of food making. At present, the Koreans eat dumpling too, but they have more foods to cook for the festival. Among them, rice cake soup is a particular Korean cuisine that has been handed to the present day. Besides, Ba Bao rice and polished glutinous rice stripes are included. Women cut rice cakes into leave-shaped pieces first and then put it into meat soup to stew with many other ingredients. If a child is asked how many bowls of soup he has eaten, that actually means how old he or she is. And every family needs to prepare honey waxy oil fruits, gui pi soup and rice sweets for the visitors.

The folklore of Koreans

Everything is new on New Year Day. Women are wearing national costumes and being busy in the kitchen from morning to night. And so is the situation for those outsiders who married Korean men.

Offering sacrifices and bowing before the ancestors is the most important part of Spring Festival celebration. The rules are fixed and strict, for example, fish is put in the east while meat is in the west; the head of fish should be laid towards the east while the tail to the west; red food must be in the east while white food in the west. Other laws include rare food and the rice are in the east while the cooked and the soup in the west. A small dinner table can be used as a contemporary altar. Then the ritual begins from the elders and the others follow them to toast and kowtow to the ancestors. When it ends, the families can enjoy sacrifice food and drinks, which is said to be lucky, or just not to waste.

The event followed is that the juniors express New Year wishes to the elders. The elders need to send back their wishes in return and give children sweets, pocket money and some solemn words related to virtues sometimes. Newly-wedded couples or distinguished guests are expected to wear traditional costumes and fell down their knees to show their respect. Boys only have a new haircut while the girls should make up and dress up.

Then the families play some games together like throwing the hub and jumping. Children like flying kite, shuttlecock kicking and skating car.

There are still some taboos for Korean Spring Festival. People are not allowed to sweep the floor, to throw the garbage or to cut the nails on the first three days. During the Festival time poultry slaying and dog meat eating are strictly prohibited. Besides, people should not be mad and quarrel with others. Men cannot cheat and eat with hats. Traditionally the Koreans neither paste the couplets nor set off fireworks, neither stick paintings nor burn paper money.

Tips for Tourism

Korean Autonomous Prefecture of Yanbian

The Prefecture is located in the Eastern part of Jilin Province, bordered by the frontier of Russia in the east, adjacent to Xianjing North Way of North Korea across the river Tumeng. It is a beautiful place with green mountains and clear waters.

Changbai Mountains are winding along wth its trees rolling over 500 kilo-meters. Rivers like Tumen, Songhua No.2, Mudan and suifen, are running forward like colorful ribbons embedded in luxuriant mountains and fields. And amazingly the Mountain area has 3 landforms:mountains,hills and basins.Specifically there are eight mountains, one river and half grass-land and field. The natural beauty impresses visitors with rolling chain of mountains,blue and dense forests.

The Prefecture,which is one of self-governed regions at the earliest, serves as the biggest colony for Koreans to settle down. 19 ethical groups lives there and Manchu, Hu, and Mongol are among them. The minority' s population accounts for 43.9 percent of the total. On the peak of Changbai Mountains, you can enjoy yourself to have a spectacular view of three nations. While on the foot of it, people there live a simple and honest life.

The best season for travel is in March and November.Visitors can walk happily across the grassland full of beautiful azalea flowers in spring, and enjoy the golden-filled boundless forests in autumn. while in hot and humid summer, it is a fine and suitable summer resort. Despite coldness in winter, it is still attractive with its icy and snowy view which prevails the north part of China. And in reality, it is not so cold with the protection of

Japanese Sea and Changbai Mountains' range. And it could not be better to take a a bath in a warm spring there.

Days for tour: two

Traffic lines:

1、by air: Yanji Airport, a medium-sized international one, is in the south west of Yanji city. People can arrive in Yanji from Soul and Qing-zhou by international airline and from Beijing, Shanghai,Shenyang and Tianjinby national line.

2、by long-distance bus: Two main road towards north-east leads to Yanji Highway. Changhu Expressway,a newly-built one, only take four hours to Changchun.

3、by train: Yanbian has some main railways connecting Russia, North Korea and the mainland of China. One in the direction of south will pass by Shenyang, the capital of Liaoning Province, to Dalian and Beijing, in the direction of south to Harbin.

4. Yi Minority

A few days before the Spring Festival, an important task of the children,besides playing with firecrackers all day, is to cut a small pine and gather pine needles in the mountains. The adult men focus on repairing gyros, leveling gyrofield and dance song field, erecting various styles of swing facilities, while the hostesses are busy with preparing the family's clothing and cleaning.

On the eve of Spring Festival, each household will erect a pine at the door, which indicates cleaning away the dirt and the old of the past year and ushering in the new, and eliminating misfortunes. The ground of the main room is covered with a thick layer of pine needles for people's sitting there to eat a festive dinner. At the eve, men must keep watch at night, when several men get together, drinking and talking about the past events of the family. Now they also play poker and have other entertainment activities. The purpose of the night watch is first of all to show respect to the ancestors; it is also for fetching the load of water to prepare the meals ready before dawn.

According to the custom, on the first day of the Spring Festival, women should rest, and all the household chores will be done by the rest of the family members, which shows gratitude for their hard work in the past year.

During the Spring Festival, there are many recreational activities. Women play different swings, while men play gyros, and these two places get very close. Playing gyro is the most popular activity. The average width of the gyro field is over 10 meters, and the length is 50 meters or so. The game is usually between two villages, with more than 20 people in each side, or more than 40. One side places the gyro, while the other side plays, with a spacing of about 15 meters. The main rule is: after hitting the other side's gyro, if the two sides' gyros are both turning, the one that goes to the last will be the winner; as long as one member in the side gets victory in the previous round, the successor can use whatever he considers suitable distance to hit the other side's gyro. The member will be sentenced to lose if the gyro stops rotation first after hitting the other side's gyro. And his successor must return to the original distance for competition. That the hitting side can maintain the right to continue "hitting" totally lies in whether the final hitter can win , when men and women, old and young will watch in the sidelines, which is extremely a lively scene. In the later period of the game, the organizers have arranged to prepare wine, dishes, rice, at the expense of the losing side. During the dinner, the two sides will discuss heatedly, and also toast each other. The winner is naturally proud, but there is no frustration

Yi people dance and sing around the bonfire

in the loser's face, and the atmosphere is very harmonious.

In the evening, there is another grand event, the dance song. The men and women, old and young, will excitedly dance song in the open space with bonfire. During the dance song, men and women in the field naturally gather around the campfire, hand in hand, and rotate counterclockwise with the rhythm of the music. The musical instruments for accompaniment are three-stringed lute, Lusheng and erhu, and the people in and off the field are all singing of Yi folk tunes. The lyrics have notional and functional words. The notional words include two parts: the first part for analogy, the second part for the blessing, with the theme "bumper harvest", "cattle and sheep fat", and the like. The dance is to "stamp the feet". People participating in the activity range from tens to hundreds; usually one village dance song, other villages gather together. Dance song normally continues to two or three o'clock in the early morning; some even dance song all through the night.

5. Zhuang Minority

Zhuang people call the Spring Festival "New Year Festival". After "sending the kitchen god" on December 23rd under the lunar calendar, Zhuang family is imbued with the atmosphere of welcoming the New Year. Each household should sweep the beam and make New Year food such as meat, Ciba, rice candy, glutinous rice cake. Among them, Zongba is surely to be made at this time. The specific approach is: use local specialty big leaves, Zongye, pack in 10 jin [a unit of weight (=1/2 kilogram)] of glutinous rice, 2 jin of pork, 3 jin of green beans, and cook in the iron pot for three days and three nights. On New Year's Eve, Zongba will be put on the altar for ancestor worship; on the third day or eighth day of the New Year, it can be served for meals after being heated. When opening Zongba, there comes out a fragrant smell, which greatly boosts the appetite. This Zongba of 10jin is not the largest. In Zhuang village of Yongning County in Guangxi, in the past, if someone passed the provincial civil service examination under the old Chinese examination system, the village would raise glutinous rice, pig's feet and other objects, and wrap up giant Zongba.

Zhuang people's Spring Festival begins from two days before the lunar January 1st, the first day called big year, the next day called small year.

On Spring Festival's Eve, each Zhuang family will paste couplets, play firecrackers, and have a happy family reunion. Also do "Ya Nian fan(food left)", for prosperity and good luck. At night, the girls do embroidery, children look forward to the fireworks, the old people teach new songs, and all people are waiting for the arrival of midnight. Each family sets up the altar in front of ancestral tablets in the main room; in front of the altar a beautiful Zhuang brocade or embroidered round-table cloth will be hung; the kitchen table is full of big Zongba, rice cakes, candied cake of popped rice and chicken, duck, fish, meat and other offerings. At the same time, in the fireplace a fire resistant hardwood will burn until the next day, indicating the descendants will go one generation after another. People sit together listening to the old people's stories, staying up until dawn.

January 1st under the lunar calendar, is the first day of Spring Festival. Before dawn, Zhuang women will go to the mountain spring or village river to collect the new water. This day's drinking or washing water cannot be that used in the day before. In the past, in some areas, the new water would be immediately weighed; if the new water weighed more than the same amount of old water, it indicates a good harvest. Back home, the new water will be poured into the pot and boil together with brown sugar, bamboo leaves, green onion, and ginger and the whole family will drink the New Year tea with the new boiled water. It is said that the New Year tea party will ensure people's every success. The elderly can have a long and healthy life, the children can be smart and capable, and the couples will live in harmony. People should also pick up a few stones similar to livestock home, and imitate the calls of them all the way. Back home, these stones will be taken into the pigsty and cowshed to bless domestic animals' thriving.

About picking up new water, there is also a custom of drinking "clever water". Early in the morning, the spring is clear, and the girls gather around the spring and in turn count the number of stars. When there is only one star left in the sky, they start to drink fresh water. The"clever woman" recognized by all villagers accompanies the girls to drink. It is said that drinking water held by the"clever woman"will make people clever; hence the saying "clever water". The first handful of water will be awarded to the first girl to the spring and the second holding the girls can race to drink. The"clever woman"holds water tempting the girls and says some amusing words, and at that time the girls' laughter rises and hangs throughout the spring. New Year's "clever water"is the girls' emotional pursuit; they all hope that in the New Year a worthy husband will be found. So,"clever water"is what the girls try to earn early on the first day of New Year.

This day, the person whoever meets outdoors will send good wishes to each other, which can ensure the whole year's good luck and happiness.

During the festival, young men and women will gather in the street or on the hillside of the village singing folk songs, and sometimes this will last three days and nights. In some areas, young people also like throwing silk balls in groups (sewn with colorful cloth, with four corners and bottom decorated with five lock of fringes, colorful strings tied in the middle, throw Hydrangea held during the festive season, filled with chaff, weighing about half a kilo) . "Spring Hall Dance" is a favorite dance of young people to celebrate the New Year and wish for the harvest. They go around the rice trough dancing and striking with the rice pole on the back or carrying pole on the shoulder, wishing the warehouse full of cereals.

From the first day to the fifteenth, all the delicious food and endless warmth depend on the stove fire. Therefore, during the Spring Festival, the stove fire in Zhuang families cannot extinguish, which symbolizes the family prosperity in wealth and descendants.

There is also the habit of celebrating Later Year, which is

called by Zhuang people "ChiLi Festival", on the 30th day in the first month. The legend goes that more than 100 years ago, a Zhuang peasant army against foreign aggressors returned triumphantly on the 30th day of the first month, but this time Spring Festival had passed. In order to welcome them, Zhuang people celebrated the festival again. Spring Festival and Later Year are equally grand festivals.

The traditional recreations during the Spring Festival are similar to those held during Zhuang people;s traditional Song Meeting on March 3rd. Other activities such as lion dancing, chicken dancing, and spring cattle dancing also attract many young people. That Lion team strikes the gongs and drums, puts up high platform, the lions cycle on more than ten square tables and to walk there freely, draws bursts of applause.

In some regions of the Western Guangxi, chicken dance, spring cattle dance passed down from the old time add to the festive atmosphere of the Spring Festival. Young man playing chicken dancing carries two fighting cocks made of wood and papaya, and strikes the gong to each household in the village to celebrate the New Year. Chicken dance song, which is auspicious and humorous, makes the hosts smile, who will not only give New Year's chicken dancer red envelope containing money, but also pull a few feathers from the " fighting cock "and plug in their own cages, to pray for domestic animals' thriving. The spring cattle dance is more interesting. The spring cattle is cleverly woven with bamboo chips, the cattle head and horns plastered up with cotton paper, cattle's eyes painted, cattle's body being a black cloth or gray cloth. The cattle dancers perform in the village by playing drums and gongs. One man in the cloth props up the cattle's head in front and the other in the cloth bends down and arches his back behind switching the tail. Another man followsthem holding the plow frame. In addition, there are alsopeople playing drums and gongs, and singer leading spring cattle song.Wherever they go, there will be songs and laughters. The dancing goes from one village to another, from the first day to the Lantern Festival on 15th. The spring cattle dance not only brings joy to every household, but also expresses their wishes of harvest and peace.

第五章 走向国际的春节

除了中国，世界上还有多个国家有过春节的习俗，主要是一些受中国文化影响的亚洲国家。春节是中国、日本、韩国、蒙古、越南、老挝、缅甸、柬埔寨、泰国、新加坡、马来西亚、印度尼西亚等东亚和东南亚国家最重要的传统节日，而且越南、韩国、新加坡、马来西亚、印尼等国家都把春节列为了法定假日。

一、春节在东南亚

在受中华传统文化影响比较深远、华人人数庞大的东南亚各国，春节在此长盛不衰，保存了全家吃团圆饭、贴春联、贴福字、吃年糕、吃粽子、挂灯笼、拜年、送红包、舞龙、舞狮等年俗。

○新加坡春节

1. 新加坡

新加坡华人约占全国人口的75%，向来重视中国农历新年。因此，新加坡华人的新年活动与饮食等习俗呈现出非常鲜明的特点，既保留着浓郁的传统风俗，又富有强烈的现代气息。新加坡政府规定春节假有两天。

过年前，新加坡华人会将住家彻底打扫干净，然后购买各种新年饰品，如财神、门神和春联等。同时，也会到花店仔细挑选自己喜爱的诸如寓意大吉大利的柑橘树、象征开运聚财的开运竹、具有吉祥与发财之意的菊花、象征财源滚滚的金钱树等。

新年期间，新加坡随处可见高高挂在屋檐下的红灯笼，大门上也都贴上了年画。由于"蝠"与"福"谐音，人们互赠的贺年卡上常常印着蝙蝠。因为"橘"与"吉"谐音，所以华人在春节期间有吃橘子的习惯。拜年时，新加坡华人会带两个橘子，进门捧向主人，象征大吉大利；客人告辞时，主人也要奉还两个橘子。新年吃鱼意味着吉利，这是由于"鱼"同汉语"富裕"的"裕"字音近。在新加坡过年，"捞鱼生"的习俗很有特色。"鱼生"是东南亚的特色新春菜式，以生鱼条为主要食材，配上各色蔬菜丝和水果丝，加上花生、腰果等干果，再撒上白芝麻、五香粉和胡椒粉等调味而成。鱼生有富贵、吉祥等能带来好兆头的说辞。吃的时候，大家一边用筷子将各种美味高高挑起，一边大声地说："捞起！捞起！捞个风生水起！"现在，随着餐饮业的发达，许多新加坡华人都会到餐馆享用年夜饭，也有叫餐送到家的。为迎合农历新年，新加坡的餐馆与酒店纷纷推出精美的各式菜肴，价格的尾数也多取与"发"的谐音"八"。

新加坡华人过春节，家家都要蒸年糕、贴春联、逛花市。但最重要的事情还是除夕全家吃团圆饭。孩子们在除夕这天直到午夜才会睡觉，大人们认为这样做可以延长孩子的生命。大年初一，晚辈纷纷给长辈拜年，长辈则要给晚辈压岁钱。大年初一，扫帚都被收起来，这一天不许扫地，以示吉祥，不然就会把好运气扫掉。大年初二以后是走亲戚的时间。

新加坡的唐人街叫“牛车水”，是新加坡庆祝春节最具代表性的地方。从腊月开始，牛车水各家老字号的商铺和年货集市就迎来川流不息的办年货的人，年货最齐全，是新加坡人办年货的首选地。大年初一前几天，一些店家会通宵营业，让忙碌的人能赶在最后一刻补办年货。临近春节的几天，入夜后牛车水街道两旁点亮五彩缤纷的彩灯和红彤彤的灯笼，为喜庆气氛再添喜庆色彩。

海滨公园是新加坡华人新年里的主要活动地点。节日里，美丽的景致中除了色彩斑斓的花灯，还有猜灯谜、传统工艺品现场制作和本地传统美食集市等。每晚，来自新加坡当地和其他国家的知名表演团体与新加坡华人和全球游客共庆新年。除夕夜，春到河畔大型倒数活动上，还有巨型烟火为即将到来的春节助兴。

妆艺大游行是新加坡华人开创的传统农历新年庆祝方式，是以舞蹈、音乐、巨型彩车、舞狮和舞龙等方式呈献的盛大游行。

旅游小贴士

新加坡“牛车水”唐人街

牛车水（Chinatown）是新加坡的唐人街。说到牛车水，其范围包括大坡、桥南路、新桥路、沙莪巷、史密斯路、登婆路、宾塔街及摩士街。大致上为北到新加坡河，西至新桥路（NewBridgeRd.）；南至"麦斯威尔"路（MaxwellRd.）和克塔艾尔路（KretaAyerRd.），东到塞西尔街（CecilSt.）。中国城被称为"牛车水"，因为原本的居民都以牛车拉水来清扫。

如今的牛车水是现代购物中心、各色小贩和百年老店毗邻而居。南桥路(SouthBridgeRoad)以西是珍珠坊、裕华国货、唐城坊等百货店，以东除了各式庙宇外，便是邻近滨海区的新兴商业区域。这里有新加坡最著名的寺庙，也有很多餐饮购物点。

牛车水最令人兴奋的莫过于农历新年期间。届时，整个地区张灯结彩；各种小店、杂铺都装修一新，还有不少节日商品和风味小吃。牛车水旁边的丹戎巴葛（TanjongPagar）小区也值得一游。这里有众多的餐馆、酒吧、艺术画廊和纪念品商店。

地址：新加坡史密斯大街335号（050335）。

市内交通：在新加坡市内，搭乘MRT东北线（North-EastLine）至牛车水站（ChinatownStation，车站编号NE4）下车即可；或者搭乘巴士C2、166、197、NR5路至SouthBridgeRoad下车。

2. 马来西亚

马来西亚的华人把春节看作一年中最重要的节日，从冬至到正月十五都算过年。这段时间，随处都可以听到华人互道“恭喜拉雅”，“恭喜”是汉语，“拉雅”为马来语，华人和马来人巧妙地把祝贺词融为一体，很是有趣。与中国内地一样，临近春节的时候，散居在各地的亲人都要想方设法回到家乡，飞机和火车常常爆满，长途汽车公司也会增开车次。

从首都吉隆坡到全国各地，每个华人聚居区都挂起大红灯笼。吉隆坡的商业区和饭店区的灯笼有时竟然多达两三万盏，烘托出浓厚的节日气氛。到了晚上，数万盏红彤彤的灯笼一齐点亮，十分壮观。

○马来西亚的春节街头

大年三十，全家在一起吃团圆饭，也会守岁到凌晨。大年初一，人们一般待在家中，接受亲友和马来西亚其他民族的拜年，并准备丰盛的饭菜招待贵客，一般有春卷、龙虾片、咖喱鸡、咖喱牛肉、椰饭等。如果是信神的人家，就不能有荤菜了，只能吃素。年初二开始人们才到亲戚朋友家拜年，初三初四开始有各种文艺娱乐活动和戏曲表演。

华人中有 20% 的天主教和基督教徒，他们也过春节。为此，教堂大年初一开放，供这些教徒做弥撒，还允许华人的舞狮队到教堂舞狮，象征兴旺发达。

由于当地华人多来自福建，受闽南文化影响，人们过春节一定要买凤梨（菠萝），因为闽南语“凤梨”与“旺来”谐音，凤梨就成了春节的吉祥水果。

3. 越南

越南，春节是最隆重的节日，也是国家法定休息时间最长的一个节日。人们在春节期间阖家团圆，拜访亲朋好友。“肥肉姜葱红对联，幡旗爆竹大粽粑。”从这句越南过年的民谣中，可以领略越南人对春节的重视程度。

过节前人们就开始准备年货了。花市是越南春节重要活动之一，春节前约 10 天，花市就热闹起来。除了鲜花、盆景，还出售各式气球、彩灯、玩具、年画、春联、年历等，把相连的几条街道装点得五彩缤纷、喜气洋洋。越南人的年货和中国人的年货差别不大，街上的年货摊上，除了出售年画和年橘外，还有各式红包封、红底金字春联等。春联上面通常都用金漆写些诸如“财源广进”等吉祥的中文字句。对于越族的家庭来说，春节期间有三样装饰品必不可少：一束含苞欲放的桃花、一盆金橘盆景和一个盛有五种水果的“五果盆”，据说这三样东西预示着新年行好运、平安顺利、欣欣向荣。在越南还有一种风俗叫“采绿”，人们在春节到来的时候采一根树枝回家，在越南语中，“绿”和“禄”同音，意味着把吉祥如意带回家。

过春节前，越南人也要在门上贴春联。以前春联用汉字书写，文字拼音化以后，现在大部分春联改用拼音文字。越南人也会在家里贴上“福”“喜”等字样和福、禄、寿星的形象，还有各种传统年画。

华人过年有除夕守岁的习俗，越南人也一样。除夕夜，人们穿上节日盛装拥上街头，年轻女子还会穿上本民族服饰。零点的时候，电台、电视台播出国家领导人春节讲话，节日气氛达到高潮。

年初一早晨，家家户户都要拜祭祖先，同时也拜土地、灶君、百艺师祖，祭品一般有粽子、红烧鱼、牛肉等。供拜完祖先后，小孩要向家中大人及老人拜年，大人们则要给他们压岁钱。春节到来时最早到家里拜年的客人特别受重视，据说这个人会给主人带来好运。因此越南人通常会要邀请自己最亲近的朋友作为来家中拜访的第一位客人。

○东南亚的春节气氛很浓，曼谷街头的节日装饰

越南人过春节最具民族特色的食品是年粽和糯米饼。年粽做法跟中国端午节吃的粽子差不多，但是年粽是方形的，而且大得多。在越南有个传说，年粽象征大地，绿色显示生机勃勃，猪肉和绿豆沙代表飞禽走兽和草木繁盛。

新春期间，街头、公园和公共娱乐场所都会举行各种文化娱乐活动，包括越南传统戏剧、歌舞、杂技、武术、摔跤、舞狮等，还有荡秋千、斗鸡等民间活动。年初一的禁忌也很多，如不能借东西、不能讨债、不能干农活（否则会惊动土地神，庄稼会遭殃）、不能扫地（即使扫了地也不能倒垃圾），等等。

二、春节在东亚

作为中国的近邻，东亚的韩国、日本都有过春节的习俗，韩国甚至将春节列为了法定节假日。

1. 韩　国

在韩国，春节是仅次于中秋节的第二大节日，一直保留着过春节的习俗。韩国称春节为“舍尔”，意思是新年之首。春节期间全国放假，人们纷纷从城市返回故乡，除夕夜全家人团聚在一起，祭祀祖先，静心祝福，祈求好运。韩国人称春节回家探亲为“归省”。

韩国据说从新罗时代(668—901)就开始过春节了。1985 年以“民俗日”的名称出现。1999 年，韩国正式恢复了春节这个节日。

每年正月三十这一天，韩国人要全家团圆吃年夜饭。每逢此时，遍布韩国各地的大小几十万家饭店，几乎全部挂上“连休停业”的牌子，也有的贴上“初三营业”的告示，形成了韩国特有的风俗。这种“三十不开门”的风俗已经有很久的历史。韩国人自古以来十分讲究年夜饭自己动手，并在家里吃年夜饭。他们认为，春节是祭奠祖先、传承孝道的大事。除夕吃团圆饭不仅难得，而且象征了家族兴旺。

韩国春节的传统风俗有很多，不仅有岁妆、岁画、福笊篱、赶夜光鬼等传说，还有祖先祭拜、岁拜、德谈、“掷木四”和跳板等习俗。过春节时，最重要的活动是祭祀祖先。祭祀了祖先，晚辈就要给长辈拜年了，长辈要给拜年的晚辈压岁钱。与中国人用红色信封包成“红包”不同，韩国人习惯用白色的信封装压岁钱。

○韩国的春节习俗与中国有很多相同之处

韩国人春节专门吃的食品，统称为“岁餐”。年夜饭很有讲究，最大的特点是饭菜必须是传统饮食，而且全部由这家的媳妇亲手做。过年最忙碌的便是各家的媳妇们。她们不仅要准备年夜饭，还要承担起春节期间全部岁餐的制作。媳妇们烹调手艺如何，已成为衡量“好媳妇”的重要标准。在岁餐中，流传至今最具代表性的春节料理是“米糕片汤”，这与古代韩国人崇尚太阳有关。白色的小圆状米糕片就代表着太阳，正月初一早晨吃米糕片汤则代表迎接太阳的光明。另外，依照原始宗教信仰，也代表着辞旧迎新、万物复活之际的严肃和整洁。

以前做米糕片汤的汤汁是用野鸡熬成，现在野鸡已经很难捕捉到了，因而改用牛肉或鸡肉汤代替。中部和北部地区还喜欢在米糕片汤里加入山鸡肉、绿豆芽、蘑菇和泡菜为馅的饺子。

按风俗，韩国人年三十的晚上不能睡觉。全家人必须同祖先一起熬夜迎接春节的到来，否则人的眉毛会变白。

韩国人春节期间一家人凑在一起玩得最多的要算从日本传进的"花牌"了。据说 90% 的成年人都会打这种牌。当然有的人也利用春节休假外出旅游。

2. 日本

日本原来也是同中国一样庆祝农历春节，日语把春节庙会中的摊贩称为"的屋"。日本明治维新后的第五年（1873 年）弃用农历，改用公历，元日随之改为格里历 1 月 1 日。虽然如此，除了日期的改变外，日本仍然依照传统方式庆祝传统节日。春节前每家都要用

○日本春节舞龙

松柏装饰房屋，除夕晚上全家人围着火炉守岁。午夜时各地的寺院响起 108 声钟声，第二天人们出门去互相拜年。在日本，新年时有一种叫“福袋”的商品。所谓福袋，就是装着商品的不透明的袋子。福袋有很多种，可以装化妆品、服装、生活杂物、电器等。

节日的庆祝活动称之为“祭”。每逢节日，均有各种庙会。但日本的庙会相对于中国的传统庙会在形式上略有不同。较大的庙会有京都三大祭（葵祭、祇园祭、时代祭）。因最初均为神道教节日，所以举办地都在神社。三大祭较为隆重，规模庞大。人们身着传统装束，有巡游、骑马、舞蹈等表演。

三、春节在其他国家

欧美国家庆祝春节的活动多局限在华人范围内，春节很少成为法定假日。随着华人影响力的增强,春节在欧美国家也日益得到重视。许多海外华人华侨虽然远离祖国，但是每到春节还是以自己的方式欢度佳节，春节在飘洒着浓浓中国味道的同时，也掺入了不少异国情调。作为中国最传统的节日，春节已经走出国门，迈向国际。春节不仅是中国人的春节，也是世界的春节。

1. 美　国

纽约从 2003 年起，已将春节纳入公共假日。不少美国人争相体验中国年，欣赏喧天的锣鼓、欢快的舞蹈以及各种色香味俱全的中国美食。春节期间，纽约的标志性建筑帝国大厦上的 1327 只彩灯就会一改往日美国星条旗的红、白、蓝三色，亮起华裔喜爱的红色和金色，表示对中国农历新年的祝贺。而在纽约的三大华人区（曼哈顿中国城、皇后区法拉盛和布鲁克林区第八大道），都会举行活动，但主要为花车游行。其中法拉盛的韩裔因同贺春节亦会加入到活动中来。

○美国纽约的春节焰火

西海岸的旧金山和洛杉矶除游行以外，还有庙会街市，出售小吃和其他小工艺品。

2. 加拿大

春节前夕，很多中国人来到多伦多华人超市“中华老字号”购物。由于此时购买年货的基本都是中国人，人们见面也都会提前拜个早年，喜气洋洋。而超市为了迎接春节，摆出了许多具有中国特色的年货，春联和灯笼是一定少不了的。春节前这里的超市总会是熙熙攘攘，人流不断。

○加拿大春节舞龙活动

在加拿大，多伦多华人春节文艺晚会已经成为一个品牌。晚会是由多伦多本地华人社团携手主办的一年一度的综合性文艺演出，包括歌舞、器乐、戏剧、相声、小品等文艺节目，是多伦多最早兴起的本地华人“春晚”，也是当地华人中最早的晚会品牌。“多伦多春晚”最早始于 1988 年春节，初期由多伦多大学中国学生学者联谊会在大学校园礼堂、图书馆等地举办，随着观众人数的逐年增多，晚会场地转至校园附近的中学礼堂举行，演出质量不断提高。后于 20 世纪 90 年代末期移师多伦多会议中心剧场等专业正规的剧院。进入

21 世纪，加拿大中国专业人士协会、多伦多华人团体联合总会也相继加入晚会主办者行列，使得春节晚会组织更为完善，成为当地华人社区携手共同举办的、富有中华民族特色的传统喜庆活动。2006 年，在多伦多春节晚会主办机构的基础上，更多的社团、机构携手合作，共同参与组织了中央电视台“同一首歌——走进加拿大”的大型春节文艺演出。20 多年来，春节晚会吸引了许多本地最优秀的华人艺术家加盟演出，推出了许多新人。现在，多伦多华人春节文艺晚会如同中国中央电视台春节晚会一样，已经成为许多华人必吃的“年夜饭”。

除了美国和加拿大以外，拉美的墨西哥城和阿根廷布宜诺斯艾利斯在节日期间也有春节庙会。

3. 法国

每逢中国春节，法国的大街小巷都焕然一新，彩旗飞扬。华人

○法国巴黎埃菲尔铁塔

聚居区挂满了彩旗和红灯笼，就连巴黎市政广场也挂上了大红灯笼，满眼看去都是喜气洋洋的中国红。春节期间，巴黎市政府广场都会燃放鞭炮，很多巴黎市民聚集在这里观赏由法国华人侨团联合举办的春节彩装游行。巴黎市市长还会为迎春狮子点睛。在锣鼓队鼓声中，舞龙、舞狮队、腰鼓队、秧歌旱船、跑驴、划龙舟分外抢眼，此时的中国年庆祝已成为巴黎最抢眼的活动。

在巴黎市 13 区、3 区、4 区和 19 区等唐人街，均有由华人社团组织的文艺游行。

4. 英国

伦敦、爱丁堡和曼城等地都有春节庙会，其中以伦敦规模最为庞大。举办地从最初的唐人街扩大到娱乐中心莱斯特广场，2002 年起更是进入大型活动中心特拉法加广场举办。2008 年起每年参与人

○英国查尔斯王子在伦敦唐人街共庆中国春节（来源：新华网）

数均超过 30 万，涵盖艺术表演及群众演出、特色工艺品小商品、各种小吃等。

5. 德国

在首都柏林，春节前夕商场里总会醒目地摆出五颜六色的中德文贺年卡。每张贺卡里都有一条孔子语句，还印有龙、凤等标志性的中国图案。德国人非常喜欢这样的贺卡。

6. 澳大利亚

在澳大利亚这个多元文化的国家，来自世界各地的移民都尽情庆祝自己的节日，中国的春节也是必不可少的。悉尼、堪培拉、昆士兰以及达尔文等城市都建有大面积唐人街。每逢春节，这些地区将举行大型的庙会，其中包括表演京剧民歌、舞龙舞狮、品尝民俗

○澳大利亚前总理吉拉德参加中国春节舞龙巡游（来源：新华网）

小吃、燃放爆竹和赛龙舟等，欢庆新年的到来。

春节正逢当地的盛夏季节，民间便以龙舟赛作为春节庆典活动的压轴戏，往往能吸引数十万观众。在墨尔本，有世界最长的“巨龙”，长 150 米，有 100 多年的历史。每年春节，200 多名健壮的澳洲人和华人扛着这条“巨龙”走街串巷，喜庆至极。

Chapter Five

The Spring Festival Abroad

Besides China, there are still many other countries celebrating the Spring Festival. These countries are mainly located in Asia. They have been influenced greatly by Chinese culture so that the Spring Festival is on their list of lawful holidays. While only overseas Chinese observe the tradition of the Spring Festival in Europe and America. In recent times, The festival has attracted more attention than ever with the development of Chinese economy. And though far away from China, many overseas celebrate the Spring Festival in both Chinesetraditional and exotic ways. This traditional Festival has thus gone abroad and becomean international festival.

1. In the Southeast of Asia

The Festival is very popular among the nations in the region as they have a large population of Chinese, and equally important, they have been deeply influenced by Chinese traditional culture. By far, Chinese people there have still kept the customs alive such as big dinner eating, couplet and Fu character pasting, lantern show and lion and dragon dance and some others.

1.1 In Singapore

In Singapore Chinese has a significant population percentage of 75%. The events related are quite characteristic due to the fact that the Festival there is both traditional and modern. People have two days off stipulated by the government.

Chinese Singaporeans clean the house and then buy some New Year products such as the couplets and god paintings before the Festival. At the same time they will pick up some flowers and plants that symbolize luck and good fortune. For instance, bamboo, chrysanthemum, orange tree and money tree are among their favorite.

The Spring Festival in Singapore

The red lanterns could be seen everywhere hung under the eaves and the paintings of door-god and fortune-god are pasted on the gates. Bat (Fu) is a homophone for fortune (fu) in Chinese, so we can always see the New Year Cards stamped by bats. And orange (Ju) sounds like luck (ji), people thus like to eat oranges. They bring only two oranges as gift and hold them to the host when they set first foot in the house on New Year Day. While when the guests leave, the hosts need to give the two oranges back. Eating fish is also auspicious as Chinese character "fish" is pronounced the same as another one "wealth".

Lo hei is a special delicacy in the southeast of Asia. It is mainly made of rare fish slices. Put in other ingredients such as vegetable shreds, fruit pieces, spicy powder, peanutsand mix them together, Lo hei will be soon ready. It is believed that the food could bring people luck and fortune when people pick up delicious delight with chopsticks while yelling out 'Lo hei, Lo hei (pick up happiness)'. At present, many ChineseSingaporeans have home delivery or enjoy their big dinner in restaurants, which win the favor of the customers by launching new and fine cuisine. Most of the price ends in lucky number '8' ('far' in Chinese means big money-making).

Besides rice cake cooking, couplets sticking and flower buying, the most important part is to have a reunion dinner with family members. On the eve children stay up till midnight and parents think this can prolong their life. The next morning, the young will send congratulations to the elders while the elders give money as gift. The groom must be taken away because floor sweeping means that good luck will be swept away. On the following days people can visit friends and relatives.

In SingaporeChinese town is renamed Niucheshui, which may be the most typical representative place to sell traditional goods. From the beginning of the 12th lunar month, flowing like rivers, product purchasers get together into the old-branded shopping malls and markets in Niuche Shui, which is regarded as the most-favored shopping area with most varieties. A few days before the Festival, some stores will be kept being open during night to meet the need of those who have no time available at daytime. The street is being illuminated with colorful lamps and red lanterns hung on both sides, which add, no doubt, more festival color.

Celebration of new year in China town of Singapore

The Seashore Park is a good place for Chinese Singaporeans to celebrate the Festival. Besides watching beautiful lanterns and solving lantern riddles, people also can see how the traditional art crafts are made on the spot, and enjoy delicious food and snack. As the night falls, the performers who are from Singapore and the rest of the world will give splendid performances. On the eve night, a large-scaled fireworks show will be held to celebrate the coming of the New Year when the countdown begins.

Chingay Parade is an ingenious celebration way that starts from ChineseSingaporeans. It is a gala parade composed of dance, music, carnival float, lion and dragon dance.

Tips for Tourism

Chinatown in Singapore

Chinatown in Singapore includes Dapo, Qiaonan Road, Xinqiao Road, Shayi Alley, Smith road,Dengpo Road,Binta Street and Moshi Street. Generally, it extends to Singapore River in the north, NewBridgeRd west,MaxwellRdKretaAyerRd in the South and CecilSt in the east.China–town in Singapore is renown as "Niucheshui" , which in Chinese means that former Chinese migrants carried water in use of oxcart to do their cleaning.

Currently Chinatown has turned into a modern shopping center, adjacent to a variety of branded stores and retail stalls.Pearl Market,Chinatown Mar–ket and Yuhua Shopping Mall are in the west part of SouthBridgeRoad, while in the east,there is a emerging commercial region next to Binhai District besides many temples.Among them visitors can go around the most famous temple in Singapore and food and beverage stores.

No other thing could be excite Chinatown people than the lunar New Year. When the new year is coming, lanterns are shinning brightly along with beautiful decoration. All the shops look new after cleaning. People can enjoy a variety of Chinese snacks with unique flavor and buy desirable products. TanjongPagar, which is close to Chniatown, is worthy of seeing around with many restaurants, bars, galleries and souvenir shops.

Address: Smith Road No.335 （050335）

Traffic:in Singapre city, Take North–East Line to Chinatown Station numbered in NE4. Or take Bus C2、166、197、NR5 to South Bridge Road.

In Malaysia

Chinese Malaysians treat the Spring Festival as the most important festival, which is a long term from the winter solstice to the fifteenth days of the first lunar month. Chinese Malaysians exchangeNew Year greetings of 'gong xi la ya', which is a combination of Chinese and Malaysian congratulations. When the Festival is coming, people will try their best to go home. Planes and trains are much more crowded than usual, and so are long-distance buses.

The red lanterns are lighting up every China town in the nation. Sometimes there are up to 20 to 30 thousand lanterns shining together in Kuala Lumpur business and hotel district. That creates a heated atmosphere and spectacular man-made scenery.

New Year celebration in Malaysia

On the eve, the families get around to eat a reunion dinner and stay up all night. The next day people will stay at home to receive the relative or Malaysian visitors and prepare delicious dishes to entertain the guests of honor. Spring rolls, lobster slice, nasi lemak, curry chicken and beef are all local-lovers and must be included on the list. However, god believers cannot eat anything but vegetables. In order not to sweep away good luck, they don't clean the floor. And on the following days, people can enjoy entertainment activities and watch opera performances.

Chinese Catholics and Christens, which covers 20% population, also celebrate the Spring Festival. The church is open for them to pray On New Year Day. Somelion dance teams are invited to perform around thechurches for sake of prosperity.

Most of Chinese Malaysians immigrated from the southern Fujian of China (Minnan Region in Chinese), so the culture of Min Nan has exerted great influence on their life. Here is an example. People must buy an auspicious fruit named Feng Li (pineapple) just because the fruit 'Feng Li' sounds like 'wang lai' (the fortune comes) in Min Nan.

In Vietnam

For Vietnamese, the Festival is the most important festival and the longest legal holiday.

People visit relatives and friendsduring the Spring Festival holidays. 'Eating fat meat and drinking ginger with red couplets on the door; tasting ZongBa and seeing big flag waving and firecrackers setting off.' From this Vietnam ballad, we mayknowhow Vietnamese pay theirattention to the Spring Festival.

Before the holidays people start to prepare New Years goods. About 10 days before the Spring Festival, the flower market begins to become crowded. In addition to fresh flowers, miniascape, people can also buy all kinds of balloons, lights, toys, posters, the Spring Festival couplet, and calendar. Streets are decorated with colorful lanterns, radiant with joy. There is little difference between Vietnamese and Chinese special purchases. The street stalls sell New Year pictures and years orange outside, and they still have various red envelope seal, red bottom gold-lettered Spring Festival couplets, etc. On Spring Festival couplets often use gold lacquer write someauspicious Chinese words.For most families, three ornaments are necessary: a bunch of sprouting peach blossom,orange miniascape and a container with five kinds of fruit.It is said that the three things can foretell good luck, safety and flourishing. Another custom is called 'green picking', people always pick up green branches home in the arrival of the Spring Festival because 'green' and 'lu' (fortune) are unisonant and it means they can bring fortune home.

As Chinese, the Vietnamese will also paste spring couplets on the door. The couplet used to be written in Chinese character and now switches to alphabet writing. Vietnamese like sticking Chinesecharacter'blessing' and 'joy'and other words, together with the image of fortune god, longevity god and all sorts of traditional New Year pictures.

Chinese have the custom of stay up on the eve, and so does Vietnamese. People put on holiday clothes andget together into the streets. Young woman like to wear theirnational costume. At 12 midnight, Spring Festival speech given by national leaders will be delivered through radio and television. And the atmosphere comes to the climax.

On New Year's Day morning, every family needs to worship their ancestors, and at the same time, they need to pay their respect to land god, fire god, and art craft god. Sacrifices are generally composed of dumplings, fried fish, beef, etc. after the worship, children will express theirhappy New Year wishes to adults and the old man, and they are given their New Year's money in return. The first guest is specially valued as it is said that this person will bring good luck to the master. And the Vietnamese will usually invite a good friend to set foot on their house as the first visitor on that big day.

Zongzi and glutinous rice cakes are two typical Vietnamese national foods to eat at the Spring Festival. The making of Zongzi is similar to that of Chinese Zongzi at Dragon Boat Festival, while Vietnamese Zongzi is square-shaped and much bigger in size. There is a legend in Vietnam in which Zongzi symbolizes earth, green leaf outside stands for life, pork and green bean fillings represent animals and birds and vegetation.

During the Spring Festival cultural and recreational activities will be held in the streets, parks and other public places including traditional Vietnamese drama, singing and dancing performance, acrobatics, martial arts, wrestling, lion dance and so on. Playing on the swing, chess, bird fighting and gamecock are popular too. There are also a few taboos on New Year's Day,

Happy New Year in Bangkok, a city in the southeast of Asia

for example, people can't borrow things and can't demand repayment of a loan. Doing farm work is also forbidden because earth god cannot be disturbed during the festival or they will bring people disaster. People are not allowed to sweep the floor. If they do it carelessly they cannot take out the trash until three days later.

2. In the East of Asia

2.1 In South Korea

The Spring Festival is the second largest after the Mid-Autumn Festival in South Korea. South Koreanscall the Spring-Festival as 'She'r', which means the beginning of the New Year. During the time people enjoy a national. They return to their hometown from big cities. On the Eve the whole family are together to worship ancestor, pray for good luck.

It is said that that the Spring Festival begins from Rochelle Era (668-901) in South Korea. In 1985 the 'folk day' festival takes its place and the Spring Festival has restored its name by 1999.

South Korean people eat family reunion dinneron the eve when thousands of restaurants hang the notice 'closure for rest days' outside, or labeled as 'open till the third day'. This particular custom has a long history out of business on the Eve. Since ancient times,the South Koreanshave been very particular about the eve dinner. They make it by hand and eat together at home. The Spring Festival is a big day to pay respect to ancestors and at the same time, to pass down filial piety tradition to the next generation. In their opinion, the reunion dinner is not only valuable to every family member, but alsoreveals the prosperity of the whole clan.

There are a lot of traditional customs observed by South

Koreans, for instance, makeup, New Year paintings, blessing strainer net, driving evil paintings and ancestral worship, ancestor's talk, throw game and the springboard. Among them the most essential part is the ancestor worship. And the followings are some strict rules for the offering way of the sacrifices, 'fish east meat west', 'fish head east and end west', 'red food east while white food west', 'dates nuts pear persimmon in their correct order', 'rare food east cooked west', 'rice left soup right' and so on. The worship procedure is also very strict. After that, the younger generation will give best wishes to the elders and the elders will give them New Year money. The South Koreans areused to putting the money into white envelopes rather than red ones as Chinese people prefer to do.

South Korea enjoys similar tradition of New Year to that of China

Korean Spring Festival food, referred to as 'New Year meal',is exquisite enough.The food must be traditional diet and have to be made in hand by the daughters -in-law of the family. These women are much occupied because they not only prepare for the reunion dinner, but are also responsible for all meals during the Spring Festival. Cooking skills has served as the most important standard to judge a woman is a good wife one or not. 'Rice cake soup' is the most representative Festival cuisine to make and this food is related to the fact that ancient Koreans adored the sun greatly. The white rice cake pieces are as round as the sun, so eating the soup on New Year's Day morning means that they meet the sun light and pay their respect. In addition it, the soup also stands for solemnity and tidiness of rebirth in accordance with some religious beliefs. The soup used to be stewed with pheasant, but now pheasantsare difficult to hunt, so people have to switch to beef or chicken soup. In the northern and central regions,people like to add dumplings to the soup and the dumplings should be filled mashed mountain chicken, bean sprout, mushroom and pickle inside. To host New Year's visitors, each family need also to prepare honey waxy, oil fruit, cinnamon soupand meat food.

Koreansusually don't sleep during the Eve night. The whole family must stay up late to meet the arrival of the Spring Festival, Together with the ancestors. Or their eyebrows would turn white in the legend.

The favorite game for the reunion family is a kind of card play which was introduced from Japan. It is said that 90% of adults can play it well. Some other people will take the holiday time to travel around and make fun.

2.2 In Japan

Japan used to celebrate the lunar New Year festival too and Japanese temple fair is called'De Wu'. After the Meiji Restoration of 1873, lunarcalendar was rejected and the Gregorian calendar was adopted. The date was changed; however, the Japanese still observed the Festival celebration in traditional way. Before the Spring Festiva,l every family decorated the house with the pine trees. On the eve the whole family sataround the fire waiting for the coming of the New Year. At midnight the temple bells would ring 108 sounds and the next day people went out to greet each other with happy New Year. There were 'blessing bags' as called selling well during the time. This bag-couldcontain cosmetics, clothing, everyday use and electric appliances, etc.

TheSpring Festival celebration was named as 'offering' in Japan. And people could get pleasure around all sorts of temple fair during the offering time. Japanese temple fairswere a little different from Chinese ones, mainly in form. In Kyoto three offerings were amongthe largest they were Kwai Offering, and Zhi YuanOffering, Times Offering. All the offerings were held in the shrines as these initiallywere Shintoism festivals. These big offerings were grand and large-scaled in which People wore national costume to patrol, ride and dance.

Dragon Dance celebration of Chinese New Year in Japan

3. In Europe and America

The Spring Festival is a holiday for overseas Chinese only

inmost European and American countries. But it has attractedincreasing attentions year by year along with the growth of Chinese influence. Some cities even have incorporated it into official holidays.

3.1 In the USA

New York made the Festival public holidays in 2003. From then more Americans have been squeezing to experience Chinese New Year. They taste well-balanced Chinese food, and enjoy deafeningdrum play and merry dance performances. During the Festival, 1327 color lamps on the State Empire have been shinning upred and golden to express ChineseNew Year congratulations to all citizens. While in three biggest China town (Manhattan, Brooklyn and Queens),a variety of celebrationactivities are held including the most famous one---flower car parade. The Koreans join Chinesecelebrations with joy as they follow the tradition of the Spring Festival too.

On the west coast of San Francisco and Los Angeles, in addition to parade, people travel around the temple fair to enjoy snacks and buysome small handmade artworks.

Skyrocket show to celebrate Chinese New Year in New York

3.2 In Canada

Before the Eve, many Chinese usually go around some Toronto Chinese 'time-honored brand'supermarkets to buy New Year products. They meet their Chinese folks with joy and exchange early greetings of happy New Year. In order to attract more customers, the supermarkets compete to display all their Chinese-styled commodities such as couplets and lanterns. As expected, they are always crowded, hustling and busting at this time.

Chinese Spring Festival evening party has become a noted event held by local Chinese communities in Toronto. The party is hosted annually and its comprehensive performances include dance, instrumental music, drama, crosstalk, and sketch show, which is regarded as the earliest local gala of Chinese Spring Festival. This 'Toronto established gala' began at first in1988 and later the parties were given by some Chinese students of Toronto University in the auditorium and library. With the audience number growing steadily every year, the party was transferred to the auditorium of a middle school near campus. And by the 1990s it has moved to the Theatres such as Toronto Conference Center Theatre as its performance qualities have been recognized widely.

After we move into the 21th century, this Spring Festival gala has been organized in a better way as more distinguished unions joined the host work like Chinese Professionals Association and Canadian Toronto Chinese Community and by far the Toronto-based gala has been a traditional celebration hosted and shared by all Chinese communities in Toronto which is full of Chinese national characteristics. In 2006, on the basis of the gala, CCTV 'Identical First Song' came to Canada and staged its first performance with joint efforts and participation of more organizers and communities. During the recent two decades, many a local best artists have been enlisted in the gala performance.At present, Toronto Chinese Spring Festival evening party,or simply the gala, is a must-watch for many overseas Chinese. In Chinese Circle it is as popular as CCTV Spring Festival Gala in China.

Besides in the USA and in Canada, we can also see temple fairs at the Festival in other places of Latin America, for example, Mexico City and Argentina Buenos Aires.

Chinese dragon dance in Canada

3.3 In France

When the Festival comes, the streets of France are fresh and colorfulwith flying flags. Banners and red lantern are also hung everywhere in China Towns. People can even see big red lanterns illuminating in Paris City Hall Plaza, radiant and full of joy and happiness. ManyParisians will get together in the Plaza to enjoy the firework show, and more excitedly watch costume parade given by French Chinese Union. The mayor is expected to finish the final draw for the eye of the dance lion, in which

Eiffel Town in the illumination of Skyrocket Show
For Chinese New Year

the lion is said to get alive and begin its dance. In the tune of drum and percussion, dragon and lion dance team, waist drum land boat team, and dragon boat team are all dancing cheerfullytogether, which has already been one of the most eye-catching events in Paris

Chinatown's celebration in Paris

In the 3th, 4th, 13th and 19th districts of Paris, there are theatrical parades hosted by some French Chinese organizations and communities.

3.4 In the UK

People could see Chinese temple fairs at the Spring Festival in London, Edinburgh and Manchester city. Andamong them,the largest is in London. The fair was first begun at China Towns and later was expanded to Leicester Square. From 2012, it has been moved into Trafalgar Square. Since 2008, there have been over 300 thousand people who have travelled around the fairs to watch art performances and to take part in participatory performances, to enjoy characteristic handicraft commodity and all kinds of snacks.

3.5 In Germany

In the capital city Berlin, the shopping malls always display colorful New Year cards in some noticeable places, with a piece of Confucius statement and dragon and phoenix design at the Festival time. Germens are all fond of these Chinese-styled cards.

Prince Charles is spending Chinese New Year in China Town of London. (Xinhua News)

4. In the Other Part of the World

4.1 In Australia

In multicultural Australia, immigrants from all over the world can celebrate their own festivals happily and so are Chinese for Chinese New Year. Most Chinese live inlarge-sized Chinatowns of Sydney, Canberra, Queensland and Darwin and other cities. So when the Spring Festival is approaching, the big temple fairs are held in these places including Beijing Opera performance, the dragon and lion dance, folk snack tasting, firecrackers show and dragon boat race to celebrate the arrival of the New Year.

Chinese Spring Festival comes whenit is midsummer time in Australia. So naturally the dragon boat race is local favorite and the main event usually attracts hundreds of thousands of people. In Melbourne, the longest dragon model in the world

Gillard, former Prime Minister of Australia, is in the parade of Chinese New Year

is as long as 150 meters with a history of over 100 years.At the Festival, the dragon will be carried around the streets by more than 200 strong Australians and Chinese and the event is extraordinary and spectacular.

附　录 Appendix

中国传统面食“饺子”的制作方法

Recipe of Mongolian Milk Tea

饺子是中国传统饮食文化中最具代表的风味特色食品之一，是我国北方民间一种带馅的面食和地方小吃，也是节令（冬至）和春节（大年三十和初一）美食。它既是主食，又兼副食；既有荤菜，又有素菜。因其选料独特，制作精细，皮薄馅嫩，味道鲜美，容易消化，老少皆宜，营养丰富，形状美观，百食不厌而深受人们的喜爱。

现以韭菜馅饺子为例，介绍饺子的制作、食用过程。

The dumpling is one of typical and traditional flour food with fillings inside, very popular in the northern China. People usually eat it at the days of Solstice and Spring Festival. Dumplings serve both as main and subsidiary dish filled with smashed vegetables and meat inside. It has gained much popularity among China, south or north, because it is made by hand with special and fresh ingredients, shaped beautifully and elegantly, delicious and easy for digestion so that it has been loved by all.

And here is the process to make and eat dumplings. To take it specific, we take leek dumplings for example.

原料：

1. 冷水面团 1 份（约 2 杯面粉量）
2. 韭菜 500 克
3. 鸡蛋 2 个
4. 高汤 1 碗
5. 香菜 1 根

Ingredients：

1.Ingredients: a dough (two cups of flour mixed with cold water)
2. 500 gram leek
3. 2 eggs
4. A bowl of soup
5.Parsley

制作步骤 /Procedures

1. 饺子馅的准备：把韭菜洗净后，切成小段状。然后把切好后的韭菜倒入容器中，一并把搅好的猪肉倒入容器里，再向里，放入适量的食盐，姜末和葱末、香菜，最好再打入 2 个鸡蛋，搅拌，混合均匀，搅拌大约 3 分钟。

1.How to make fillings first: Wash leek first and cut into pieces.Then put it and smashed pork into a container. After that, put in a certain amount of salt, parsley and ginger and onion powder, and possibly two eggs for best. Mix them for three minutes till they well-blended by churning.

2. 饺子皮的制作：先将面粉和水揉成团 ，加保鲜膜静置 15 分钟。再将面团分成四份，每份揉成长条形状，切成大小相等的若干份。把每份小面团按扁，然后用面棍擀成圆形，中间厚边簿。

2.How to make the flour covering: Pour water into flour and rub to dough.Cover plastic film onto it for 15 minutes. Divide the dough into four parts and rub each part into bars and cut into dices evenly. Press each dice flat and roll it into round slice with thick in the middle and thin on the rim.

3. 一切都准备好后，开始包饺子。包饺子时最好在旁边放半碗清水，以便在饺子皮周围粘上水，这样饺子容易紧紧的黏在一起，不易散。

3.When everything is ready, we may begin to wrap dumplings. we had better put a bowl of some water aside so that we could get some water on the covering to make it sticky. And in this way dumpling are not easy to get open when it gets being cooked.

4. 饺子包好后，就可以下锅，用大火烧开；烧开后在向里面倒入点清水，盖上锅盖，大概 2 分钟左右，再次烧开后就可以捞起，食用。

4.When dumpling wrapping is finished, it is time to cook it quick in the hot water. Put in some cold water when the water is boiling and put the cover of the pot to stew for about 2 minutes. You can enjoy it when the water is boiling again.

5. 饺子包好后，就可以下锅，用大火烧开；烧开后在向里面倒入点清水，盖上锅盖，大概 2 分钟左右，再次烧开后就可以捞起，食用。

5.Last but not least, make some sauce juice. First get two bowls ready. One is for sauce and diced onion and the other for vinegar. One could dip dumpling in the sauce bowls to satisfy one ' s taste.

注意事项 /Cautions

1. 包饺子的时候，要捏紧，防止火烧时散开；

1.Wrap dumplings tight lest they would be loose in boiling water.

2. 饺子开始烧开后，不能及时捞上来，要放点清水，再次烧开；
2.Dumpling could not be got out when water first boils. It should be done when water is boiling again after some new cold water is put into the pot.

3. 捞饺子时，要一并乘出一些饺子汤。
3.Get some soup when get dumplings.

丛书后记

上下五千年的悠久历史孕育了灿烂辉煌的中华文化。我国地域辽阔，民族众多，节庆活动丰富多彩，而如此众多的节庆活动就是一座座珍贵丰富的旅游资源宝藏。在中华民族漫长的历史长河中，春节、清明、端午、中秋等传统节日和少数民族节日，是中华民族优秀传统文化的历史积淀，是中华民族精神和情感传承的重要载体，是维系祖国统一、民族团结、文化认同、社会和谐的精神纽带，是中华民族生生不息的不竭动力。

春节以正月为岁首，贴门神、朝贺礼；元宵节张灯、观灯；清明节扫墓、踏青、郊游、赏牡丹；端午节赛龙舟、包粽子；上巳节祓禊；七夕节乞巧，牛郎会织女；中秋节赏月、食月饼；节日间的皮影戏、长安鼓乐；少数民族的节日赶圩、歌舞美食……这一桩桩有趣的节日习俗，是联络华人、华侨亲情、乡情、民族情的纽带，是中国非物质文化遗产的“活化石”。

为了传播中华民族优秀传统文化，推进中外文化交流，中国人类学民族学研究会民族节庆专业委员会与安徽人民出版社合作，继成功出版《中国节庆文化》丛书之后，再次推出《多彩中国节》丛书。为此，民族节庆专委会专门成立了编纂委员会，邀请了国际节庆协会（IFEA）主席兼首席执行官史蒂文·施迈德先生、中国文联原执行副主席冯骥才先生、第十一届全国政协民族和宗教委员会副主任周明甫先生等担任顾问，由《中外节庆网》总编辑彭新良博士担任主编，16位知名学者组成编委会，负责从书的组织策划、选题确定、体例拟定和作者的甄选。

出版《多彩中国节》丛书，是民族节庆专业委员会和安徽人民出版社合作的结晶。安徽人民出版社是安徽省最早的出版社，有60余年的建社历史，在对外传播方面走在全国出版社的前列；民族节庆专业委员会是我国节庆研究领域唯一的国家级社团，拥有丰富的专家资源和地方节庆资源。这套丛书的出版，实现了双方优势资源的整合。丛书的面世，若能对推动中国文化的对外传播、促进传统民族文化的传承与保护、展示中华民族的文化魅力、塑造节庆的品牌与形象有所裨益，我们将甚感欣慰。

掩卷沉思，这套丛书凝聚着诸位作者的智慧，倾注着编纂者的心血，也诠释着中华民族文化的灿烂与辉煌。在此，真诚感谢各位编委会成员、丛书作者、译者以及出版社工作人员付出的辛劳，以及各界朋友对丛书编纂工作的鼎力支持！希望各位读者对丛书多提宝贵意见，以便我们进一步完善后续作品，将更加璀璨的节庆文化呈现在世界面前。

为了向中外读者更加形象地展示各民族的节庆文化，本丛书选用了大量图片。这些图片，既有来自于丛书作者的亲自拍摄，也有的来自于民族节庆专委会图片库（由各地方节庆组织、节庆主办单位报送并授权使用），还有部分图片是由编委会从专业图片库购买，或从新闻媒体中转载。由于时间关系，无法与原作者一一取得联系，请有关作者与本书编委会联系（邮箱：pxl@jieqing365.com），我们将按相关规定支付稿酬。特此致谢。

《多彩中国节》丛书编委会

2018年3月

Series Postscript

China has developed its splendid and profound culture during its long history of 5000 years. It has a vast territory, numerous nationalities as well as the colorful festivals. The rich festival activities have become the invaluable tourism resources. The traditional festivals, such as the Spring Festival, the Tomb-Sweeping Festival, the Dragon Boat Festival, the Mid-Autumn Festival as well as the festivals of ethnic minorities, represent the excellent traditional culture of China and have become an important carrier bearing the spirits and emotions of Chinese people, a spirit tie for the national reunification, national unity, cultural identity and social harmony, and an inexhaustible motive force for the development of Chinese nation.

The Spring Festival starts with Chinese lunar January, when people post pictures of the Door Gods and exchange gifts and wishes cheerfully. At the Lantern Festival a splendid light show is to be held and enjoyed. On the Tomb-Sweeping Festival, men and women will worship their ancestors by sweeping the tombs, going for a walk in the country and watching the peony. And then the Dragon Boat Festival witnesses a wonderful boat race and the making of zongzi. Equally interesting is the needling celebration on the Double Seventh Festival related to a touching love story of a cowboy and his fairy bride. While the Mid-Autumn Festival is characterized by moon-cake eating and moon watching. Besides all these, people can also enjoy shadow puppet shows, Chang'an drum performance, along with celebration fairs, songs and dances and delicious snacks for ethic groups. A variety of festival entertainment and celebrations have formed a bond among all Chinese, at home or abroad, and they are regarded as the "living fossil" of Chinese intangible cultural heritage.

In order to spread the excellent traditional culture of China, and promote the folk festival brand for our country, the Folk Festival Commission of the China Union of Anthropological and Ethnological Science (CUAES) has worked with the Anhui People's Publishing House to publish *The Colorful Chinese Festivals Series*. For this purpose, the Folk Festival Commission has established the editorial board of *The Colorful Chinese Festivals Series*, by inviting Mr. Steven Wood Schmader, president and CEO of the International Festival And Events Association (IFEA); Mr. Feng Jicai, former executive vice-president of China Federation of Literary and Art Circles(CFLAC); Mr. Zhou Mingfu, deputy director of the Eleventh National and Religious Committee of the CPPCC as consultants; Dr. Peng Xinliang, editor-in-chief of the Chinese and foreign Festival Website as the chief editor; and 16 famous scholars as the members to organize, plan, select and determine the topics and the authors.

This series is the product of the cooperation between the Folk Festival Commission and Anhui People's Publishing House. Anhui People's Publishing House is the first publishing house in Anhui Province, which has a history of over 60 years, and has been in the leading position in terms of foreign transmission. The Folk Festival Commission is the only organization of national level in the field of research of the Chinese festivals, which has experts and rich local festival resources. The series has integrated the advantageous resources of both parties. We will be delighted and gratified to see that the series could promote the foreign transmission of the Chinese culture, promote the inheritance and preservation of the traditional and folk cultures, express the cultural charms of China and build the festival brand and image of China.

The Colorful Chinese Festivals Series is bearing the wisdoms and knowledge of all of its authors and the great efforts of the editors, and explaining the splendid cultures of the Chinese nation. We hereby sincerely express our gratitude to the members of the board, the authors, the translators and the personnel in the publishing house for their great efforts and to all friends from all walks of the society for their supports. We hope you can provide your invaluable opinions for us to further promote the following works so as to show the world our excellent festival culture.

This series uses a large number of pictures in order to unfold the festive cultures in a vivid way to readers at home and abroad. Some of them are shot by the authors themselves, some of them come from the picture database of the Folk Festival Commission (contributed and authorized by the local folk festival organizations or organizers of local festival celebrations), and some of them are bought from Saitu Website or taken from the news media. Because of the limit of time, we can't contact the contributors one by one. Please don't hesitate about contacting the editorial board of this series (e-mail: pxl@jieqing365.com) if you're the contributor. We'll pay you by conforming to the state stipulations.

Editorial Committee of *The Colorful Chinese Festivals Series*

March, 2018